CITIES AND VISITORS

Studies in Urban and Social Change

Published by Blackwell in association with the *International Journal of Urban and Regional Research*. Series editors: Harvey Molotch, Linda McDowell, Margit Mayer, and Chris Pickvance.

Published

Fragmented Societies
Enzo Mingione

Free Markets and Food Riots
John Walton and David Seddon

Post-Fordism
Ash Amin (ed.)

The People's Home? Social Rented Housing in Europe and America
Michael Harloe

Cities After Socialism: Urban and Regional Change and Conflict in Post-Socialist Societies
Gregory Andrusz, Michael Harloe and Ivan Szelenyi (eds)

Urban Poverty and the Underclass: A Reader
Enzo Mingione

Capital Culture: Gender at Work in the City
Linda McDowell

Contemporary Urban Japan: A Sociology of Consumption
John Clammer

Globalizing Cities: A New Spatial Order?
Peter Marcuse and Ronald van Kempen (eds)

The Social Control of Cities? A Comparative Perspective
Sophie Body-Gendrot

Cinema and the City: Film and Urban Societies in a Global Context
Mark Shiel and Tony Fitzmaurice (eds)

The New Chinese City: Globalization and Market Reform
John R. Logan (ed.)

Understanding the City: Contemporary and Future Perspectives
John Eade and Christopher Mele (eds)

Cities and Visitors: Regulating People, Markets, and City Space
Lily M. Hoffman, Susan S. Fainstein, and Dennis R. Judd (eds)

Forthcoming

European Cities in a Global Age: A Comparative Perspective
Alan Harding (ed.)

Urban South Africa
Alan Mabin and Susan Parnell

Urban Social Movements and the State
Margit Mayer

CITIES AND VISITORS

REGULATING PEOPLE, MARKETS, AND CITY SPACE

Edited by

Lily M. Hoffman,
Susan S. Fainstein, and
Dennis R. Judd

Blackwell
Publishing

350 Main Street, Malden, MA 02148-5018, USA
108 Cowley Road, Oxford OX4 1JF, UK
550 Swanston Street, Carlton, Victoria 3053, Australia

First published 2003 by Blackwell Publishing Ltd

Library of Congress Cataloging-in-Publication Data

Cities and visitors : regulating people, markets, and city space / edited by Lily M. Hoffman,
Susan S. Fainstein, Dennis R. Judd.
    p. cm. — (Studies in urban and social change)
  Papers generated by a research collective, the International Tourism Research Group (ITRG),
funded by the Council for European Studies, whose member scholars first met in Amsterdam in
April 1998 and subsequently in Montreal and in Barcelona.
   Includes bibliographical references and index.
   ISBN 1-4051-0058-3 (alk. paper) — ISBN 1-4051-0059-1 (pbk. : alk. paper)
   1. Tourism. 2. Cities and towns. 3. Tourism—management. I. Hoffman, Lily M.
II. Fainstein, Susan S. III. Judd, Dennis R. IV. Series.
  G155.A1C487 2003
  338.4'791'091732—dc21

                                  2003044370

A catalogue record for this title is available from the British Library.

Set in 10½ on 12 pt Baskerville
by SNP Best-set Typesetter Ltd., Hong Kong
Printed and bound in the United Kingdom
by MPG Books Ltd, Bodmin, Cornwall

For further information on
Blackwell Publishing, visit our website:
http://www.blackwellpublishing.com

Contents

List of Illustrations   vii

List of Tables   ix

List of Contributors   xi

Series Editors' Preface   xv

Preface   xvi

Introduction   1
Susan S. Fainstein, Lily M. Hoffman, and Dennis R. Judd

Part I: Regulating Visitors   21

1   Visitors and the Spatial Ecology of the City
     Dennis R. Judd   23

2   Cities, Security, and Visitors: Managing Mega-Events in
     France
     Sophie Body-Gendrot   39

3   Sociological Theories of Tourism and Regulation Theory
     Nicolò Costa and Guido Martinotti   53

Part II: Regulating City Space   73

4   Amsterdam: It's All in the Mix
     Pieter Terhorst, Jacques van de Ven, and Leon Deben   75

5   Revalorizing the Inner City: Tourism and Regulation in
    Harlem
    Lily M. Hoffman   91

6   Barcelona: Governing Coalitions, Visitors, and the Changing
    City Center
    Marisol García and Núria Claver   113

7   The Evolution of Australian Tourism Urbanization
    Patrick Mullins   126

Part III: Regulating Labor Markets   143

8   Regulating Hospitality: Tourism Workers in New York and
    Los Angeles
    David L. Gladstone and Susan S. Fainstein   145

9   Shaping the Tourism Labor Market in Montreal
    Marc V. Levine   167

Part IV: Regulating the Tourism Industry   185

10 Mexico: Tensions in the Fordist Model of Tourism
    Development
    Daniel Hiernaux-Nicolas   187

11 The New Berlin: Marketing the City of Dreams
    Hartmut Häussermann and Claire Colomb   200

12 Museums as Flagships of Urban Development
    Chris Hamnett and Noam Shoval   219

Part V: Conclusion   237

13 Making Theoretical Sense of Tourism
    Susan S. Fainstein, Lily M. Hoffman, and Dennis R. Judd   239

Index   254

List of Illustrations

Plates

1.1	Times Square, New York, entertainment complex	28
2.1	Paris sports fan	44
3.1	The Grand Canal, Venice	64
4.1	Legalized prostitution in Amsterdam	77
5.1	The Apollo Theater, Harlem's cultural icon	101
6.1	Doing business in Barcelona's medieval center	118
7.1	Beachfront property on Australia's Gold Coast	139
8.1	Waiter dressed as action hero at restaurant in Universal City Walk, Los Angeles	157
9.1	Tourists in Old Montreal	176
10.1	Mexican beach scene	192
11.1	"The largest building site in Europe"	205
12.1	Inside the Musée D'Orsay, Paris	226
13.1	Resistance to plans for a stadium to house Olympic competition on Manhattan's West Side	240

Figures

7.1	Location of Australia's 14 largest urban areas, including the three major tourist centers, and other selected tourist centers	129
12.1	Museum building and commercialization process: a conceptual framework	229

List of Tables

5.1 Repositioning of the US inner-city minority community   105
6.1 Number of hotels by category, Barcelona, 1999–2001   122
7.1 Australia's 14 largest urban areas at the 2001 Census (ranked) and population change, 1991–2001   127
7.2 Australia's top ten tourism destinations for international and domestic tourists (percentage of overnight visitors)   130
7.3 Employment in tourism industries: Gold Coast, Sunshine Coast, and Cairns compared (1996) (percentages)   131
8.1 New York City visitor arrivals and expenditures, 1991–2002   149
8.2 Los Angeles visitor arrivals and expenditures, 1991–2000   149
8.3 New York City tourism-related employment, 1977–1997   152
8.4 Los Angeles County tourism-related employment, 1977–1997   154
9.1 Average annual employment income in key tourism occupations in metropolitan Montreal, 1990–1995   172
9.2 Work, status, and gender composition of key tourism occupations in metropolitan Montreal, 1995   172
9.3 Income in tourism occupations as proportion of average employment income, Canada's three largest metropolitan areas, 1995   173

9.4 Average wages in tourism occupations as proportion of
average annual pay, selected US metropolitan areas, 1997   173
9.5 Unionization rates in selected North American
metropolitan areas   175
12.1 The ten most visited attractions (millions of visitors) in
London, Paris, and New York, 1997   224

Contributors

Sophie Body-Gendrot, a political scientist, is Professor of American Studies at the Sorbonne, Paris, and a researcher at CNRS. She is the Director of the Center of Urban Studies in the Anglophone World at the Sorbonne and of a European network of researchers focusing on the dynamics of violence in Europe. She has written and co-edited a dozen books and numerous articles published in Europe and in the US. The author of *The Social Control of Cities? A Comparative Perspective* (Blackwell, 2000), she has just completed a book (in French) on American society after 9/11.

Núria Claver holds a degree in sociology from the Universitat de Barcelona. Her MA dissertation was on Barcelona's old city regeneration. She is currently involved in two European research projects: "The socio-economic performance of social enterprises in the field of integration by work" and "Transformations des structures familiales et évolution des politiques sociales."

Claire Colomb will complete a PhD in Town Planning at the Bartlett School of Architecture and Planning, University College London (UCL) in 2003. Her dissertation is entitled "City marketing and urban planning in the new Berlin: urban policy-making between the global and the local." She is currently working as Project Developer in the European Union Programme on Transnational Co-operation in Spatial Planning, while teaching part-time at the Bartlett School of Planning, UCL.

Nicolò Costa is Associate Professor of the Sociology of Tourism at Milano Bicocca University and Director of the Observatory on Religious and Cultural Tourism in Italy. He has published a number of papers on tourism and tourism education.

Leon Deben is Associate Professor and Chair of the Department of Sociology and Anthropology at the University of Amsterdam. He has written about the culture of the working class in the Netherlands, urban renewal, homelessness, and changes in the use of urban public space.

Susan S. Fainstein is Professor of Urban Planning in the School of Architecture, Planning and Preservation at Columbia University, New York. With Dennis Judd she is co-editor of *The Tourist City*. Among her other books is *The City Builders*, now in a second edition. In her various published works she has written about urban redevelopment, planning theory, comparative public policy, and urban social movements.

Marisol García lectures at the University of Barcelona. She is a member of the editorial board of the *International Journal of Urban and Regional Research*, and has been a Visiting Fellow at St Antony's College (Oxford), a Research Fellow at the Royal Institute of International Affairs (London), and a Visiting Fellow at the European University Institute (Florence) and the University of Amsterdam. Among her recent publications is *Does a Southern European Model Exist?* (2001) (with various authors).

David L. Gladstone is an Assistant Professor at the College of Urban and Public Affairs, University of New Orleans. He has written on urban tourism and economic development and is currently writing a book on the nature and impact of tourism in developing countries.

Chris Hamnett is Professor of Geography at King's College London. He was previously Professor of Urban Geography at the Open University. Among his publications are *Winners and Losers: The Housing Market in Modern Britain*, *Unequal City: London in the Global Arena*, and *Shrinking the State: Privatization in Comparative Perspective*. He has held numerous visiting appointments including Nuffield College Oxford and the Netherlands Institute of Advanced Studies. He currently holds an advisory professorship at East China Normal University, Shanghai.

Hartmut Häussermann was Professor for Urban Sociology and Local Administration at the Universities of Kassel and Bremen. Since 1993, he has been teaching at Humboldt-University of Berlin. President of Research Committee 21 of the ISA, his research interests include changes and restructuring of the united Berlin, new forms of social and spatial segregation and exclusion in European cities, and urban governance.

Daniel Hiernaux-Nicolas is the Director of the Human Geography Program at the Metropolitan Autonomous University of Mexico City, Campus Iztapalapa. He is a specialist in tourism studies and urban and regional questions in Mexico and the author of numerous books about these topics. His latest work is *Metropolis and Ethnicity* (in Spanish), published by El Colegio Mexiquense, 2000. His most recent research is a study of social tourism in Mexico, financed by the Federal Ministry of Tourism.

Lily M. Hoffman is Associate Professor of Sociology and Director of the Rosenberg/Humphrey Program in Public Policy at City College/CUNY, and a member of the sociology faculty at the CUNY Graduate Center. She has written (with Jiri Musil) about urban tourism in post-Communist Prague. She is interested in how restructuring economies affect formerly marginalized inner-city communities with a focus on issues of social and spatial inclusion/exclusion. She is the author of *The Politics of Knowledge: Activist Movements in Medicine and Planning* (SUNY Press).

Dennis R. Judd is a Professor in the Department of Political Science, University of Illinois at Chicago. He is editor of the "Globalization and Community" book series for the University of Minnesota Press. He has published extensively on urban politics, urban development, urban tourism, and related subjects. Most recently he co-edited with Susan S. Fainstein *The Tourist City* and edited *The Infrastructure of Play: Building the Tourist City* (M. E. Sharpe, 2003).

Marc V. Levine is Director of the Center for Economic Development and Director of the Center for Canadian-American Policy Studies at the University of Wisconsin-Milwaukee, where he is Professor of History and Urban Studies. He also holds a visiting professorship at l'Institut National de la Recherche Scientifique-Urbanisation at l'Université du Québec in Montreal. He is the author or co-author of four books, including, most recently, *La Reconquête de Montréal*, and he has written numerous articles on urban development, economic policy, and social inequality. He is currently working on a book comparing the impact of tourism-based urban redevelopment in Baltimore and Montreal since the 1960s.

Guido Martinotti holds the Chair of Urban Sociology at the Università degli studi di Milano-Bicocca, in which he is also currently Pro-rector. Since 1985 he has been annually Visiting Professor at the Department of Sociology of the University of California at Santa Barbara. He has been

Chairman of the Standing Committee for the Social Sciences of the European Science Foundation, member of the board of the European Science and Technology Assembly and is currently Chairman of the Social Science Committee of Academia Europaea. He has written extensively on urban social change and the sociology of knowledge.

Patrick Mullins is Reader in Sociology at the University of Queensland. He has had a long-standing interest in the way tourism effects new urban forms, with his research focusing empirically on Australia's two major tourist centers, the Gold Coast and the Sunshine Coast. Currently he is involved in an international study of urban quality of life, as a member of the Australian research team that is examining quality of life in South East Queensland, a rapidly growing urban region that includes the Gold Coast and the Sunshine Coast.

Noam Shoval is a lecturer in the Department of Geography of the Hebrew University of Jerusalem. He conducted his post-doctoral research at the Department of Geography, King's College, University of London (2000–1). He was the recipient of the Lord Goodman Chevening Post-doctoral fellowship (2000) and a Fulbright post-doctoral award (2000). His main research interests are tourism and culture as tools for urban regeneration, models of hotel location, spatial activity of tourists and tourism management in heritage cities.

Pieter Terhorst is Associate Professor of Urban and Economic Geography at the University of Amsterdam, Department of Geography and Planning. His published works concern housing, the informal economy, and regimes and urban trajectories.

Jacques van de Ven is Associate Professor of Economic Geography at the University of Amsterdam and Professor of Urban Affairs at the College of Professional Education at The Hague.

Series Editors' Preface

The Blackwell *Studies in Urban and Social Change* series aims to advance theoretical debates and empirical analyses stimulated by changes in the fortunes of cities and regions across the world. Among topics taken up in past volumes and welcomed for future submissions are:

- Connections between economic restructuring and urban change
- Urban divisions, difference, and diversity
- Convergence and divergence among regions of east and west, north, and south
- Urban and environmental movements
- International migration and capital flows
- Trends in urban political economy
- Patterns of urban-based consumption and symbolic systems

The series is explicitly interdisciplinary; the editors judge books by their contribution to intellectual solutions rather than according to disciplinary origin.

Proposals may be submitted to members of the series Editorial Committee:

Harvey Molotch
Linda McDowell
Margit Mayer
Chris Pickvance

Preface

This book had its genesis in a research collective, the International Tourism Research Group (ITRG), funded by the Council for European Studies. Although tourism had become an increasingly important sector of the global economy and shaper of cities, scholarship had yet to treat it with the seriousness accorded to other urban topics. Our aim was to place tourism within a theoretical perspective so as to enable comparative research. Our group, made up of eminent urban scholars from a number of countries, met three times. Our first meeting was held in Amsterdam in April 1998; we subsequently met in Montreal and in Barcelona. The meetings were considerably enhanced by the tourism opportunities presented by the three cities in which we conferred and the stimulating company of our conferees.

At our last meeting we decided to place tourism and travel within the framework of regulation theory. We struggled together to fit empirical data within a theoretical framework that would allow the complexities of scale and the multidimensionality of factors with which we were engaged to remain intact. The individual chapters of this book, which originated as papers presented at this conference, reflect our ongoing effort toward analytic clarity.

We wish to thank the Council for European Studies for its initial grant, and City College of the City University of New York, the University of Missouri at Saint Louis, the University of Amsterdam, and the University of Illinois at Chicago for their ongoing support. Many individuals also contributed to this book. We appreciate the able assistance of Núria Claver, Gina Neff, Grace Han, Roosmarijn Gerritsma, Aitor Gómez and Daniel Bliss.

Lily M. Hoffman
Susan S. Fainstein
Dennis R. Judd

Introduction

Susan S. Fainstein, Lily M. Hoffman, and Dennis R. Judd

In recent decades cities have fought hard to insert themselves into the "space of flows" of global tourism (Castells 2000). The scale of investment has been significant: In only two or three decades, the infrastructure of travel has transformed cityscapes, prompted the construction of airports, mass transportation systems, and urban amenities, and even forced governments to address long-standing environmental problems (Judd et al. 2002). Urban regimes have especially focused on the competition for tourists because, unlike other economic sectors where central cities lose out to peripheral areas, in the case of tourism, the urban core dominates the metropolitan area. Their history, architectural heritage, inimitable cultural assets and qualities, and clusters of amenities give older central cities built-in advantages as tourist destinations. Even within resort areas where travelers may be seeking beauty and solitude, major agglomerations boasting multiple sites for shopping and dining typically spring up. Though some aspects of urban tourism may be suburbanizing, the advantages that favor cities are not likely to disappear.

Cities have attempted to attract tourists by persuading national governments to finance large tourism-related infrastructure projects and by promoting such projects on their own. Many of the bitterest political issues in recent decades have revolved around the question of whether disproportionate resources should be devoted to the promotion of middle-class leisure when poverty and its attendant social problems are neglected

(Harvey 2001: 345–68; Eisinger 2000). Despite criticisms about its effects, however, the high priority afforded to tourist development by city leaders will undoubtedly continue, in light of its character as an export industry that offers opportunities for unskilled workers.

Tourism, as well as comprising a major economic sector within cities, carries important symbolic weight. It depends on imagery for its appeals, and tourists bring with them a set of perceptions that filter and refract the urban scene. Their expectations then combine with the indigenous culture as well as the strategic considerations of urban regimes and tourism firms to reshape the city.

Theoretical Framework

A useful approach to understanding the impacts of tourism is through recognizing that, like other economic sectors, it is governed by regulatory frameworks constituted at different geographic scales. Within cities local regimes of accumulation specify, within the limits of their context, "the broad relationships between production, consumption, savings and investment" (Lauria 1997a: 6). Regulation, broadly conceived, refers to the institutional structures that support and stabilize a given regime of accumulation (i.e. of capitalist profitability) – both the formal rules imposed by institutions as well as the informal norms and expectations that arise from social and cultural patterns (Amin 1994a). Usually applied to the national level, arguments about regulation can be extended to the urban regime (see Lauria 1997b). Doing so raises the following questions:

- Do the institutions, rules and regulations of a globalized tourism industry increasingly reduce difference and variation in urban tourism?
- Alternatively, does urban tourism vary significantly from place to place because it reflects local political realities and local cultures?

As we shall indicate, the chapters in this volume point to both phenomena. International flows of capital, multinational corporations, and imitative marketing produce standardization, even while differing local regimes, cultures, and conscious efforts at differentiation produce distinctive tourism locales. Moreover, because the tourism experience is produced by the tourist as well as by the service provider, the character of the interaction between the two is more open that that of most other relationships between purchaser and supplier and in some ways compares to the relationship between artist and viewer.

What is tourism?

Studies of travel and tourism tend to take their subject matter for granted. Thus, the "travel" literature implies that people go on trips to seek the exotic – sometimes the distinction is made between traveler and tourist, with the former occupying the more honored status. The tourism industry's trade literature, on the other hand, focuses on those pursuing such mundane activities as attending meetings, visiting clients, or going shopping, while sociological and anthropological studies usually limit themselves to consumers of leisure and entertainment. We, however, make no assumptions about the purpose of travel and do not privilege one type of visitor over another.

Our principal concern is the way in which cities are shaped by efforts to attract and control visitors and by the economic, spatial, and cultural impact of non-residents living within them for limited times. We have thus entitled this volume *Cities and Visitors* rather than *Cities and Tourists*. We shall employ the term tourist interchangeably with visitor and traveler, because that is the common usage, but the reader should keep in mind that we intend the most expansive meaning in regard to the tourist's motivation. We take this position because, in terms of urban development, different types of tourists may use the same facilities (e.g. hotels) and because many trips are multi-purpose. Thus, the business traveler may well shop or visit a museum and will almost certainly dine out. In fact, in the year 2000, an estimated 60 percent of frequent travelers took time out for leisure while on business trips (Collins 2001: 7). The impacts of tourism on cities would be fundamentally different if cities were responding to travelers whose only purpose was to consume entertainment and culture. Although a voluminous travel literature plays upon the distinction between mere tourists and intrepid souls on the path of discovery, surely such people are exceedingly rare. Moreover, the literature produced by self-styled adventurers (who are often professional travel writers) feeds into commodification by becoming a source of images mined by the tourism industry, thereby blurring the initial differentiation between tourists and adventurers.

Our definition of tourism is consonant with that of the World Tourism Organization (WTO), which defines a tourist as any person who stays away from home overnight for a limited time (WTO 1995). It encompasses people traveling to visit relatives, make a deal, inspect a branch facility, attend a meeting, install a computer system, search for a job or another home, as well as those seeking cultural enrichment or entertainment. Nevertheless, while we do not narrowly restrict our definition of tourism, we remain interested in the motives of visitors, which are shaped by and respond to industrial sectors dedicated to satisfying and manipulating their needs. Because we wish to understand the interaction between cities and visitors, we must examine the principal intermediary in this relationship – the industries that produce the desires, images, products, infrastructure, and venues that they consume. This task is difficult, however, since the boundaries between industries serving tourists and those providing services to residents and commuters are extremely permeable and ambiguous.

The tourism industry

A global tourism production system maintains a commanding position in directing and influencing tourist flows (Ioannides 1995). The principal players at this scale are international firms such as airlines, credit card companies, hotel and resort chains, and tour operators. These organizations achieve economies of scale through the delivery of standardized services and products to masses of tourists (Barber 1995: 130–1), although techniques of flexible specialization make it simultaneously possible to project a contrived sense of variation (Britton 1991). At the same time, there is genuine variation in the interaction between global institutions and the places of tourism. When global suppliers of products and services penetrate into local environments, even highly standardized products may be modified (McDonald's serving wine in Paris, for example, or lamburgers – the "Maharaja Mac" – in India).

Except for long-distance transportation services, no supplier exclusively serves tourists. Even hotels receive an important part of their revenues from acting as venues for events with local clienteles (ranging from the purely local, like Rotary Club meetings, to more mixed, like weddings and other celebrations). As a result, obtaining accurate data on the economic effects of tourism is difficult and depends heavily on estimates concerning the proportion of shoppers, diners, museum-goers, sports fans, etc. that come from out of town. The term "tourism-related" applies to industries that attract substantial numbers of tourists without being dominated by them. Consequently, the regulatory structure within which tourism functions also has vague boundaries.

Global and local

The institutions, rules, and regulations that govern urban tourism are constituted at different scales. Moreover, the relationships between the global and the local are complex and highly contingent. For example, most of the consumer products sold to urban tourists (such items as logo cups and Tshirts) travel global circuits of manufacture and distribution, and companies with global reach provide the amenities and services (such as atrium hotels, gourmet cuisine, and fine wine) demanded by an affluent middle class with cosmopolitan tastes. Still, the leveling tendencies of globalization are mediated by state regulations, local initiatives, and an "urban imaginary" composed of "the set of meanings about the city that arise in a specific historical and cultural space" (Hannigan 1998: 195). In sum, the relative mix of the global and the local cannot simply be assumed.

As with other global flows, the effect of tourists on specific places is shaped powerfully by the particularities of history, culture, politics, and social relations (Abu-Lughod 1999). In some cities tourism has exerted a powerful presence over a long period. Venice, for example, has drawn visitors for more than 200 years, and, of course, from its founding it was shaped fundamentally by traders from distant places. In contrast, in a process that Mullins (1991) has called tourism urbanization, cities built expressly for tourists have sprung up all over the globe in the recent past. New resort cities have urbanized previously undeveloped areas such as the Gold Coast of Australia and both coasts of Mexico (Hiernaux-Nicolas 1999).[1] Cities like Las Vegas tend to deny local flavor and history lest they distract visitors from the main event, gambling. Tourist-historic cities, on the other hand, promote a unique architectural and historical legacy. A subset of this type, cities of culture, exists in Europe, where large investments in festivals, amenities, mega-events, and infrastructure have been used to revive and secure historic centers in cities like Barcelona (van den Berg et al. 2003). Older industrial cities have converted themselves into tourist destinations by building an infrastructure for the purpose of attracting visitors. Because these cities remained mostly unattractive or were even repellent to visitors, a specialized and often fortified tourist space was typically inserted into the old industrial and slum landscape.

The different types of tourist city are governed by different regulatory strategies. Resort cities conform most purely to the image of cities as theme parks, though much of the literature on urban tourism expresses the fear (or conviction) that all cities are traveling down the same path (Sorkin 1992; Hannigan 1998; Reichl 1999). Cities dominated by tourism enterprises are characterized by a hierarchical, coordinated, standardized control of nearly all aspects of the tourist experience (Judd, ch. 1, this volume). Tourist-historic cities manage tourist flows while preserving the architectural and historical features that give them their particular character. As in Venice and Bruges, tourist flows represent both a danger and the lifeblood for tourist-historic cities. A significant amount of formal planning and administration is devoted to promoting and preserving such places, both to keep them from becoming overwhelmed by the crush of visitors and to preserve the qualities that make them distinctive.

Industrial cities that have converted to tourism have their own peculiar set of problems. In addition to the imperative of insulating tourists from areas outside tourist enclaves, these cities – especially in the United States – must also find a way to finance expensive new infrastructure within the context of tight fiscal constraints and, often, in the face of political opposition. New institutional arrangements – business improvement districts, tax increment finance districts, specialized development authorities, etc. – have grown up to finance and manage the various components of tourism. The Cities of Culture designated by the European Union have also utilized public/private authorities, but these have normally been much more inclusive and have engaged in planning on a larger scale than is possible in US cities (van den Berg et al. 2003).

In sum, though much work remains to be done to tease out the details, we can assert that a rich institutional structure has emerged to regulate local tourism. To theorize urban tourism, it is useful to understand how these institutions create tourism as a product, how they manage the processes of accumulation, how they regulate the relationship between capital and labor, and how they are situated in urban space.

Types of Regulation

Economic production in tourism as in other industries proceeds within a mode of regulation that governs industrial structure, workforce participation, customer relations, and the broader socio-political context within which the industry operates. Approaches to describing the ways in which attitudes and behavior make for predictability and trust have flourished in recent years under the rubrics of both regulation theory and the "new institutionalism" (Healey 1999; North 1990). We have chosen to employ the vocabulary of the former approach, but the set of explicit rules and implicit understandings surrounding tourism could as well be expressed in terms of the latter. Investigating tourism within either analytic framework requires insights into the relationship between various scales of tourism development.

The extent to which regulation constructs the character of tourism becomes strikingly evident when we compare it to other economic sectors. Very little of the tourism infrastructure is physical – only transportation vehicles and the buildings in which tourism activities take place. Most of tourism production and consumption is perceptual and intangible. Purchasing a tourist experience differs from buying other items like furniture and cars, where, even though sales depend somewhat on associated fantasies, objective performance tests exist. Relations between buyer and seller also deviate from those in other service industries. Unlike, for example, bank clients, who also display high levels of trust (Giddens 1990), tourists operate in unfamiliar surroundings and are negotiating non-routine circumstances. Much of the tourism regulatory system aims to reduce strangeness and impose predictability, thereby providing the visitors with a feeling of safety. The paradox, however, is that total achievement of this goal diminishes the lure of participation, at least for that segment of the consumer base seeking adventure.

At the same time, as has become especially noticeable after September 11, 2001, places need protection from travelers. The threat of terrorism frightens residents and scares away potential visitors. This newly perceived risk overlays earlier problems presented by strangers, who frequently posed as tourists in order to overcome barriers to immigration. The need to monitor visitors, however, presents challenges for an industry and for places that must present an inviting ambiance to achieve their economic goals. Furthermore, efforts to restrict threats from potential terrorists and to block illegal immigration, as well as posing difficulties for the industry, impinge on the most fundamental of civil rights, that of free movement.

Because for visitors the object of consumption is place itself, and because tourists interact with place and industrial producers more intensely than do purchasers of other goods and services, tourism operates within a more entangling web of regulations than do other industries. As will be discussed below, it is in the regulation of the city and of the visitor that the formal and informal rules governing travel and tourism differ from those affecting other industries, at least in extent, if not in kind. In contrast, within the areas of labor-management relations and industry operations, regulatory functions resemble those conducted elsewhere.

There are four types of regulatory frameworks that structure relations within the tourism milieu, of which the first two are distinctive: (1) regulation of visitors to protect the city; (2) regulation of the city for the benefit of visitors and the tourism industry; (3) regulation of labor markets for the benefit of capital, labor, and place; and (4) regulation of the industry for the benefit of place, consumers, and labor. The chapters in this book use qualitative case studies of tourism in different locales to show how these different types of regulation operate singly and in combination to create particular tourist settings, with different chapters emphasizing different aspects of the regulatory framework.

Regulating the visitor to protect the city

Before September 11, 2001, the principal danger that tourists presented was environmental degradation caused by their swamping and Disneyfying the sites to which they flocked. Only a few touristic places (e.g. London,

Jerusalem, Srinagar) had long coped with the menace of terrorism. Although some (e.g., undocumented aliens) were considered undesirable, most places had only weak apparatuses for sorting out acceptable from unacceptable visitors. Principal responsibility for ensuring that visitors were not threatening or unwanted lay with national authorities operating at national borders. Now, however, urban governments are pulled between the contradictory needs to be welcoming to travelers and wary that outsiders may intend harm. Formerly the surveillance cameras primarily focused on residents who might injure visitors; now the possibility of visitors with hostile motives has swung the security apparatus toward the newcomer (see Body-Gendrot, ch. 2, this volume). And, as Martinotti (1999) points out, visitors, even when they are citizens of the same country, have only limited political and civil rights. When they are foreigners, they have almost no rights.[2]

Regulating the city

The commercial leadership and government of some cities – for example, Venice, Italy, and San Diego, California – have recognized the importance of tourism to their economies for more than a century. What distinguishes the present era is that virtually every city sees a tourism possibility and has taken steps to encourage it. They have done so through city marketing, spatial reconstruction, and establishment of secure spaces. These actions result from a recognition that few visitors come to a place because of its unmediated appeal. Rather, its attractions need to be packaged and advertised so that potential customers will perceive their attractiveness.

MacCannell (1976: 10), in his well-known book *The Tourist*, argues that tourists desire "a more profound appreciation of society and culture . . . All tourists desire this deeper involvement with society and culture to some degree." MacCannell's argument, however, is tautological, since for him tourists are only those who travel with this motivation in mind. But, if we consider all those who visit a city, then he is probably not describing the motive of most. MacCannell is disturbed that the commodification of place undermines the goal of the anthropologically-minded visitor. But if we employ our broader definition of tourist as any outsider who visits a city, then the kind of commodification he rues may well be welcome to many. The created image of the city, or at any rate its purpose-built tourist venues, may be precisely what the visitor seeks. This is particularly true for the most economically rewarding type of visitor, the business traveler, and standardized facilities are devised to meet his or her needs.

The images and structures of the tourist's city are the product of deliberate social and physical construction; thus, their character embodies the mode of regulation characterizing any place or era. From the perspective of those promoting the city's economic growth (i.e., the urban regime), the need is to attract travelers, which is accomplished through the provision of both appropriate material structures and expected symbolic referents or markers. MacCannell (1976: 113) contends that "more important than the sight [itself] . . . is some marker involvement." Thus, "sightseers do not, in any empirical sense, *see* San Francisco. They see Fisherman's Wharf, a cable car, the Golden Gate Bridge, Union Square, . . . [etc.] As elements in a set called 'San Francisco,' each of these items is a symbolic marker" (ibid.: 111, italics in original).

The extent to which attracting visitors requires physical reconstruction of the city depends on the segment of the tourism market that the city is addressing and on its social and material conditions. Tourist-historical cities may rely primarily on symbolic constructions, but converted cities, where the presence of low-income residents and unappealing structures could repel visitors, develop new infrastructure and at times "tourist bubbles" to make tourists feel secure (Judd 1999). The visitor may receive further protection in the form of surveillance cameras, visible security guards, and defended perimeters (Flusty 2001). Until recently the principal security concern in most cities was protection of the visitor from unsightly premises and criminal behavior (Goldstone 2001).

Labor market regulation

The tourism labor market has a double-edged quality for unskilled workers. On the one hand, it offers easy entry, even for people who do not speak the native language or possess documentation. On the other, it is an extreme example of labor market flexibility, providing low-wage, insecure employment with few benefit programs or career ladders. In the United States, as protection for labor under federal law has decreased, the mode of regulation has increasingly favored employers; elsewhere, even where labor laws are stricter than in the US, tourism workers have likewise suffered the loss of secure employment. Moreover, as pressure to limit the flow of illegal migrants has increased, restrictions on employment have grown. Most recently, for example, airport screeners in the United States have become federal employees, and non-citizens, who had previously dominated this category of employment in many cities, have been excluded from these jobs.

The kinds of regulation surrounding labor markets vary substantially from country to country, and within the United States, from city to city. Unionization, living wage legislation, and laws affecting wages, hours, and safety all constitute aspects of the regulatory or institutional framework surrounding work within tourism and tourism-related industries. The character of work life depends on numerous variables ranging from the political power of labor to the level of demand for tourism services to whether the job is "front of the house" or "back of the house," and whether workers and management are connected through kin relations. Therefore, much is contingent in terms of the situation of tourism workers. Nevertheless, while their situation varies, the rewards of the typical hotel and restaurant workers studied in this volume (Levine and Gladstone and Fainstein) are generally considerably less than those of workers in knowledge-based sectors. Knowledge-based tourism employment is emerging, however, related to conventions, business travel, events planning, and marketing.

Regulation of the industry

The extent to which suppliers of services and products to tourists are promoted and constrained by formal regulation differs according to whether the firm is small or big and whether or not it is locally owned. Regulators include national and local economic development and tourism offices, city governments, industry chains, and booking systems. The Internet, in a short period of time, has changed the institutional framework of tourism, diminishing the gatekeeper role of travel agents, increasing the power of the individual consumer, and offering small providers direct access to consumers. Thus, while information technology may reduce the need for travel by facilitating communication without proximity, it also encourages travel by making arrangements easier.

The industry itself is characterized by both Fordist and post-Fordist elements. Some sectors of the industry possess a particular marketing problem – they are inherently local but must sell their product to strangers. Consequently, franchising, branding and standardization are employed to create a commodity recognizable outside the local environment. As discussed above, however, standardization is desirable for certain categories of travelers, even while it goes against the wishes of others. Thus, operators within the industry must simultaneously differentiate themselves and appeal to potential consumers by offering familiar comforts. To a large extent firms rely on their context – the city in which they are located – to provide the basis for this differentiation and to act as marketing media.

Scale, Disaggregation, Difference

Examining cities and tourism only at the aggregated urban level obscures both the global forces at work and the intra-urban differences. We need to disaggregate and to make scale explicit. For example, the factors that draw visitors to New York City, when that metropolis is equated with Manhattan south of 96th Street, may differ from those that bring them to an area within the city such as Harlem, and these differences may in turn have differing consequences for the metropolitan area. Furthermore, assessment of the social and spatial effects of economic restructuring may vary depending upon what scale is used. To maximize the scaling potential of a regulation framework – its ability to help us examine the impact of larger economic and social forces on place – we need to identify the global forces and the specific local conditions at the appropriate level of analysis.

Global forces

In the past few decades we have seen the rise of new modes of production and integration together with new markets and market forces. Mass production has given way to flexible specialization (Amin 1994b); vertical hierarchy and concentration to more horizontal arrangements coordinated by a powerful information technology (Storper 1994). In advanced economies, saturated mass markets have resulted in the production of non-standardized goods and services for an increasingly differentiated population of consumers, corresponding not only to demographic variables of income, education, gender, and age, but also to lifestyle and cultural factors (Amin 1994b). This restructuring of production, management, marketing, and consumption has been characterized as post-Fordist in contrast to the Fordist paradigm of mass production for mass markets. In addition, the opening of formerly closed societies such as Russia and China has also transformed the global economy by providing new sites for production and consumption. Taken together, these large-scale global trends have stimulated flows of capital, people, and culture, with consequences for cities and tourism.

Much has been written about financial flows and the emergence of global cities as command centers, but less has been said about either the contributions of tourism to these flows or about the effect of flows of visitors on place. Multinational capital shapes localities in a variety of ways: designating and marketing local sites; linking them in regional and global networks; as well as influencing the planning process and physical layout of metropolitan areas (Roost 1998; Beauregard and Haila 2000; Häussermann and Colomb, ch. 11, this volume). The flow of financial capital itself has increased the overall movement of people, with visitors coming for work, trade shows, and training programs. Overall, the city's function as a center for entertainment, culture, and consumption is reinforced by the flow of business travelers.

Along with business travelers, immigrants and migrants are part of the stream of people, pushed and pulled by political as well as economic forces, heading towards cities, building ethnic enclaves of commerce and culture. Retaining their transnational identities and linkages (Smith 1997), these areas of difference and "otherness" quickly become attractive to both residents and visitors, as the general population – through work, study, leisure, and the media – becomes more cosmopolitan in taste.

Cultural flows not only result in the cultural standardization protested by the critics of globalization and represented by McDonald's or the Gap; they are also two-way streets that increase cultural differentiation as a greater diversity of cultural products and consumers enter the global marketplace. These products and services are purveyed not only by multinational corporations but also by small businesses and individuals who can directly access the global consumer via the Internet. In newly opening societies, tourism offers a relatively easy entrepreneurial start-up for individuals and an economic development strategy for localities (Hoffman and Musil 1999). Moreover, a large, easily forgotten segment of the tourism market consists of low-income travelers. These include religious pilgrims and "drifter tourists" (Edensor 1998; Gladstone 2001). This flow, which has grown rapidly as a consequence of cheap airfares, is much more likely to patronize small guesthouses and informal restaurants than chain establishments. While individually these travelers may spend little, in the aggregate their expenditures are substantial and support a vast array of small-scale businesses.

Tourism, a service sector industry which has experienced exponential growth over the past few decades, exemplifies many of these ongoing processes – from new modes of production and changing uses of technology to the development of new markets and demands. This, in turn, affects the social and spatial geography of cities and metropolitan areas. The emergence of urban tourism as a leading market niche is itself an example of these larger trends, illustrating the synergy of tourism with business networks and economic development in general.

Local variation

Discussion of whether the spatial impact of economic restructuring is the strengthening or weakening of localities typically refers to cities and regions in general (inter alia, Storper and Scott 1989; Amin and Malmberg 1994). Yet differentiation exists among cities and regions as well as within metropolitan areas, reflecting differences in demography (household composition, education, income, ethnicity); political economy (presence and size of specific industries, products and services, mix of public and private enterprise, mix of formal and informal economic activity); and regulatory practice (provision of security and cleanliness; planning practices such as zoning). At a time of economic restructuring, specific local conditions make a given area more or less attractive to the flows of capital, people, and culture that make for tourism.

Cities have traditionally been culturally and ethnically diverse – home to strangers – and their demography has been related to their dynamic and innovative potential. Yet, this has not always made for a positive assessment. In the US, urban diversity has contributed to a negative image (Beauregard 1993); cities have historically been associated with immigrants, minorities and the poor, and social mobility has meant moving to the suburbs.

The increasing centrality of culture and consumption to the economy of the city has raised the question of whether these trends exacerbate existing forms of social and spatial inequality or provide new opportunities for marginalized areas and populations. Overall, urban scholars have tended to agree that the city has been transformed from a place of production to a vast consumption mall with negative consequences for minorities and the poor, e.g. the loss of manufacturing jobs, the loss of public space, gentrification of neighborhoods (Harvey 1994; Zukin 1991, 1995). Such assumptions, however, may be misleading. The breakdown and differentiation of mass markets, and the other global forces which have brought cultural diversity to the fore, are giving rise to new forms of cultural capital, to phenomena such as niche marketing, and to the enhanced attractiveness of previously non-marketable places. This has affected urban tourism in general and specific metropolitan areas in particular, as illustrated by the case study of tourism development in Harlem (Hoffman, ch. 5, this volume). Whether cultural capital translates into social, economic, and/or political clout for formerly marginalized groups and the places with which they are identified, or becomes appropriated by traditional elites, must be examined empirically. We cannot merely assume that the same groups and places will remain in control.

In sum, this book seeks to provide a unifying and synthesizing framework for the study of urban tourism. Many of the major works on globalization have omitted tourism from their discussion. At the same time, urban scholars have treated visitors as marginal to the development of cities despite the current focus on tourism as an urban economic development strategy (except see Martinotti 1999). We believe that understanding the interaction between visitors and the city is fundamental to understanding twenty-first-century urban life – and even more so after the events of September 11, 2001.

Organization of the Book

The chapters that follow explore the interaction between global forces and particular local conditions in constructing, modifying, and maintaining the images and structures of urban tourism regimes. Although each chapter may describe several types of regulation, we have grouped them in terms of their main thrust – whether it is visitors, the city, labor markets, or the tourism industry.

Except for the chapters on Mexico and Australia's Gold Coast, we have focused on old cities in Europe and the United States. Thus, we have focused on places where catering to visitors required a transformation of urban space and customs. Broadening our scope to include developing countries was not possible within the confines of a single volume. We hope, however, that eventually such a companion work will appear.

In Part I, the authors take up the question of whether visitors are being subjected to regulation regimes that increasingly monitor and direct their movements. Dennis Judd in chapter 1 examines the assumption that urban tourists are controlled through the construction of fortress-like tourist enclaves. While agreeing that such controls operate in some places, he makes a case for the complexity and diversity of urban tourism. Not only does regulation take many forms, it can even be evaded. In chapter 2 Sophie Body-Gendrot addresses this issue through her analysis of the World Soccer Cup of 1998 and the Millennium celebration of 1999 in Paris. She argues that such mega-events make social control and security a major regulatory issue for historic cities, leading to a zero-tolerance mentality; empowering the national state (due to the need to plan at national, regional, and international levels); encouraging public/private partnerships; and introducing technologically sophisticated surveillance equipment that undermines civil liberties. In chapter 3 Costa and Martinotti who look at Venice, argue that it is essential to find ways to control and direct tourist numbers and activities – to create a sustainable tourism; otherwise, the city will simply become overwhelmed.

In Part II, the authors provide evidence that the spaces of urban tourism vary significantly and, indeed, that urban diversity is itself a draw. They do not confirm the worst fears of many critics that cities are being reduced to theme parks or transformed into standardized corporate environments; they even suggest that residents and local culture may benefit. Terhorst, van de Ven, and Deben in chapter 4 find that Amsterdam has achieved a style of tourism that combines the concerns of residents with the desire of tourists to consume urban culture. They examine how the city has attempted to maintain this "mix" in the face of a variety of challenges. Lily Hoffman's case study of central Harlem in chapter 5 analyzes the forces that make a seemingly unlikely inner-city area a tourism site. She describes how a restructuring post-Fordist economy, which valorizes cultural diversity as well as under-served markets, is making this formerly marginalized inner-city area marketable, thus repositioning Harlem in relation to New York City, New York State, and the region. In Barcelona, García and Claver in chapter 6 describe how a great deal of planning has gone into upscaling tourism because it is recognized as a critical economic sector for the city. Nevertheless, planning has sought to preserve and enhance those elements, such as its early twentieth-century modernist culture, that make Barcelona unique. Finally, Patrick Mullins, who developed the notion of tourism urbanization in regard to Australia, looks at trends in the phenomenon over time in chapter 7. In contrast to the emphasis on diversity in Amsterdam, New York, and Barcelona, he finds that cities developed specifically for tourism, as one would expect, tend to emphasize uniformity. Furthermore, since visitors come to the Gold Coast for access to nature, environmental regulation is the central concern.

Part III on labor markets introduces one of the more controversial issues associated with a tourism economy – that it is universally a low-wage, unstable labor market, and that tourism development should be shunned for this reason alone. Evaluation of this claim is hampered by the complexity of gaining an accurate statistical picture of the industry, given its overlap with entertainment, food, retailing, etc. In chapter 8 Gladstone and Fainstein compare capital-labor relations in New York City and Los Angeles to find that local labor rates and practices are dependent upon local political culture, particularly regarding labor organizations and community groups. They attribute the differences in labor-market outcomes to unionization in New York's hotel industry and the community-labor coalition for a living wage in Los Angeles. In chapter 9 Marc Levine shows that in Montreal the tourism labor market is constrained by a comparatively high level of unionization relative to US cities. Nevertheless, he concludes that, because of locally high unemployment and management strategies, outcomes are not radically different from those in the US. Like Gladstone and Fainstein, Levine finds that, generally, tourism and tourism-related activities produce low-wage, insecure jobs.

Part IV takes up the topic of regulating the tourism industry. States attempt to regulate tourism along with other industries by intervening in market processes and directing and mediating social, cultural, and environmental effects. Planning, public relations and promotional activities, taxation policies, and public/private partnerships are among the means to these ends. Overall the case studies show that as the economic and symbolic importance of tourism grows, state activity increases. Daniel Hiernaux-Nicolas in chapter 10 discusses the promotion of tourism in Mexico. He argues that state-directed mass tourism organized primarily along Fordist lines developed intensively after World War II, with the urging of international development institutions. More recently, in line with global trends toward privatization and the openness of national economies, tourism has become more flexible in its organization. In chapter 11 Haüssermann and Colomb recount the deliberate construction of "the New Berlin" as a post-industrial service center after the fall of the Berlin Wall in 1989, by a collaboration between investors and urban marketing professionals, local policy-makers, media, and cultural institutions. Examining the central role of tourism in the process, they state that even the construction sites were marked for visitors. In chapter 12 Hamnett and Shoval take up the museum – transformed through commodification from an elite institution to a "fun palace" with shops, restaurants, blockbuster exhibits, franchising, and branding – and tie this development to the central place of culture and arts in the post-industrial city. Economic prominence, they argue, has made the museum a "flagship of urban development and an important part of inter-urban competition."

Considered together, these chapters reveal that tourism may be a force for diversification and difference as much as for uniformity, and indicate some directions for systematic comparative study, while pointing to more progressive tourism policies. By using the paradigm of regulation as a unifying theme, they indicate the constraints on the interaction between cities and visitors, the forces that shape the operations of tourism and tourism-related industries, and the effect on urban form of a tourism-oriented economy.

NOTES

1   In an earlier work, Fainstein and Judd (1999) described three types of cities visited by tourists: (1) resort cities created expressly for tourism, like Las Vegas or Cancun; (2) tourist-historical cities that claim an inherited historic and cultural identity; and (3) converted cities with an infrastructure expressly created for tourism that is insulated from the larger urban milieu. Judd (1999) has coined the term "tourist bubble" to characterize areas marked off by "a well-defined perimeter [that] separates the tourist space from the rest of the city."

2   The case of Abdallah Higazy illustrates this point. An Egyptian student visiting New York was arrested and held incommunicado for more than a month. FBI agents claimed he had an aviation radio in his hotel room with a view of the World Trade Center on September 11. Eventually a private pilot, who had occupied a different room, claimed the radio (Fritsch 2002).

REFERENCES

Abu-Lughod, J. L. 1999: *New York, Chicago, Los Angeles: America's Global Cities*. Minneapolis, MN: University of Minnesota Press.

Amin, A. (ed.) 1994a: *Post-Fordism: A Reader*. Oxford: Blackwell.

—— 1994b: Post-Fordism: models, fantasies and phantoms of transition. In A. Amin (ed.), *Post-Fordism: A Reader*. Oxford: Blackwell, 1–40.

—— and Malmberg, A. 1994: Competing structural and institutional influences on the geography of production in Europe. In A. Amin (ed.), *Post-Fordism: A Reader*. Oxford: Blackwell, 227–48.

Barber, B. 1995: *Jihad vs. McWorld: Terrorism's Challenge to Democracy*, new introduction, 2001. New York: Ballantine Books.

Beauregard, R. A. 1993: *Voices of Decline*. New York: Blackwell.

—— and Haila, A. 2000: The unavoidable continuities of the city. In P. Marcuse and R. van Kempen (eds.), *Globalizing Cities: A New Spatial Order?* Oxford: Blackwell, 22–36.

Britton, S. 1991: Tourism, capital and place: towards a critical geography of tourism. *Environment and Planning D: Society and Space*, 9: 451–78.

Castells, M. 2000: *The Rise of the Network Society*, 2nd ed. Oxford: Blackwell.

Collins, R. 2001: Escaping the grind: work business travel for pleasure. *International Herald Tribune*, July 6, B1.

Edensor, T. 1998: *Tourists at the Taj: Performance and Meaning at a Symbolic Site*. New York: Routledge.

Eisinger, P. 2000: The politics of bread and circuses. *Urban Affairs Review* 35 (3): 316–33.

Fainstein, S. S. and Judd, D. R. 1999: Cities as places to play. In D. R. Judd and S. S. Fainstein (eds.), *The Tourist City*. New Haven, CT: Yale University Press, 261–72.

Flusty, S. 2001: The banality of interdiction: surveillance, control and the displacement of diversity. *International Journal of Urban and Regional Research* 25 (3): 658–64.

Fritsch, J. 2002: Grateful Egyptian is freed as US terror case fizzles. *New York Times*, January 18, 1.

Giddens, A. 1990: *The Consequences of Modernity*. Stanford, CA: Stanford University Press.

Gladstone, D. L. 2001: From pilgrimage to package tourism: a comparative study of travel and tourism in the Third World. PhD dissertation, Rutgers University, New Brunswick, NJ.

Goldstone, P. 2001: *Making the World Safe for Tourism*. New Haven, CT: Yale University Press.

Hannigan, J. 1998: *Fantasy City*. New York: Routledge.

Harvey, D. 1994: Flexible accumulation through urbanisation: reflections on 'postmodernism' in the American city. In A. Amin (ed.), *Post-Fordism: A Reader*. Oxford: Blackwell.

—— 2001: *Spaces of Capital: Towards a Critical Geography*. New York: Routledge.

Healey, P. 1999: Institutionalist analysis, communicative planning, and shaping places. *Journal of Planning Education and Research* 19: 111–21.

Hiernaux-Nicolas, D. 1999: Cancun bliss. In D. R. Judd and S. S. Fainstein (eds.), *The Tourist City*. New Haven, CT: Yale University Press, 124–42.

Hoffman, L. M. and Musil, J. 1999: Culture meets commerce: tourism in post-communist Prague. In D. R. Judd and S. S. Fainstein (eds.), *The Tourist City*. New Haven, CT: Yale University Press, 179–97.

Iaonnides, D. 1995: Strengthening the ties between tourism and economic geography: a theoretical agenda. *Professional Geographer* 47 (1): 49–60.

Judd, D. R. 1999: Constructing the tourist bubble. In D. R. Judd and S. S. Fainstein (eds.), *The Tourist City*. New Haven, CT: Yale University Press, 35–53.

——, Winter, W., Barnes, W., and Stern, E. (eds.) 2002: *Tourism and Entertainment as a Local Economic Development Strategy*. Washington, DC: National League of Cities.

Lauria, M. 1997a: Introduction: reconstructing urban regime theory. In M. Lauria (ed.), *Reconstructing Urban Regime Theory: Regulating Urban Politics in a Global Economy*. Thousand Oaks, CA: Sage, 1–10.

——1977b: *Reconstructing Urban Regime Theory: Regulating Urban Politics in a Global Economy*. Thousand Oaks, CA: Sage.

MacCannell, D. 1976: *The Tourist*. New York: Schocken.

Martinotti, G. 1999: A city for whom? Transients and public life in the second-generation metropolis. In R. A. Beauregard and S. Body-Gendrot (eds.), *The Urban Moment*. Thousand Oaks, CA: Sage, 155–84.

Mullins, P. 1991: Tourism urbanization. *International Journal of Urban and Regional Research* 15: 326–42.

North, D. 1990: *Institutions, Institutional Change, and Economic Performance*. Cambridge: Cambridge University Press.

Reichl, A. 1999: *Reconstructing Times Square*. Lawrence, KS: University Press of Kansas.

Roost, F. 1998: Recreating the city as entertainment center: the media industry's role in transforming Potsdamer Platz and Times Square. *Journal of Urban Technology* 5 (3): 1–21.

Smith, R. C. 1997: Transnational migration, assimilation, and political community. In M. E. Crahan and A. Vourvoulias-Bush (eds.), *The City and the World: New York's Global Future*. New York: Council on Foreign Relations, Inc., 110–32.

Sorkin, M. (ed.) 1992: *Variations on a Theme Park: The New American City and the End of Public Space*. New York: Hill and Wang.

Storper, M. 1994: The transition to flexible specialisation in the US film industry: external economies, the division of labour and the crossing of industrial divides. In A. Amin (ed.), *Post-Fordism: A Reader*. Oxford: Blackwell, 195–226.

——and Scott, A. 1989: The geographical foundations and social regulation of flexible production complexes. In J. Wolch and M. Dear (eds.), *The Power of Geography: How Territory Shapes Social Life*. Winchester, MA: Unwin Hyman.

van den Berg, L., van der Borg, J., and Russo, A. P. 2003: The infrastructure of urban tourism: a European model? In Dennis R. Judd (ed.), *The Infrastructure of Play: Building the Tourist City*. Armonk, NY: M.E. Sharpe.

World Tourism Organization 1995: *Compendium of Tourism Statistics, 1989–1993*. Madrid: World Tourism Organization.

Zukin, S. 1991: *Landscapes of Power: From Detroit to Disney World*. Berkeley, CA: University of California Press.

——1995: *The Cultures of Cities*. Oxford: Blackwell.

Part I
Regulating Visitors

1   Visitors and the Spatial Ecology of the City
    Dennis R. Judd

2   Cities, Security, and Visitors: Managing Mega-Events in France
    Sophie Body-Gendrot

3   Sociological Theories of Tourism and Regulation Theory
    Nicolò Costa and Guido Martinotti

1

Visitors and the Spatial Ecology of the City

Dennis R. Judd

In the post-structuralist urban literature,[1] enclaves represent local nodes of international circuits of capital and culture, though each of them may masquerade as a local space: gated communities, through the magic of marketing, become neighborhoods; malls are said to be the new marketplaces; and tourist bubbles offer simulacra of the cities they are replacing. As Michael Sorkin describes it, the "new city replaces the anomaly and delight of [local] places with a universal particular, a generic urbanism inflected only by appliqué" (1992: xiii). In his account, this new city is characterized by "rising levels of manipulation and surveillance" and "new modes of segregation," all put in the service of a "city of simulations, television city, the city as theme park" (Sorkin 1992: xiii–xiv). David Harvey echoes the frequently expressed concern that cities are being turned into sanitized, monotonous copies of one another, "almost identical from city to city" (1989: 295). Similarly, Chris Rojek describes a "universal cultural space" that "provides the same aesthetic and spatial references wherever one is in the world" (1995: 146).

By now an overwhelming consensus has emerged around the assertion that these enclaves are different from the public spaces of the past. Enclosure, it is said, facilitates new forms of domination. Tim Edensor proposes that the tourist enclave is a "total institution" of regulation that "materializes an ideology of consumption and regulates the performances of tourists" (1998: 52). Edensor echoes Lefebvre's observation that tourist spaces "are planned with the greatest care: centralized, organized, hierar-chized, symbolized and programmed to the nth degree" (1991: 384). Tilling the same ground, John Hannigan asserts that the uniformity of the spaces they inhabit subjects tourists to "a measured, controlled and orga-nized kind of urban experience" (1998: 6) that eliminates the unpredictable quality of everyday street life. Such views seem to inexorably confirm Daniel Boorstin's complaint, expressed as early as 1961, that tourists have become passive consumers of pleasure "isolated within tourist facilities" whose promoters specialize in sponsoring pseudo-events and performances (1961: 94, 97, 109).

In this chapter I contest the vision that foresees the future city as little more than an assemblage of fortified spaces colonized by global capital and affluent residents and visitors. Predictions of such a dismal urban dystopia seem warranted only if one's focus is restricted to a few cities. Some older manufacturing and port cities in the United States and England have shared a trajectory that seems to confirm the direst predic-tions: a steep decline during the deindustrialization of the 1970s and 1980s, followed by a style of revitalization that sharply segmented urban space, to the benefit of the affluent middle class and the detriment of the poor (Judd and Parkinson 1990). Baltimore may be taken as emblematic of this type of redevelopment; its famed Harborplace is a virtual reservation for visitors who rarely experience the rest of a troubled city (Hula 1990; Harvey 2001: 128–57). It makes sense that Los Angeles should inspire the "LA School" of urban geographers to theorize a fragmented and center-less city, because it is one (Dear 2002). Las Vegas has also become an object of fascinated scrutiny because it seems to provide a voyeuristic glimpse into a city that has been constructed as a façade of carnival and spectacle (Rothman and Davis 2002).

But it is hazardous to treat these and cities like them as harbingers of what all cities are destined to become. The fractured character of Baltimore, Los Angeles, and Las Vegas may be exceptional rather than archetypal. Despite the effects of globalization, cities vary significantly from one another, and they are not necessarily converging. Boston, for example, is a walking city for residents and visitors alike, notwithstanding the presence of the world's first Rouse mall at Faneuil Hall and an inter-connected mall and hotel complex at Copley Plaza (Ehrlich and Dreier 1999). The streets outside these enclosures are crowded with local residents and visitors, and visitors spill over into business and residential areas far more freely than a decade ago. Likewise, tourists are not confined within barricaded spaces in New York, San Francisco, or Chicago, despite the presence of tourist bubbles such as South Street Seaport, Ghirardelli Square, and the Magnificent Mile.

Tourist enclaves have become ubiquitous features within cities, but they do not inexorably overwhelm them. In assessing the spatial character of urban tourism, the scale of analysis is fundamental. Within tourist enclaves, a non-democratic, directive, and authoritarian regulation is attempted and generally achieved. But when urban tourism is considered at the scale of the city, enclaves generally capture only some of the visitors some of the time. Urban tourism does not operate, in most cities, as a "total institution" of regulation, and it is not likely that it will do so in the future. I pursue this line of argument in the remainder of this chapter.

The Construction of Tourist Enclaves

Until the rise of mass tourism in the latter half of the nineteenth century, cities held a special status as travel destinations. The cities of the Grand Tour of the fifteenth through the eighteenth centuries – mainly Paris, Geneva, Rome, Florence, Venice, Naples – were visited as a rite of passage by young men of the British upper class, who were expected to come of age by seeing "the ruins of classical Rome as well as the churches and palaces and art collections of the great Continental capitals" (Withey 1997: 7). The Grand Tour cities offered a veneer of high culture as well as abundant worldly diversions, but they were also often reviled. As the historian Lynne Withey has observed, the signs of poverty, social disorder, and physical decay were everywhere apparent in Rome, Naples, and Venice, and Paris was a warren of overcrowded streets filled with careening horses and wagons, strewn with garbage and running with sewage (Withey 1997).

Whatever the drawbacks of the Grand Tour cities, travelers were willing to brave weeks of discomfort to negotiate rutted roads and nearly impassable mountains, if necessary, to get to them. The hazards and inconvenience of travel sharpened a widely shared disdain for nature and the natural. Mountains were considered ugly and forbidding, seacoasts generally inaccessible and dangerous. By the mid-eighteenth century, however, such attitudes began to change. Nature was discovered as a vast repository of sublime views and vistas. The Romantic poets reinterpreted nature as a tamed backdrop of leafy bowers, stately trees, and placid lakes. With the rise of the industrial cities of the nineteenth century, the worship of nature reached full bloom, now interpreted through Thoreau, Wordsworth, and their contemporaries as the repository of the human spirit, as opposed to the meanness and gloom of the cities.

The "American Grand Tour" of the post-Civil War years provided a sharp contrast with its earlier European counterpart, with trips up the Hudson and Connecticut river valleys as "prime examples of the picturesque," and the Catskill Mountains and Niagara Falls as iconic examples of the "sublime" (Withey 1997: 117). But Europeans also visited such places as St Louis, Cincinnati, and Chicago to see the dramatic evidence of bustling progress and industry. They noted the grand hotels and mansions, riverboats, and steamships; recently arrived immigrants and even sometimes the occasional Indian, all combined into "a curious mixture of the civilized and the primitive" (Withey 1997: 131). Urban elites were convinced that visitors' perceptions might determine a city's economic prospects, and so they assiduously promoted (real and imagined) cultural, educational, and artistic accomplishments (Wade 1959).

European cities were reborn as tourist destinations by becoming stops on a democratized version of the Grand Tour. Beginning in the 1850s, Thomas Cook began the age of mass tourism by leading package tours to the continent. Cities promoted themselves as well, but as centers of industry more than of culture. The glorification of technology and progress supplied the common thread running through the fairs and exhibitions of the nineteenth and first decades of the twentieth centuries: London's Crystal Palace exposition of 1851 and the Paris Exhibition of 1867; across the ocean, the World's Fairs of Chicago in 1893, St Louis in 1904, and New York in 1938.

But such promotional activities were not sufficient by themselves to transform cities into tourist destinations. The cities of the industrial age were as often noted for their squalid slums and social problems as for their architectural and cultural treasures (Hall 1996: ch. 2). A visitor who chose to travel a city's streets randomly might well have many adventures, but not all would likely be welcomed. Urban tourism grew in tandem with the signposting of the sites and sights that visitors should seek out. When Thomas Cook began offering package tours to European cities, he took his charges to significant historical sites and to cultural attractions, arranged lodging, and provided essential information and assistance (Urry 1990: 24). By 1869 he was leading the first tourists to Jerusalem and the Holy Land, a business that mushroomed (through Thomas Cook and Son) to 5,000 visitors a year within a decade (Brendon 1991: 120–3).

Package tours demystified the place being visited by breaking it into manageable parts, each of which carried significance and meaning. By the turn of the century most major European cities had been thus interpreted through guidebooks, and guiding services had sprung up to compete with Cook. In the United States, a parallel process evolved, but local tourism entrepreneurs took the lead. Guidebooks, sketches, drawings, and photographs "coached" visitors about what to see and do. The representations and the physical spaces "played a key role in both making cities appealing to tourists and conveying a sense of social unity" (Cocks 2001: 144). Local tour operators translated the descriptions and representations found in guide books into physical reality by providing tourists with fixed itineraries, which reduced the cities they saw to a mélange of monuments, historical sites, and cultural facilities. The tourist experience on mass transportation and guided tours reduced the city to a panorama of a "passing city" seen in a "spectatorial, fascinated manner" (ibid.: 164). World's Fairs and exhibitions embellished the habit of seeing cities as a collage of stylized urban images and set scenes. As one visitor observed about the World's Columbian Exposition at the Chicago World's Fair of 1893, "The Fair is a world . . . in which ugliness and useless[ness] have been extirpated, and the beautiful and useful alone admitted" (ibid.: 128). The City Beautiful movement derived much of its inspiration from the Chicago World's Fair, with its focus on monumental architecture, parks, and public spaces.

Half a century later, a similar process of image-making and spatial reconstruction unfolded. By the 1960s in the United States the older industrial cities were faced with the physical dilapidation of downtowns and the spread of blight through miles of neighborhoods surrounding the core. The massive clearance projects financed by urban renewal failed to bring a renaissance, and any improvements from the federal grant programs of the 1960s and 1970s were overshadowed by crime, riots, and social unrest. Republican candidates and the media portrayed cities as outposts of violence and racial problems, so that terms like *ghetto, welfare, the underclass, crime,* and *the inner city* became conflated into interchangeable images (Edsall and Edsall 1991). As a result, a narrative of urban decline entered the national consciousness that mostly erased the positive images that cities might have inherited from the past (Beauregard 1993).

A generation of "Messiah mayors" burst onto the American scene in the 1980s, proclaiming a gospel of self-help and renewal (Teaford 1990). By using tax breaks and subsidies and new public/private partnerships, they stimulated a remarkable period of regeneration. Especially in older cities, a tourist bubble took form around a cluster of facilities and amenities (new waterfronts, atrium hotels, festival malls, convention centers, sports stadiums, entertainment districts), a space or series of spaces segregated from the remainder of the city. By building fortress spaces, even the most crime-ridden cities were able to carve out islands and reservations that could comfortably be inhabited by tourists and middle-class city residents.

In the ensuing years, enclavic tourist spaces have multiplied throughout the world. Stephen Graham and Simon Marvin predict the global proliferation of fantasy cities that bundle together retailing, restaurants and bars, performance halls, cinemas and IMAX theatres, hotels, video and virtual reality centers, and other diversions into an all-consuming environment of consumption and entertainment (2001: 265). Even now, a world traveler can find versions of these entertainment complexes scattered all over the globe (Iyer 2000).

Plate 1.1   Times Square, New York, entertainment complex. *Source*: Corbis

Tourist Enclaves as "Total Regulation" Regimes

Baudrillard's analysis of sites of consumption as cultural fields composed of "a sign-consuming totality" is helpful in understanding how the managers of tourist enclaves may attempt to regulate their users. Baudrillard writes that shopping centers are places in which "art and leisure mingle with everyday life" and constitute, in effect, subcultures of their own that establish a perfect context for consumption through "the total conditioning of action and time" (Baudrillard 1998: 28, 29). They allow desire and satiation to be blended into a super-heated mixture in which all sensations become overwhelmed by a pandemonium composed of a "sweeping vista of perpetual shopping" (ibid.: 30). Enclavic tourist spaces may operate similarly, by enveloping visitors within an environment that floods their senses with the signs and symbols of consumption and play.

Such experiences may be conceived as comprising a totalizing environment that filters the tourists' perceptions, experiences, and desires. This is akin to Bourdieu's *habitus*, a constellation of the dispositions and attitudes, practices, and representations that organize everyday life (Bourdieu 1990a), or (in Aboulafia's excellent summary) "the home of our non-reflexive engagement with the world" (Aboulafia 1999: 166). As a constellation of behaviors, *habitus* can, in effect, act as an agent protecting itself from change and disruptions, but "it" can also make choices to deflect challenges to its continued existence:

> Early experiences have particular weight because the *habitus* tends to ensure its own constancy and its defence against change through the selection it makes within new information . . . Through the systematic "choices" it makes among the places, events and people that might be frequented, the *habitus* tends to protect itself from crises and critical challenges by providing itself with a milieu to which it is as pre-adapted as possible. (Bourdieu 1990b: 60–1)

The tourists who inhabit enclavic spaces are encouraged to act, essentially, like factory workers subjected to "the time-sheet, the timekeeper, the informers, and the fines" (Thompson 1967). Because they are bounded by physical barriers and are designed for specialized activities, venues such as sports stadiums, convention centers, and malls may accomplish an almost total regulation of the body. Sports stadiums and convention centers, for example, are designed for the sole purpose of performance, and users who have other activities in mind are apt to be thrown out. Likewise, shopping malls are built as palaces of consumption; aimless loitering is discouraged or forbidden. Though they sometimes masquerade as public spaces, such confining environments project a "finite, or finished, aspect" that directs everything inward (Lefebvre 1991: 147). As Edensor has noted, these spaces may become as subject to the "remorseless surveillance through panopticon visual monitoring" as the carceral networks described by Foucault (Foucault 1977; Edensor 1998).

Enclavic tourist spaces are designed to regulate their inhabitants through the control of four principal aspects of agency: desire, consumption, movement, and time. Desire and consumption are regulated by promotion and marketing. Time and movement are strictly confined (by corridors, turnstiles, escalators, tunnels and tubes) and monitored (by security cameras and security guards). The use of time is also constrained by the scheduling of staged spectacles and performances and by physical features such as the availability or absence of seating and gathering places. The experiences and products on offer combine homogeneity and heterogeneity – enough of the former to give a sense of comfort and familiarity, enough of the latter to induce a sense of novelty and surprise.

Activities except those encouraged by corporate sponsors are often intercepted or forbidden. Malls routinely prohibit political activities of any kind, and security forces are quick to escort conspicuous non-consumers off the premises. The way that this works can be discerned in the opening of the World Financial Center in New York City in October 1988. The advertising agents for the developer, Olympia & York, staged five days of celebrations, all intended to convey (in the advertising firm's language) "a progressive understanding of the uses of public space." As it transpired, the celebrations were tied closely to the marketing needs of the businesses located in the Center. The sponsored activities defined and strictly limited the activities of the participants, who were reduced to the status of passive observers (Boyer 1994: 468).

If cities were composed mainly of archipelagos of enclaves, visitors and local inhabitants would scarcely be able to escape the close surveillance and control that enclavic space facilitates. However, enclaves constitute only one component of an increasingly complex spatiality of urban tourism. The environments inhabited by city visitors run the gamut from spaces built specifically for the production of spectacle and consumption, to public spaces such as waterfronts, parks, and plazas, to business and residential streets. This complex geography provides plenty of opportunity for visitors to escape the confines of enclosure.

The Complex Spatiality of Urban Tourism

Visitors to some cities find it difficult to move freely about. Most visitors to Detroit quickly exhaust the attractions of the Renaissance Center and Greektown, but they walk into the surrounding city at their own peril. Visitors to Baltimore are generally advised to avoid the "other Baltimore" that lies outside the Harborplace development, with its broad marble and stone plazas, Rouse mall, aquarium, restaurants and bars, and luxury hotels (Hula 1990; Harvey 2001: 128–57). In Las Vegas virtually all visitors are confined within casinos, hotels, and malls. But these cities lie at the extreme of a continuum. Typically, enclaves inhabited by visitors coexist with downtown business districts, streets populated with local small businesses and shops, neighborhoods, and public buildings, and public spaces.

Enclaves are generally incorporated into an urban texture which has itself become an object of fascination and consumption. As Sassen and Roost have observed, "the large city has assumed the status of exotica. Modern tourism is no longer centered on the historic monument, concert hall, or museum but on the urban scene or, more precisely, on some version of the urban scene fit for tourism" (1999: 143). The "scene" that visitors consume is composed of a kaleidoscope of experiences and spaces devoted to work, consumption, leisure, and entertainment (Featherstone 1994: 394–7).

The areas in cities inviting tourists to wander about may not be places normally inhabited by tourists at all; they may be "edgy" – transitional neighborhoods or zones where people are on the margins of urban society

– places where ethnic minorities, non-whites, immigrants, and poor people may live and work. Such areas may be attractive precisely because they have not been constructed for and do not provide for tourists. Outside of the usual comfort zone, the tourist can stroll into an interesting and unpredictable intellectual and physical space. As expressed by an artist living in such a neighborhood, "Along with the danger there's a vitality . . . when you're sure of personal safety there's a certain edge goes away. And there's something exciting having that edge" (Lloyd 2002: 528).

In European cities that do not have the extremes of segregation, crime, racial tensions, and social problems of some older cities in the United States and of cities in developing countries, visitors tend to be absorbed into the urban fabric. Leo van den Berg and his collaborators have proposed that there is a "European Model" that emphasizes the "harmonious development of the city" rather than the construction of segregated tourist spaces (van den Berg et al. 2003). Their studies of Rotterdam, Amsterdam, Lisbon, and Birmingham show that planners and policy-makers in those cities weigh the costs of tourism by taking into account "displacement of resident-oriented activities, gentrification, and cultural friction" (van den Berg 2003).

Such a balancing of local needs and economic development projects requires an over-arching political vision that is rarely possible in cities where leaders feel desperate for development at almost any cost. In European cities, the unique architectural and cultural heritage of urban cores has been understood to be the main attraction for visitors; as a consequence, tourism development has been aimed at enhancing the character of each city. Similarly, planners in Vancouver, Canada, have regarded tourism as a natural by-product of policies that emphasize neighborhoods, urban amenities, and the environment (Artibise 2003). Even in Montreal, a city that has emphasized mega-projects such as Expo 67 (the 1967 World's Fair) and the 1976 Summer Olympics, as well as other large projects, no tourist bubble has developed; visitors to the city often wander through the downtown and the neighborhoods (Levine 2003). Mexico City is an especially interesting case because it has focused its energies on the development of an enclave in the historic center – a strategy virtually forced on the city by its high crime rates. But despite these conditions, planners are trying to make the enclave a place desirable for local residents as much as for visitors (Hiernaux-Nicolas 2003).

The changing geography of urban spatial structure reflects the rise of an urban culture that revolves around "quality of life" concerns (Clark et al. 2002; Lloyd 2002). It is increasingly difficult to distinguish visitor from "local" spaces because leisure, entertainment, and cultural sectors are sustained as crucially by local residents as by out-of-town visitors. When not traveling elsewhere, local residents frequently engage in activities that are indistinguishable from what tourists do: dine out, go to the mall, walk along the waterfront, attend a concert. The rise of a new urban culture devoted to aesthetic pursuits has remade cities into places that provide the consumption opportunities of travel right at home: "Consumers no longer travel vast distances to experience a magnificent diversity of consumption opportunities. For their convenience, flourishing districts of urban entertainment concentrate objects, or at least their facsimiles, [gathered] from the world over . . . Residents increasingly act like tourists in their own cities" (Lloyd 2000: 7).[2] The resulting "localization of leisure" has stimulated, as much as has tourism, the conversion of cities or parts of cities into specialized venues for entertainment (Hannigan 1998: 61).

A globalized consumer culture has spread to embrace the middle classes in developing and developed countries, and the bundles of consumer goods they desire have become remarkably similar. Sassen has documented the concentration of a class of highly paid workers in the services sector in global cities; however, in actuality the new global class of privileged "symbolic analysts" has spread to nearly all corners of the globe (Reich 1991; Sassen 1994; Lury 1997: 90). The rise of a global cosmopolitan class can be discerned in the proliferation of urban lifestyle magazines (Greenberg 2000: 5). In the 1960s, lifestyle magazines were launched in 60 US metropolitan areas, a number that grew to more than 100 by the end of the century (Greenberg 2000). These magazines are similar from city to city because the target audience is unvarying: an affluent new middle class made up disproportionately of empty-nest baby boomers and their highly educated and well-paid progeny. In her study of *New York*, *Atlanta*, and *Los Angeles* magazines, Miriam Greenberg found that since the early 1990s, people in this strata share a preoccupation with "narrowly-defined, consumer-oriented, and politically conservative urban lifestyles" (ibid.: 25). The new middle-class consumer can acquire instant sophistication by eating the cuisine, drinking the wine, smoking the cigars, and buying the cars and art recommended by a new breed of writers and critics who specialize in giving lifestyle advice. Though Greenberg's study only examines magazines published in the United States, similar magazines can be found on the newsstands of major cities throughout the world.

Tourism overlaps with – indeed, is a product of – a globalized culture of consumption sustained by highly mobile workers and consumers. It makes sense to assume that the members of this class will tend to demand and therefore to reproduce similar urban environments wherever they go. This tendency is not difficult to observe. New York's Soho, like warehouse districts elsewhere, has been invaded by a predictable mix of themed stores. Likewise, ethnic cuisine has not only been internationalized but also fetishized, so that the same varieties of ethnic nouvelle cuisine can be found in almost any city. These developments suggest a provocative question: Will a globalized culture of affluent consumption eventually reduce all cities to a monotonous monoculture?

In fact, it is far from clear that cosmopolitans want the same thing everywhere they go. Because many residents and visitors seek out the unique, and numerous visitors come for other purposes than sightseeing, a tendency towards homogeneity is not inevitable, and it may even be unlikely. Richard Lloyd discerns the rise of a new culture of "neo-bohemia" led by urban residents who associate "gritty spaces with creative energy" (2000: 1). This new class, he argues, is responsible for the reclaiming of "apparently anachronistic spaces" in inner cities such as old warehouse and industrial districts (ibid.: 5), a development much like the gentrification of London's city fringe, where designers and artists have colonized old market halls, storefronts, and workshops (Fainstein 2001).

Richard Florida has shown that the group he calls "the creative class" – highly educated professionals with rarified intellectual, analytic, artistic, and creative skills – frequently regard lifestyle as more important than a particular job in choosing a place to live (2002: 224). The members of this class demand social interaction, culture, nightlife, diversity, and authenticity, the latter defined as "historic buildings, established neighborhoods, a unique music scene or specific cultural attributes. It comes from the mix – from urban grit alongside renovated buildings, from the commingling of young and old, long-time neighborhood characters and yuppies, fashion models and 'bag ladies'" (ibid.: 228). Florida indicates that the creative class tends to reject "canned experiences": "A chain theme restaurant, a multimedia-circus sports stadium or a prepackaged entertainment-and-tourist district is like a packaged tour: You do not get to create your experience or modulate the intensity: it is thrust upon you." What the members of the creative class demand is "to have a hand in creating the experience [of the city] rather than merely consuming it" (ibid.: 232). These preferences have spawned a globalized movement demanding a higher level of urban amenities, both public and private (Clark et al. 2002).

Modes of Resistance

It is difficult to anticipate the kinds of places and experiences to which tourists will be drawn. Harlem, for example, has become a popular destination for German tourists fascinated by African-American religious services and by other tourists attracted by "ethnic" New York (Hoffman 2000). Some proportion of tourists and local residents seek out such places as an alternative to the contrived atmosphere of enclavic tourist spaces. Feifer has proposed that these people be called post-tourists (after "post-modern"). Unlike ordinary tourists, post-tourists do not wish to gaze upon officially sanctioned tourist sites, partly because they have already weathered a continuing barrage of tourist objects and images projected by television, film, magazines, and other media. They are jaded by travel before they even leave home. Having ceased to regard any particular "gaze" as privileged, the post-tourist seeks out a multitude of experiences, as an antidote to boredom (Feifer 1985: 269).

City visitors possess a significant capacity to resist the totalizing regulation intended by the managers of enclavic tourist spaces. Post-tourists, jaded by a lifetime of exposure to marketing and theming, are apt to adopt an *ironic stance* within the confines of Disneyfied environments. What post-tourists seek in festival malls and entertainment multiplexes is pure fun and escapism; they are likely to find criticisms that these spaces are inauthentic to be ill-tempered, meaningless, or beside the point (Fainstein 2001: 210). Their ironic stance allows them to seek their own experiences even within a confining environment.

A second mode of resistance is *a refusal to conform* to expected uses of tourist spaces. As de Certeau has observed, "space is a practiced place"; as, for example, when "the street geometrically defined by urban planning is transformed into a space by walkers" (1984: 117). Because the developers of enclavic spaces must respond to changing tastes and preferences, the practices within them may be less static and unchanging than is sometimes supposed. Even in cities splintered into enclaves and fragments, Stephen Graham and Simon Marvin identify several modes of resistance: Residents of gated communities regularly ignore or defy their common-interest associations; young people find ways to evade the strict regulations within malls; and the rules imposed by the owners and managers of enclaves are sometimes met by well-organized protests (2001: 389, 394–5). The refusal to conform may even be asserted in extremely confining circumstances. In his study of tourism in India, Edensor found that despite the best efforts of the guides on package tours to shield their charges from unanticipated encounters, the intermingling of spaces often promoted casual wandering and walking and lounging about on streets, in markets, and at outdoor cafés. The members of packaged tours sometimes freely wandered about, occupying the liminal zone of anonymity of the *flâneur* (Urry 1990: 138).

This suggests a third mode of resistance: *escape* from closely regulated tourist enclaves. Escape is easy in all but the most specialized resort cities or crime-ridden urban cores. In fact, escape is often encouraged; cities that offer a wide range of amenities and interesting urban experiences advertise their enclaves as only one option in a range of experiences. The franchised brand-name outlets associated with festival malls (such as Banana Republic, the Gap, Victoria's Secret, etc.) have spilled out from the malls and into shopping districts such as the Magnificent Mile on Michigan Avenue, Chicago, and in London's Chelsea precisely because their customers have refused to stay confined. The institutions of "high culture" – museums, performing arts centers, playhouses, and art galleries – may be found not only in their traditional settings, but, increasingly, within entertainment enclaves (presumably the plays staged at the Shakespeare theatre on Chicago's Navy Pier are no less authentic because of its location). It is also evident that cities on both sides of the Atlantic have been investing heavily in such public amenities as parks, fountains, formal gardens, and public art, which contradicts dire predictions that the public realm is disappearing (Clark et al. 2002).

The disorder of urban life, the unpredictable mélange of the local and vernacular with the global, is expressed in the variety of experiences available to a typical city's residents and visitors. All in the same day a visitor may sample Disneyfied entertainments, go to a Monet exhibit, walk through a historic neighborhood, and end up at Mexican restaurant (which may be a cheap local *taqueria* or a restaurant serving a globalized, nouvelle Mexican cuisine). The city is a crucible melding circuits of globalized capital and culture with the local and the eccentric, the cosmopolitan with the parochial. Walter Benjamin's delight in the exuberant anarchy of city life can still be experienced, even by the casual visitor:

> Not to find one's way in a city may well be uninteresting and banal. It requires ignorance – nothing more. But to lose oneself in a city – as one loses oneself in a forest – that calls for quite a different schooling. Then, signboards and street names, passers-by, roofs, kiosks, or bars must speak to the wanderer like a cracking twig under his feet in the forest, like the startling call of a bittern in the distance . . . in the midst of asphalt streets of the city I felt exposed to the powers of nature. (Benjamin 1978: 8–9)

It should be noted that even when they leave enclaves and indulge in the unpredictable adventures of the *flâneur*, visitors are subjected to a variety of regulations in the form of official surveillance, legal strictures, spatial configurations, and the limited range of options and choices available to them. Complete escape from regulation is not an option, but the visitors encounter many different modes of regulation in contemporary cities. The spatial ecology of cities is becoming more, not less, complex and varied. As Graham and Marvin have observed, "urban life is more diverse, varied and unpredictable than the common reliance on US-inspired urban dystopias suggests" (2001: 392). The obituaries pronouncing the imminent demise of the public city may be greatly exaggerated.

NOTES

1 I follow Susan Fainstein's example (*The City Builders* 2001: 204–13) in employing this term to denote a body of scholarship that emphasizes what is often labeled the "post-modern geography" of the city, which is described as a landscape fractured by walls, barriers, and a geography of difference and separation, a form of development brought about by the economic and political influences of globalization. This view constitutes a sharp departure from a "modernist" twentieth-century geography of comprehensive planning, large-scale development, and the goal of achieving order and harmony in the urban environment The post-structuralist interpretation of urban development is rather self-consciously represented in the self-styled LA School (cf. Michael J. Dear (ed.), *From Chicago to LA*).
2 Richard Lloyd's concept of the "as if" tourist is brilliant, and if there is any justice, this felicitous term will become a mainstay in the literature on tourism and urban tourism.

REFERENCES

Aboulafia, M. 1999: A (neo) American in Paris: Bourdieu, Mead, and pragmatism. In R. Shusterman (ed.), *Bourdieu: A Critical Reader*. London: Blackwell, 153–74.

Artibise, A. 2003: Tourism infrastructure of a post-industrial city: a case study of Vancouver, British Columbia. In D. R. Judd (ed.), *The Infrastructure of Play: Building the Tourist City*. Armonk, NY: M. E. Sharpe.

Baudrillard, J. 1998: *The Consumer Society: Myths and Structures*. Thousand Oaks, CA: Sage Publications.

Beauregard, R. A. 1993: *Voices of Decline: The Postwar Fate of American Cities*. New York: Blackwell.

Benjamin, W. 1978: *Essays, Aphorisms, Autobiographical Writings*. New York: Harcourt Brace Jovanovich.

Boorstin, D. J. 1961: *The Image: A Guide to Pseudo-Events in America*. New York: Vintage.

Bourdieu, P. 1990a: Structures, habitus and practices. In *The Polity Reader in Social Theory*. Cambridge: Polity Press, 95–110.

——1990b: *The Logic of Practice*. Stanford, CA: Stanford University Press.

Boyer, C. 1994: *The City of Collective Memory: Its Historical Imagery and Architectural Entertainments*. Cambridge, MA: MIT Press.

Brendon, P. 1991: *Thomas Cook: 150 Years of Popular Tourism*. London: Secker and Warburg.

Clark, T. N., Lloyd, R., Wong, K. K., and Jain. 2002: Amenities drive urban growth. *Journal of Urban Affairs* 24 (5): 493–516.

Cocks, C. 2001: *Doing the Town: The Rise of Urban Tourism in the United States, 1859–1915*. Berkeley, CA: University of California Press.

Dear, M. J. (ed.) 2002: *From Chicago to LA: Making Sense of Urban Theory*. Thousand Oaks, CA: Sage Publications.

De Certeau, M. 1984: *The Practice of Everyday Life*. Berkeley, CA: University of California Press.

Edensor, T. 1998: *Tourists at the Taj: Performance and Meaning at a Symbolic Site*. New York: Routledge.

Edsall, T. B. and Edsall, M. D. 1991: *Chain Reaction: The Impact of Race, Rights, and Taxes on American Politics*. New York: W. W. Norton.

Ehrlich, B. and Dreier, P. 1999: The new Boston discovers the old: tourism and the struggle for a livable city. In D. R. Judd and S. S. Fainstein (eds.), *The Tourist City*. New Haven, CT: Yale University Press, 155–78.

Fainstein, S. S. 2001: *The City Builders*, 2nd ed. Lawrence, KS: University Press of Kansas.

Featherstone, M. 1994: City cultures and post-modern lifestyles. In A. Amin (ed.), *Post-Fordism: A Reader*. Oxford: Blackwell, 387–408.

Feifer, M. 1985: *Going Places*. London: Macmillan.

Florida, R. 2002: *The Rise of the Creative Class*. New York: Basic Books.

Foucault, M. 1977: *Discipline and Punish: The Birth of the Prison*. London: Allen Lane.

Graham, S. and Marvin, S. 2001: *Splintering Urbanism: Networked Infrastructure, Technological Mobilities and the Urban Condition*. London: Routledge.

Greenberg, M. 2000: Branding cities: a social history of the urban lifestyle magazine. *Urban Affairs Review* 36 (2): 228–63.

Hall, P. 1996: *Cities of Tomorrow*. Cambridge, MA: Blackwell.

Hannigan, J. 1998: *Fantasy City: Pleasure and Profit in the Postmodern Metropolis*. New York: Routledge.

Harvey, D. 1989: *The Condition of Postmodernity*. Oxford: Blackwell.

—— 2001: *Spaces of Capital: Towards a Critical Geography*. New York: Routledge.

Hiernaux-Nicolas, D. 2003: Tourism and strategic competitiveness: infrastructure development in Mexico City. In D. R. Judd (ed.), *The Infrastructure of Play: Building the Tourist City*. Armonk, New York: M. E. Sharpe.

Hoffman, L. M. 2000: Tourism and the revitalization of Harlem. In *Research in Urban Sociology*, vol. 5. Greenwich, CT: JAI Press, 207–23.

Hula, R. C. 1990: The two Baltimores. In D. R. Judd and M. Parkinson (eds.), *Leadership and Urban Regeneration: Cities in North America and Europe*. Thousand Oaks, CA: Sage Publications, 191–215.

Iyer, P. 2000: *The Global Soul: Jet-Lag, Shopping Malls and the Search for Home*. London: Bloomsbury.

Judd, D. and Parkinson, M. (eds.) 1990: *Leadership and Urban Regeneration: Cities in North America and Europe*. Thousand Oaks, CA: Sage Publications.

Lefebvre, H. 1991: *The Production of Space*. London: Blackwell.

Levine, M. V. 2003: Tourism infrastructure and urban redevelopment in Montreal. In D. R. Judd (ed.), *The Infrastructure of Play: Building the Tourist City*. Armonk, NY: M. E. Sharpe.

Lloyd, R. 2000: Grit as glamour: neo-Bohemia and urban change. Unpublished manuscript, University of Chicago.

—— 2002: Art and neighborhood redevelopment in Chicago. *Journal of Urban Affairs* 24 (5): 517–32.

Lury, C. 1997: The objects of travel. In C. Rojek and J. Urry (eds.), *Touring Cultures: Transformations of Travel and Theory*. London: Routledge, 75–95.

Reich, R. B. 1991: *The Work of Nations: Preparing Ourselves for 21st Century Capitalism*. New York: Knopf.

Rojek, C. 1995: *Decentering Leisure*. London: Sage.

Rothman, H. K. and Davis, M. (eds.) 2002: *The Grit beneath the Glitter*. Berkeley, CA: University of California Press.

Sassen, S. 1994: *Cities in a World Economy*. Thousand Oaks, CA: Pine Forge Press.

—— and Roost, F. 1999: The city: strategic site for the global entertainment industry. In D. R. Judd and S. S. Fainstein (eds.), *The Tourist City*. New Haven, CT: Yale University Press, 143–54.

Sorkin, M. (ed.) 1992: *Variations on a Theme Park*. New York: Hill and Wang.

Teaford, J. 1990: *The Rough Road to Renaissance: Urban Revitalization in America, 1940–1985*. Baltimore: Johns Hopkins University Press.

Thompson, E. P. 1967: Time, discipline, and industrial capitalism. *Past and Present* 38, as quoted in S. Zukin [1991], *Landscapes of Power: From Detroit to Disney World*. Berkeley, CA: University of California Press, 17.

Urry, J. 1990: *The Tourist Gaze: Leisure and Travel in Contemporary Societies*. London: Sage Publications.

van den Berg, L., van den Borg, J., and Russo, A. P. 2003: The infrastructure of urban tourism: a European model? In D. R. Judd (ed.), *The Infrastructure of Play: Building the Tourist City*. New York: M. E. Sharpe.

Wade, R. C. 1959: *The Urban Frontier: Pioneer Life in Early Pittsburgh, Cincinnati, Lexington, Louisville, and St Louis*. Chicago: University of Chicago Press.

Withey, L. 1997: *Grand Tours and Cook's Tours: A History of Leisure Travel 1750 to 1915*. New York: William Morrow and Company.

2

Cities, Security, and Visitors: Managing Mega-Events in France

Sophie Body-Gendrot

Violence always strikes by surprise. By its very nature, it exceeds our expectations, disturbs our practices, upsets our daily life. Security is therefore a formidable task faced by authorities in every country. In France, it has been the first concern of citizens since 2000.

Cities are especially susceptible to the threat of violence. Guaranteeing safety is a formidable task when mega-events are staged in cities, where the social context provides ample cover for potential trouble-makers and the built environment makes security difficult. Mega-events attract large numbers of visitors and high-profile dignitaries, as well as hoodlums, hooligans, and potential terrorists. Managing risk is an issue of governance as much as the specific policies that might be applied. Techniques of social control and security are mobilized within a context of the organization and capabilities of the state apparatus, but, as this study of French security policy reveals, mega-events globalize the security apparatus. Actors at all levels, from the international to the local, become involved in what must be understood as a governance structure, however temporary it may be. This observation probably holds for mega-events in all countries, but it has been reinforced by the events of September 11.

The French state is highly centralized, with cities at the bottom of a pyramid of power of an internal security apparatus. The French police are considered as archetypal of a centralized police force. Some have argued that France, and especially Paris, are over-policed, and yet there is no local police force. Whereas the average ratio in Europe is one policeman per 300 inhabitants, in France, the ratio is one for 243, compared with one for 380 in the UK and one for 432 in the US (Meyzonnier 1994). To deal with potentially dangerous mega-events, the French state is perceived as the only entity capable of (1) expressing authority across the whole territory; (2) mounting safety operations in cooperation with neighboring states; and (3) coordinating the security policies and activities of local authorities in a comprehensive way. The state in France has few competitors and its interventions into many processes are seen as legitimate and even required by public opinion. Many French mayors are only too happy not to be accountable on matters of safety.

But despite their apparent monopoly over security policy, the French police increasingly must cooperate and negotiate with a variety of local and international participants. Globalization has introduced new actors who are involved in maintaining security in two ways. First, the privatization of safety has introduced a competition between private and public policing in urban spaces (Body-Gendrot 2000a). Second, international organizations have become closely involved in security policy governing mega-events. Third, cities have become more active participants because security is one aspect of overall urban development and local promotion. Because they gather such large crowds in circumscribed places and because so many investments and resources are at stake, a colossal security apparatus is mobilized by the central state, but its activities are closely coordinated with global and local actors.

Partnerships involving various institutional actors and cooperation with private interests guided security policies on the occasion of the World Cup, held in Paris in 1998. The *principle of precaution* that guided Great Britain's response to the crisis of "mad cow" disease was adjusted to a new context, and it was internalized by all decision-makers in assessing new risks that threatened safety. A narrow, technical approach to policing was not possible because the principle of precaution breaks the traditional link between expertise and action. Rather than responding to events, continuous resources were necessary to evaluate risk, and ambiguity became embedded within every action and policy (Latour 2000). Therefore, security policy, rather than involving mere policing, became redefined as a mode of governance.

The two case studies presented in this chapter, security policy for the World Soccer Cup in 1998 in Paris and a few other cities, and the Millennium celebrations of December 31, 1999 and January 1, 2000 in many French cities, highlight the special nature of security arrangements for mega-events, which draw hundreds of thousands of international visitors and residents into circumscribed spaces. Such was the case with the World Soccer Cup of 1998. Paris took center-stage both as a historic city and as the capital of a powerful state. The commitment of the central state, which deployed colossal resources, did not raise any objections from the French public. It was understood that it is the duty of the state to protect cities and that costs should not be a matter of debate. Public opinion polls showed that most French citizens agreed with the sentiment that "the state should be the main actor to organize the celebration."

The celebration of the Millennium in 1999–2000 was different from the World Soccer Cup. There was less of an international presence, no global audiences and fewer media crews. But each city hosting Millennium events saw itself as in a competition, with each city hoping to outdo others. Therefore, local culture played a definitive role, including in security policy. Accordingly, even in the context of a national police force, policing and security policy reflected the influence of local culture. The variations between cities illustrated the principle that "regulation has a highly complex geography," because "social practices are situated into [political, economic, social] spaces which vary in form and process" (Lauria 1997: 14, 21).

The World Soccer Cup of 1998

The last time France hosted a World Soccer Cup (WSC) was in 1938, but much had changed in the intervening 60 years. The globalization of the media has turned the Cup into a truly international event with audiences all over the world simultaneously watching the matches, while air travel has made it possible for hundreds of thousands of fans to converge on the games. Soccer has become better organized; indeed, it has become an object of attention and funding by many national governments. The budget of the International Federation of Football Associations (FIFA) exceeds the total French budget. Accordingly, for Paris and for France the stakes were enormous, in both symbolic and material terms.

France as a country and Paris as a site for some of the matches were very attractive to the WSC organizers. Six months before the games, the demand was such that a lottery was organized for the 200,000 remaining tickets, and an incredible 25 million phone inquiries for tickets were received.[1] FIFA delegated the organization of the French games to the Comité Français d'Organisation (CFO), a private organization of 650 employees which supervises soccer games in France. The CFO was sponsored by hundreds of national public and private firms.

The state and its neighbors: an international partnership

The border police had to control the entry of six million soccer supporters. There was a serious chance that high-risk soccer fans might cause
trouble. The difficulty of monitoring this group was made more difficult
by the fact that there was the usual flow of travelers across the borders.
Travelers with a stadium ticket were allowed entry (the number was
checked by the Schengen computerized system),[2] but soccer fans without
proper documents and identified trouble-makers were escorted out through
airports, railway stations, and seaports. Mobile security forces were present
at all transit sites and in railway stations, and on trains.

The global nature of the soccer games and of the threats associated
with them meant that security had to become globalized as well. Four
phases marked transnational cooperation. First, international agreements
about how to handle high-risk fans were signed. Second, foreign police personnel were invited to share space at police headquarters within France.
Third, staff members assigned to nine joint police forces were given special
training. Finally, in France, the UK and Germany, the instantaneous transmission of information was given priority both in matters of hooliganism
and of internal security. On almost 80 percent of the trains carrying British
fans, uniformed and unarmed British police officers provided close surveillance of high-risk fans. With German authorities, the cooperation
arrangement was slightly different. For each game involving German
teams, the Bundensgrenzschutz (BGS) confiscated travel documents from
high-risk nationals, while the French border police denied entry to additional fans identified as dangerous. Close communication between the
French central command and the police forces of 31 countries was established.[3] The scale of the transnational effort was remarkable: 60,000
supporters coming by air and 58,000 train travelers were checked. Of
these, 1,539 were denied entry on security grounds. Nineteen special
escorts were conducted under absolute emergency measures.

In addition to hooliganism, terrorism appeared as a serious threat. In
1995 and in 1996, France had experienced very damaging terrorist
attacks. In the six months leading up to the games, a variety of potential
threats were identified. The most serious were thought to be from groups
that opposed sports for ideological reasons, hit teams that might target
officials from certain countries, and radical Islamic terrorist networks.
From May to July 1998, several incidents caused concern, especially the
arrest of some Islamists in Belgium who were preparing an attack on
France, and an attempted bomb attack in Paris in May. Criminal inquiries
led to the investigation of over one hundred people in several European
countries.

The length of time the event would take – 32 days from June 10 to July 12, 1998 – meant that security forces had to be on alert for a long period. And because the matches would take place at ten sites, a huge organizational and logistics effort was required. Security was organized in a pattern of concentric circles. A central command post was to supervise the regional and local units while it simultaneously cooperated with international police forces. A perimeter around the stadiums was established to fit in with details of local topography. A police precinct was established on each site with a prosecutor ready to act on the spot and forbid trouble-makers further access to the stadium. Another perimeter encompassed the crowds and French visitors on streets further from the stadiums. In nearby barracks, 1,800 army soldiers stood ready to intervene. Specially trained riot police,[4] motor squads, anti-terrorist forces, and border police were also on alert. Teams of bomb disposal experts checked team accommodation and training sites as well as the stadiums. At all sites, ambulance helicopters and reserve aircraft were positioned in case of emergency. Overall, 3,000 fire-fighters, doctors and emergency staff were on alert during the 32 days of the games. This impressive display of force seemed to work. In Lens, German hooligans fatally assaulted a gendarme. Though tragic, this incident took place far from the Cup sites, showing that the bubble of security immediately surrounding the matches would be difficult to penetrate.

A blueprint law signed into law in January 1995 gave sports organizers the responsibility for ensuring public order inside sports areas; accordingly, private security companies monitored the crowds within the stadiums. The St. Denis stadium near Paris was equipped with 125 surveillance cameras which could be used to immediately spot trouble-makers. The cameras ran tapes at all times, which could be shared with anyone in the security system. The privately hired stadium stewards (one for each hundred participants) were permitted to conduct searches with the assistance of public police officers. The logistics inside the stadiums as well as the use of material devices such as mobile barriers, turnstiles, gates, and emergency exits were submitted to the national police's chiefs for authorization. It was agreed that the police would have 1,000 uniformed or plainclothes officers in the stadiums during high-risk games. The blurring of the public/private boundaries was obvious at every turn: Part of the private security teams hired by the organizers consisted of former or retired police officers; and many policemen were present in the stadium, in their position as official authorities. But it can be surmised that the policemen exerted surveillance not only over the crowds, but also over the stadium stewards as well.

When examined in its entirety, the security apparatus was, in essence, a governance structure, *albeit* one brought together temporarily. An interac-

Plate 2.1 Paris sports fan. *Source*: Corbis

tive regulation regime was composed of national police, prefects, event organizers, mayors, public prosecutors, and local authorities. In each city, the national police were backed up by gendarmes, the riot police, and emergency staff. Within the stadiums, a combination of private security and public policing provided the final locus of control within a complex structure.

Local variations

Maintaining a festive atmosphere within the context of an enormous security apparatus presented a major challenge to cities. The members of the Organizing Committee of the WSC placed a premium on maintaining an entertainment atmosphere; "We did not wish to transform whole cities into bunkers," remarked R.-G. Querry, the official in charge of security for the WSC. But it was a daunting task to avoid this outcome. On the one hand, regional and local authorities had to face the potential risks related both to hooligans and to inner-city youth and on the other, they had to control multicultural crowds of visitors. They also needed to ensure that daily life would continue uninterrupted despite the magnitude of the event. Residents expected a minimum freedom of movement and protection at the same time. The media, on the lookout for the slightest occurrence of disturbance, exerted considerable pressure as well.

Security worked well inside the stadiums because of the multiple layers of defense outside. On June 14 and 15 in Marseilles, for instance, three sites were under surveillance simultaneously for the Tunisia–UK game: the stadium, the beach area and the Old Port. Three factors explain disturbances which took place on the beach involving fans from different countries: the arrival of several hundred category "B" British fans within two days, non-stop drinking, and the joining in of thousands of people in an atmosphere of "boozy festivity." Moreover, Marseilles has its own culture: Minority youths from the housing projects have the reputation of being tough and restless. At the slightest provocation, they sometimes overreact. It may be that the police decided to intervene too late, after fights had begun. At the same time, the Old Port nearby was also a vulnerable site with crowded bars, stores, and restaurants. A display of too many police in such an area would have threatened the festive atmosphere desired by the WRC organizers and by local officials. Lessons were drawn from the problems in Marseilles. In other southern cities such as Montpellier and Toulouse, police forces anticipated trouble outside the stadiums. The cities decided to close bars early and to defer music festivals, with little protest from residents.

If the World Soccer Cup was a great success on the whole, this was not entirely due to the massive involvement of the French state and to the *savoir faire* of police forces. Local residents also contributed to the success of the event. About 12,000 volunteers were involved in staging the WSC, and they sometimes participated in surprising ways. Take St. Denis, a tough working-class locality (Body-Gendrot 2000b, 2000a: ch. 5). The reformist mayor seized the WSC as an opportunity to convince national and international sports authorities that a new stadium had to be built in St. Denis, and he managed to grab two-thirds of the 1,500 new jobs created for the event. Moreover, he convinced the high-risk kids from various public housing projects that they could be winners too. With this aim in mind, he invited teenagers from other countries to come and play soccer, in parallel with the big world players. Star players took part for charity in their shows. The mayor asked these teenagers to involve themselves in preserving the security of the community, and no incident marred the sports events. Collective efficacy and positive moral reinforcement significantly lowered the threat of violence, via a positive contagious effect. In other words, the WSC was used to address the inner-city's social problems such as juvenile delinquency and racism and to displace daily frustrations. Linkages and new forms of communication were observed among various components of the community and its organizations. Both the imagination and the social expectations of the community were mobilized.

The Millennium Celebrations[5]

The Millennium celebrations in France had been planned for more than a year by public authorities at the national and local levels. Many tourists were expected to come to Paris for the celebrations and not a single hotel room was available in the city that night. Two main events – the fireworks from the Eiffel Tower and the operation of eleven Ferris wheels along the Champs-Elysées – presented several types of risk: the possibility of an accident occurring with the Ferris wheels; crowd panics; brawls due to heavy drinking; muggings, and assaults. Previous events had allowed authorities to test their management capacity for mass events. So many checks of the Ferris wheels were made that no accidents happened despite an enormous storm in the early morning of January 1, 2000, which devastated parts of the country and destroyed ancient trees at Versailles.

New regulations had been established after a tragedy in 1992 in Bastia, Corsica, when a metal structure collapsed during a soccer game, causing 18 deaths and 1,300 injuries. Technical investigations before mega-events are now mandatory. Architects, technicians, and engineers were thus mobilized to check the Ferris wheels and their supports. The principle of precaution determined respective public and private responsibilities. As with the WSC, private organizers submitted their proposal to public authorities for authorization. Some creative but risky ideas were immediately discarded, and the number of wheels was reduced from fifteen to eleven. For each theme wheel, all sorts of potential dangers had to be imagined by the experienced organizers. Barriers circumscribing the sites were erected to prevent endangering the crowds in case of a mishap.

Anticipating over one million people moving at the same time from the Eiffel Tower to the Champs-Elysées, an increased surveillance apparatus was deployed that involved 20,000 police officers and 12,000 community police officers, backed by 3,500 officers from the anti-riot squads, and 1,800 soldiers operating in the subway, railway stations, and public spaces.[6] Seven thousand firemen and numerous paramedical personnel also stood by.

The Police Prefect of Paris was in charge of an established Defense Zone via an Operation Center, located near the command and information rooms. This structure had already functioned for the WSC. It linked the Home Secretary to regional prefects, to Army forces, and to the heads of public services. The main goal of the structure was to establish a continuous liaison between public decision-makers which could be preserved even if, as many experts predicted, a possible Y2K bug disrupted computer systems. (The same concern was also expressed in New York City on the occasion of its Millennium celebrations.)

The considerable autonomy given to 35 precinct commanders was a somewhat new arrangement. While a chain of command linked them to a control room where images from 300 cameras appeared on the screens (no helicopters and no completely dark places in the city were consequently allowed), they communicated on their radio with one another. These precautions were not useless. That night, 1,500 high-risk individuals were identified thanks to the cameras from suburban train stations and hundreds of plainclothes police officers.[7] In Paris, 113 people were arrested and kept in custody (220 nationally) for carrying weapons or for theft. At the stroke of midnight, despite the failure of the countdown, the seven-minute fireworks from the Eiffel Tower and the thousand silver bulbs suddenly lit on the Tower drew delirious applause and cheers from the crowds. Then the crowds stayed on for hours, entertained by more events and spectacles.

Between 30 and 40 French cities organized celebrations for the Millennium, attracting crowds ranging from 40,000 to 200,000. Each city organized its own celebration, according to its local culture and history, and mobilized its own security. In Lyon, the city invented four symbolic doors dedicated to fire, earth, air, and water. Dozens of thousands of people gathered in various public spaces without incidents. In other cities, the Millennium was just a night like any other, with cars set on fire and petty delinquency. In Strasbourg a 20 percent increase in police numbers helped prevent disorders. Car-burning hit only a few dozen cars, a spectacular drop on previous years.[8] However, clashes between youths from immigrant and ethnic neighborhoods and firemen and the police could not be avoided, damaging the border city's efforts to improve its image as an international city and the site of the European Parliament (Body-Gendrot 2000a).

In other large cities around the world, an emphasis on heavy security was also evident. In New York City, there was widespread concern that a bomb might be planted at Times Square. Tough security measures were consequently undertaken. A three-block-wide stretch of midtown was closed to traffic and parked cars removed. Bomb-sniffing dogs patrolled underground tunnels, police helicopters were used for surveillance overhead, officers were placed on roofs, while others stopped and searched pedestrians for weapons and other suspicious objects. The entire Port Authority police force of 1,250 members was added to 8,000 regular police forces assigned to the blocks around Times Square. The 1993 terrorist bombing at the World Trade Center still lived vividly in the memories of witnesses and survivors. Officials took no risks. No New York mayor could allow disorders to tarnish the celebration viewed by millions of television gazers. But, as in France, city authorities were not acting alone. In Washington, DC, intelligence and law enforcement officials kept vigil at command posts for any sign of trouble. A response center inside the Central Intelligence Agency's counterterrorism offices was operating 24 hours a day, while the FBI's command center was placed on alert status.

Other cities took different approaches, depending on their resources and assessment of local risks. Seattle cancelled the Millennium celebration altogether. The city was still recovering from an eruption of violence during the World Trade Organization meeting in December, and local officials said that they could not take the risk of new disorders.

The Risks and the Benefits of Mega-Events

The WSC has been labeled a "historical ecstasy" by philosopher Edgar Morin. A big "Us" seized youths, adults, immigrants, tourists, nationals into a phenomenon of fusion, identity-sharing, poetry and non-military patriotism. There was indeed no aggression, contempt or ethnocentrism accompanying defeats or victories during the games. The cultural integration of brown, black, and white players into one plural action came out visibly and marked the triumph of the French team trained by an underdog upon whom the media had looked with contempt for months. The local revealed the global in the most satisfactory way. This may explain why local residents did not mind the heavy security apparatus in their city. They had more to gain than to lose. The feeling of unity and pride they felt when all the eyes turned to their stadium had lasting effects.

However, the risks in staging the WSC should not be minimized. An unanticipated risk came from the crowd of 900,000 fans who spontaneously erupted onto the Champs-Elysées after the final victory by the French team. Police forces had to be quickly deployed and kept on alert. How to monitor a large crowd, especially when so many people are drunk? How to identify those who came with the purpose of attacking others? How to spot potential terrorists?

Like other large cities, Paris is becoming accustomed to bearing risks. As the world's leading tourist city, it cannot allow its reputation to be tarnished by a major disaster. The stakes involve both the present and the future of the city. The French Secretary for tourism had feared that the WSC would deter other tourists from coming to France. However, in the months following the WSC, a 20 percent increase in the number of tourists was registered, probably as a consequence of the Cup. Twenty million tourists came to the Paris region (Ile de France) between January and August, with 9.6 million coming to Paris with a record number of 6 million visitors coming to the Eiffel Tower.

A comparison with the Atlanta Olympic Games of 1996 confirms that for any city hosting a mega-event, security will command enormous organizational and fiscal resources. At first blush, it might seem that the games in Atlanta demonstrated the advantages of private-sector activity. In Atlanta, the application for the games was submitted by a private organization. Then the games made use of thousands of volunteers and employees from various firms and sponsors. Thousands of private agents were hired for security. A firm monitored surveillance cameras and integrated electronic systems and alarm points. But most of the money to pay for all this came from public funds. Security costs amounted to $70 million for the organizer and to $100 million for the State of Georgia. What is striking here is the massive deployment of public resources. Though the distinction between public and private forces was frequently blurred in Atlanta, there was involvement of local forces (2,500 police officers added to county sheriffs and staff), of the Georgia police force, the National Guard, the police transit system, port and airport authorities, highway patrols, SWAT teams, the Immigration and Naturalization Service, the US Marshalls Office, the Drug Enforcement Agency, the armed forces, as well as the White House. More than 35,000 agents from many agencies and all levels of governments were involved (Bauer 1996: 140). Pressures were brought by Washington on the Atlanta mayor and the State of Georgia to commit ever more law enforcement personnel for the games. One thousand federal recruits were sent to Atlanta in the last three months before the games. This demonstrates that, even in a country that valorizes small government and privatization, when it comes to security during a mega international event, public authority and resources remains essential. The reason is simple: The potential costs of disruption are forbidding.

These cases reveal that national differences matter, but not nearly as much as one might expect. Mega-events impose their own logic, and one of these is that security cannot be achieved strictly by national and local efforts. Privatization is more developed than before in France, and international cooperation is now a component in the making of French security policies. The WSC case reveals the continued presence of a strong French state, but one that cooperates with several other actors to achieve security. In Atlanta, the large security presence was relatively uncoordinated until an explosion occurred in the Centennial Olympic Park, a site which was not anyone's specific responsibility. After that, attempts were made to achieve closer coordination. The WSC involved extensive co-production of security with private organizers, though the entire apparatus was organized with tight state control. A comprehensive and integrated approach with international and sophisticated technological components can more easily be provided by the state in a country like France.

The size and the scope of mega-events impose a logic of their own which dictates a carefully coordinated security apparatus involving actors at several levels, including the global, and extensive use of surveillance technologies and information networks. In nations less historically centralized than France, state intervention in the organization of security remains critical. For certain types of cultural events such as the Millennium celebrations, each city pursues its strategy according to its resources and know-how. For mega-events like the World Soccer Cup, the internationalization of the spectacle, the magnitude of investments, and the enormous stakes for the host country and cities change the game fundamentally. The threat to cities posed by soccer thugs requires an organizational response similar to that required by the threats of terrorists. In the United States, the Department of Homeland Security will surely become involved in protecting mega-events from risks, and we can therefore expect a very rapid convergence – in the case of security organization and policy – between a strong, centralized state such as France, and a decentralized state such as the US. For mega-event organizers, the climate of fear provoked by the events of September 11 makes an internationalized security apparatus a priority; the events become almost secondary.

NOTES

1 Some people would have paid any price to get tickets for the final games. Three FIFA executives were indicted for organizing a swindle involving fake tickets.
2 The technical information comes from the Home Secretary's Information and Public Relations Bureau and from the author's interviews with F. Labrousse, General Comptroller and Technical Adviser within the Paris Police Prefect Cabinet and with R.-G. Querry, General Inspector of the National Police, Head of the International Cooperation Service.
3 Concerning the computerized system ACROPOL, the lack of complete fact files on the system generated frustrations among foreign visitors.
4 The CRS – Compagnies républicaines de sécurité – are supervised by the Home Secretary. They are called on to maintain and restore order during public disorders, and they conduct surveillance missions.
5 These observations are based on interviews with Mr. Querry.
6 For the whole country, 65,000 police officers and 5,000 anti-riot squads were on alert that night.
7 At the end of January 2001, between 150 and 250 youths from two housing projects at the periphery of Paris decided to meet at La Défense to solve their perennial conflicts on a Saturday afternoon when crowds of people were shopping at the mall. The mayors from the two localities had warned the prefects about the possible clash a few days before. Yet there seems to have been no anticipation of the kind we describe for the Millennium on the part of the Home Secretary. Was it deliberate, due to election time in order to show public opinion how the police are necessary? Was it a lack of communication within the pyramidal organization, an inability to respond right on time or a lack of anticipation from the Home Secretary's staff? The contrast between the Millennium preparation and the lack of it at La Défense is striking.
8 Incidents of car burning in Strasbourg reached 20 once more in December 2000 and may have caused the defeat of the incumbent mayor in the following elections.

REFERENCES

Bauer, A. 1996: Quelques enseignements des J. O. d'Atlanta 1996. *Cahiers de la sécurité intérieure* 26, 140–2.
Body-Gendrot, S. 2000a: *The Social Control of Cities? A Comparative Perspective*. Oxford, Blackwell.
——2000b: Marginalization and political response in the French context. In P. Hamel, H. Lustiger-Thaler, and M. Mayer (eds.), *Urban Movements in a Globalizing World*. London: Routledge, 59–79.

Latour, B. 2000: Prenons garde au principe de précaution, *Le Monde*, January 4, 15.

Lauria, M. 1997: *Reconstructing Urban Regime Theory: Regulating Urban Politics in a Global Economy.* London: Sage.

Meyzonnier, P. 1994: Interpol. In P. Meyzonnier, *Les forces de police dans l'Union européenne.* Paris: L'Harmattan.

3

Sociological Theories of Tourism and Regulation Theory

Nicolò Costa and Guido Martinotti

This chapter tries to relate regulation theory (Boyer 1990) and its applications to urban politics (Lauria 1997) to some of the established social theories of international tourism.[1] Now is a fruitful moment for a theoretical reassessment of tourism sociology, particularly as it is concerned with organized spaces. We can call this the new theoretical approach to tourism. "New," as it is frequently used in the titles and subtitles of articles in major journals in the field as well as books, refers to issues and approaches that have come to the fore since the rise of social movements in the 1960s. These recent concerns, as they refer to tourism, touch on the transformation of Third World communities, environmental effects, and urban impacts, in particular.[2]

We can summarize the results of the new theoretical and empirical investigations within four major theoretical categories:

- critical theory;
- relational theory;
- theory of sustainable tourism;
- theory of city-users and hypertourists.

We briefly review each theory from the point of view of regulation theory as a "new" sociological contribution better able to explain the forms, structures, and dynamics of tourism. The case study of Venice that follows is important, because the approaches to tourism policy embodied in the four theoretical frameworks compete with each other to structure the tourism planning of the city. The final paragraph proposes the use of "collaboration theory and community tourism planning" (Murphy 1985, 1988; Jamal and Getz 1995) as an opportunity for the better regulation of tourism and tourist spaces.

Critical Theory

The theory of pseudo-events and the falsity of bad taste transmitted by mass tourism[3] and the theory of pseudo-spaces or ephemeral simulacra[4] have in common a radical aversion toward the tourist as a banal and frivolous consumer of spaces that he/she visits without any seriousness or depth. The tourist is manipulated by the vacation marketeers. For Boorstin (1961), tourist events are not spontaneous but fictitious; for Turner and Ash (1975) tourists are golden hordes that ruin the local cultures; for Augé (1992, 1997), tourist spaces are kitsch and unreal, while for MacCannell (1992), they are empty meeting grounds. The critical representation of tourism is contemptuous of places dedicated to tourism pursuits, and the critique has the mission of unmasking the positive representations of the operators engaged in making profits without scruples. The authors cited are more or less nostalgic. Boorstin, Adler (1989a, 1989b), and Augé explicitly regret the lost art of traveling, replaced in their view by illusions. The comparative method adopted is mainly or implicitly diachronic as critics choose to compare the worst of today's travels with the best of yesterday's. The language is similar to that used by satirical writers that picture the tourist in embarrassing situations to caricature him, exaggerating the stereotype. Such critique leads to the denial of a sociological understanding of tourist spaces, substituting a theorization of the absurdity of tourist locations and the "impossible travel" (Augé 1997).

Critical theory is important, as it yields information regarding intellectuals and their audience. Indeed, books within this tradition have had great success with a learned public – the members of the intellectualized middle class, engaged in differentiating themselves from mass tourists through the construction and presentation of an ideal self, that of intelligent travelers who differentiate themselves through the exhibition of refined and expensive cultural tastes (Munt 1994).

Through critique, the intellectualized middle class has elaborated a distinctive poetic and policy of taste and distaste in the form of the "romantic gaze," which is opposed to the "collective gaze" of the general public (Urry 1990). Critical intellectuals do not have among their primary objectives the intergenerational transmission of the art of travel, and their books lack any indication of how to fill vacations with acceptable content. They have provided a critique which contrasts standardized recreation and the rule of money with authentic experience. They have failed, however, to describe a content different from that generated by the market. The "critical" middle class is composed of snobbish individuals. Graburn and Barthel-Bouchier (2001: 149) observe: "These commentators, snobs or anti-tourists are sure of two things: tourists are not us and they are inherently bad, the regressive detritus of burgeoning affluence in modernity."

Consequently, critical intellectuals have not had any practical impact on the regulation of the negative environmental and social-equity effects of mass tourism. They have delineated the aestheticism of the anti-tourist in everyday life with considerations regarding taste and distaste in order to contrast the vulgarity of the masses that have crowded beaches and ski slopes and invaded cities. The ideal visitor, remembered nostalgically, is the learned traveler who knows ancient languages, proceeds at a leisurely pace, learns neither useful nor practical things, and belongs to a complex high culture. We hypothesize that the critics of the welfare-state-consumer-society-mass tourism trinomial belong to the intellectual type that Bauman (1987) defines as legislators. They set the rules for good taste, exhibit certainties from top to bottom, and are surrounded by aura and timorous respect.

Regulation theory should identify the professional profile of the interpreter-intellectuals operating between the local culture, the tourist culture and the culture imported through tourism. In fact, the advent of the interpreter-intellectuals creates uncertainty even among the professional image-makers (hotel managers of multinational chains, tour guides, niche tour operators, restaurateurs, etc.) who, through the 1990s, were trying to improve their performances by developing the most advanced techniques in personal services. They are responding to the spreading of a new international middle class of interpreters, engaged in imposing the customs of its hegemony over tourist spaces in cities of culture. But the process is not yet completed. The model of post-modern tourism or post-industrial tourism is still neither fully formed nor wholly adopted – indeed some tourist companies are still introducing repetitive work and the assembly line according to the industrial model (Ritzer 1996). Thus, the professional uncertainty of those working within tourism is destined to grow. The hotel manager or the tourist guide is subject to de-differentiation – specialization inhibits his or her role of broker-interpreter (Urry 1990). This broader professional role is in demand among the local population as well as within the tourist system and the cultures imported through tourism.

Within this context, regulation theory can provide guidelines to orient the management of human resources within tourism organizations directly involved in the intellectualization of traveling. In fact, regulation theory can reorient the cultural critique toward problem-solving, at developing a policy of taste and distaste different from that proposed up until today by nostalgic intellectuals and anti-tourists.

Relational Theory

Under this name we regroup two theories developed during the 1970s and 1980s: the theory of ritual inversion[5] and the theory of staged authenticity.[6] They have in common the idea that experiencing difference (experience through time and space) is the central issue of tourism sociology and that structural factors are active over the long run. The analysis of interpersonal relational dynamics, according to the classical individual-society approach, is considered essential to give a holistic sense to tourism in the contemporary society. Symbolic interactionism, phenomenology and Durkheimian theory are fused in a single descriptive model of tourism. The theory of ritual inversion, as we shall see, falls within the scenario of industrial tourism, while the theory of staged authenticity fits within the scenario of the service economy.

Ritual inversion is expressed through the overturn of habits: idleness versus work, nude body versus covered body, effervescence versus routine, sacred nature versus pollution, tanned skin versus pale skin, etc. Ritual inversion is the anthropological aspect of the festival (Falassi 1987): it periodically returns in specific moments of the yearly cycle, it favors the dissipation of part of the resources accumulated through work; it has a regenerative function compared to working time, it allows the gratification of pleasures otherwise denied. Workers can enjoy the feast of industrial society, taking summer vacations within the framework of Keynsian policies intended to sustain consumer demand (Costa 1989). With the advent of mass tourism, two moments of life are condensed into one: the rural (rest is concentrated between Christmas and New Year's Day) and the industrial (rest is concentrated in the month of August). This explains why, in high-consumption societies, the following ritual inversion occurs: the industrial cities are emptied, and the tourist cities are filled up. The latter are the locations where the liminal experience of the feast is enjoyed, which Costa (1989) and Shields (1991) compare to Carnival.

The rules of social control are entrusted to the autonomy of the private sphere guaranteed by the State (the family nucleus as agent of tourist socialization) and by consumption (the worker deserves to become a consumer as he has done his duty as a producer, but if he does not, he will lose the pleasures of enjoyment). The summer feast celebrates the supremacy of the economy within the social policies of the welfare state.

Actually, after the crisis of 1929, the carnival-feast, which excites the lowest instincts through confusion and noise, is not understandable through aesthetics: It celebrates the integration of contract workers, the joyous belonging to the Fordist factory and industrial capitalism. Workers have the security, coming back from vacation, of finding their job waiting. The unemployed, on the other hand, are the cast-offs, the unwanted; they have no income and too much leisure time, but they do not know what to do with it as they cannot guarantee the pleasures of tourism to themselves and their families.

Deregulation stands in the same relation to Fordist control as the intellectual interpreter does to the intellectual legislator: they both point to the crisis of modes of regulation based on hierarchy and functionalism. An evolved regulation theory, however, should not just emphasize the limits and the insufficiencies of deregulation but should concern itself with the development of appropriate public controls. Even during the long season of triumphant Fordism, tourism claimed creative activities not reducible to formal regulation through State control. It was, however, indirectly controlled by Keynesian and Fordist economic policies, which subordinated the educational potential of tourism (democratic recreation) to recreational and evasive consumptions, which satisfied better than associationism the search for a balanced relationship between a tight work organization and freedom of movement and choice. A public pedagogy of tourism was not taken into consideration.

MacCannell (1976) in his early work develops a theory of authenticity in opposition to those critical theories which emphasize the ephemeral aspects and hetero-directed behavior of mass tourists. The tourist is "today's pilgrim" as he celebrates the transcendence of nature or of a cultural asset over the fragments, the discontinuities, and the innovations of modernity. The tourist industry satisfies such motivation with the organization of spaces characterized by "staged authenticity." Cohen (1988, 1995), however, notes that not all tourists seek authenticity. He proposes a typology of tourist demand in which he identifies only one, narrow category – the existential tourist – that conforms to MacCannell's profile of the traveler. Costa (1989) argues that in any case authenticity is not a permanent characteristic of a location or of a segment of travelers but is negotiated among the participants – between guests and hosts – and it is constantly built and rebuilt through discourses in competition. In MacCannell's perspective the regulation of tourism does not operate only in a competitive arena but can also involve cooperation. For the cooperative tourist, who presupposes cultural equality, locals will open their back region for visitors who truly wish to know it. There is a sensitive tourist who changes behavior, choosing cultural respect over intrusiveness. We may define this kind of traveler as a de-consumer. MacCannell contributes to the formation of a "new" tourist conscience, and to the cultural organizer of responsible or aware tourism, which refuses certain consumer choices even though there is a certain income to be obtained.

A direct consequence of this sensitivity is changes within tourist marketing, and more generally speaking, within the industry of hospitality. The quality of service encounters requires the humanization of the service (Krippendorf 1987). Certain tourist companies, flight companies and hotel chains adopt a marketing strategy that does not require receptionists to be repetitive and does not assume that there should only be one best way to interact with a guest. Skills are modeled on the clients' perceptions in order to customize the service and earn the trust of the client. As the multi-motivated client replaces the mass consumer, the tourism worker is flexible and acquires skills that do not belong to his or her traditional role.

E-commerce emphasizes relational marketing through one-to-one communication as service encounters re-created in a virtual environment: Commercial negotiations have a high content of interactivity and allow the negotiation of the package of custom tourist services. Industrial marketing, based on mass advertising transmitted by passive media like network television or periodicals (broadcasting one-to-many communication), is overcome by an on-demand direct relationship (Ellsworth and Ellsworth 1995). More generally speaking, a new conception of tourism is asserting itself (Poon 1994): the demand is no longer hetero-directed, unspecific and celebrative but is active, mature, and relational; time is no longer cyclic but more malleable – more vacations over the year, less differentiation between work and leisure time.

As a result, the scenario changes: from economic growth to restoration and especially from regulation to deregulation. Not the 1980s type of deregulation, but rather one concerning agencies operating between State and civil society (cultural and tourist associations, professionals of the service class with a special life style, small tour-operators proposing unpackaged or flexible travels, intellectuals-interpreters, etc.) who have de-structured mass tourism and freed the daemon of information technology, stretching local boundaries.

The new relational paradigm, expressed through the search for authenticity, has broken the Fordist rigidity. Integrating with the service economy, it delineates a new scientific conception and a new practice of tourism, albeit so far only partially and in response to demand. What then should be the role of the State and of local institutions in promoting forms of uncontrolled control within tourism? Certainly, we may think about international cooperation through professional skilling, re-skilling, up-skilling policies so that local elites could promote innovation and creativity in collaboration with middle-class travelers coming from wealthy countries and experts in relational marketing in a virtual environment. What international regulation may be elaborated in order to develop the deregulation/reregulation of responsible and aware tourism?

Sustainable Tourism

Sustainable tourism emerges:

- with the diffusion of environmental and ecological topics induced by the "verdi" (ecologists) movement. The practices of "alternative" and counter-cultural tourism do not only express an aesthetic critique against mass tourism but also deploy a differentiated life style and operative models for territorial planning.
- as a consequence of inquiries into the environmental impact of tourism at the local level and on consequent management techniques;[7]
- in relation to the diffusion of codes of ethics developed by international organizations like the Catholic Church (in its Encyclical *Peregrinans in Terra* of 1969), the United Nations (at its World Tourism Organization Conference in Manila 1980), and UNESCO (at its 1999 conference in Santiago).

We now briefly recall some crucial institutionalization phases of sustainable tourism. The Brundtland Commission, which defined sustainable development in its report *Our Common Future* (1987) represent the starting point of a world commitment to development that responds equitably to the social and environmental needs of both present and future generations. The commitment emphasizes the need to introduce a sustainable use of natural resources. Applying the principles of the Rio Declaration (1992) to tourist development, Agenda 21 emphasizes the urgent need to promote "the formulation of ecologically rational and culturally viable tourism programs." According to Ryel and Grasse (1991), the conservationist ethic provides several basic components: increasing public awareness of the environment, maximizing economic benefits for local communities, fostering cultural sensitivity, and minimizing the negative impacts of travel on the environment.

With Agenda 21 sustainable tourism has entered the planning of tourist development in European cities. Increasingly, master plans contemplate the adoption of specific measures aimed at promoting tourist sites compatible with the environment. Funds granted to non-governmental organizations engaged in international cooperation impose models compatible with environmental protection. During the 1990s, the magazine *The Journal of Sustainable Tourism* supported this approach, while the *Annals of Tourism*

Research and *Tourist Management* dedicated many articles to the environmental impact of tourism.

The concept of sustainable tourism emphasizes community-based planning (Murphy 1985), which connects the decommodification of mass tourism to specific targets of ecologically motivated tourism. In this approach the territorial "trademark" prevails over the dominant discourse of the international big players' company "trademark" (tour operators, hotel chains, airlines). Pearce, Moscardo and Ross (1991; 1995) have developed a method based on representation of all actors engaged in tourist-community relationships.

Sustainable tourism is the first regulation theory after mass tourism. As discussed above, sustainable tourism is characterized not just by a voluntary ethical commitment but also by coded rules within the legal regulations of national states applied at municipal and regional planning levels. It has affected tourist programs and facilities, thereby correcting erroneous evolutionary conceptions of tourist development theorized by economists like Kurt Krapf. One of the pioneers of the economic theory of tourism during the 1960s, he simplistically assumed that developing nations would benefit from international mass tourism on the Fordist model. There are close relations between relational theory and sustainable tourism. In fact, Cohen (1995), studying trends and challenges in contemporary tourism, coined the expression "sustainable authenticity" to outline those situations where demand is interwoven with conservation of the authentic culture of the local populations.

As sustainable tourism has grown, can regulation theory point the way toward rules and policies aimed at institutionalizing this new mode? Or instead does it have a mainly critical function, as stated by Mowforth and Munt (1998)? Is it possible that sustainable authenticity only represents a legitimation – the subtle and devious politics of external influence enhancing the friendly image of Western tourism? If so, is there a need to watch over it? And who should carry out this task?

City Users and Hypertourists

This theory (Martinotti 1993; Costa 1995) has developed in relation to the disembedding and re-embedding processes analyzed by Giddens (1990) and the advent of a mix within the service economy, represented by the productive use of visual culture (cinema, cartoon, television, etc.) in order to create tourist attractions for tourists.

City users (Martinotti 1993) form the consuming population that passes in a transitory way through the second-generation metropolis.[8] This population consists of cultural and recreational tourists, metropolitan businessmen, international students, athletes following their teams, suburban day-trippers, visitors crowding the historical centers for certain feasts or for shopping sprees, etc. No systematic data exists on the flows of city users.[9]

Hypertourists (Costa 1995) are city users or vacationing visitors strictly defined. They come for short periods, crowding multifunctional cities like Venice in certain periods of the year but also artificial places like Las Vegas or Rimini, defined "amusement factories" or fantasy cities (Hannigan 1998). From the socio-demographic point of view, there is hypertourism every time that the city users or vacationer visitors exceed the number of residents and therefore the city is defined as a place with a basic tourist vocation, or the artificial site attracts permanently such a number of visitors that it becomes a non-resident city similar to a theme park. The social morphology of the hypertourist city represents a transformation in contemporary capitalism. Studying the Disney theme parks, the international exhibitions, the malls and recreational cities, Costa argues that cities dominated by a single recreational function are the consequence of modern capitalistic companies employing visual culture as a productive factor within a context of expressive, market-oriented megalomania.

While the tourism economy is territorialized (the site has its unrepeatable uniqueness, where even authenticity can be found), the hypertourism economy is deterritorialized (the site has a repeatable, clonable exceptionality, effects programmed by the multimedia industry). While the museum or the beach was originally pre-tourist or extra-tourist, they become resources for corporations seeking profits; tourism companies expressly devise the hypertourist artifice as a magnet for visitors. While the collective or romantic tourist gaze is a first sight, the gaze of the hypertourist is a replay of the images forming his mental maps as a consumer of visual culture (cinema, cartoons, television, fashion).

The metropolitan businessman can also become an hypertourist when he visits a city to carry out convention activities or to meet exhibitors or buyers in a specialized fair: he lives inside an artificial, mono-functional and self-referential bubble as he crosses the multifunctional city, where the destination of his trip is located, without seeing it. He must reach, as soon as possible and in the most comfortable way, the deterritorialized magnet of the exposition hall. Then he returns, again as soon as possible and in the most comfortable way, to the city of residence. Urban spaces of the multifunctional city are evaluated as uncomfortable limits to the programming of his trip towards the specialist fair or convention. Many components of the "tourist bubble" observed by Judd (1999) as typical of hypertourist locations are the consequences of disembedding city users and hypertourists.

The sociological literature on tourism generally consists of empirical research grouped by issues (Law 1993; Jansen-Verbeke 2000), even in the publications of social scientists who define themselves as "critics" (e.g. Shaw and Williams 1994). The argument concerning city users and hypertourists is one of the few sociological theories of urban tourism. It provides information on the historic roots of the scientific attention towards urban tourism. Within consumer society and mass tourism, the city is considered as an original place (site of production) or as a destination place of all the flows (site of consumption), connected to each other through the dynamics of the ritual inversion (as explained above, the reversal of social activities). The offer of cultural services (museums, art galleries), convention centers, theme parks or mixes of leisure activities as in the mega-malls (cinemas, hotels, sport, shopping, etc.) characterizes this new urban landscape. Urban tourism has acquired a strategic function in the policies for local development. As had already happened with the Fordist factory in the mass consumer society, there is a hope that it can produce new employment.

The theory of city users and hypertourists allows an interpretation of urban policies from an original point of view. Multi-functional cities do not have a strong political subject capable of regulating local development in relation to the economic power established by the new transitory populations; they lack a meta-manager responsive to the needs of multi-motivated users who are not members of the local community and therefore do not elect local leaders. The political situation of urban tourism is contradictory: supporters of regulations work toward decommodification in order to apply principles of sustainable, responsible tourism; at the same time local entrepreneurs counterpoise policies stretching seasonal tourism in order to maintain patronage. If urban marketing policies are aimed at the attraction of city users or external capital for the realization of artificial attractions, the critical intellectual complains while local entrepreneurs resist so as to block the entrance of competitors; the result is the reproduction of the center-suburb dynamics typical of traditional tourist colonization.

The sports, exhibition, and cultural mega-events that occurred during the 1980s and 1990s in cities with international or global aspirations seem strategic factors allowing meta-managers to define local actions aimed at urban development and connecting them to a strong idea of the hospitable city. Once more the power was outside the local communities. These were media events: the main business was connected to visual culture (advertisement, television shows, sponsors, etc.). Popular media drive local elites to develop aggressive urban marketing policies that are able to catch mega-events. These events represent an instrument to win the support of residents, who may be involved directly or indirectly in the event or have expectations from it.

The acquiescence of residents derives from the promise of displaying the city on television screens or through other mass media, Internet included. Thus, the "baroque" policy of mega-events stimulates the development of tourism services and therefore a revitalization of urban functions. In any case, competition is the regulating agent of these urban policies: cities try to acquire the mega-events organized by non-governmental international organizations whose decision makers are bonded by a supra-national loyalty. They proceed through global lobbying activities, working through local firms and the municipal government, which is transformed into an entrepreneurial enterprise competing in a global contest under conditions of apparent fair play (the best one wins).

Can a progressive regulation theory qualify as a limit to baroque capitalism? And if so, why? Does it develop a "sustainable authenticity" according to an aesthetic and political choice? We present the case of Venice to illustrate our arguments and answer our question concerning the potential of regulation.

Hypertourism and Venice

Venice attracts around 12 million visitors a year. With Florence and Rome, it is a typical example of an Italian multi-functional and historic tourist city. Cultural assets and historic centers form a magnet which attracts multi-motivated visitors. Like Florence and Rome, Venice has been subjected to regulation of the tourist flows according to the spatial dynamics of mass tourism. In fact, the global coordinators of the flows are the tour operators: the big players on an international level and the small players on a local level like bus operators. In comparison to the other two cities, Venice has stronger leaning towards hypertourism, towards deterritorialization due to the prevalence of city users over residents and to the growing predominance of the big tourist players' "trademark" images. In fact, only a small proportion of the city users actually visit the most famous sights. By the second half of the 1980s, Brosio and Santagata (1992) found that only 25 percent visit St Mark's and only 20 percent the Galleria dell'Accademia. There is no direct correlation between the growth of urban tourism and the consumption of art and culture. Most people visit the city for its "atmosphere."

Statistics confirm that Venice is visited largely by day-trippers. Oggiano (1992) and Di Maria (2000) highlight the fact that the typical visitor is a commuter who resides in the neighboring areas of Mestre and Cavallino and tours the "lagoon" city both quickly and fleetingly. In fact, hotels situated within the historic center contain only 12,000 rooms. Within an

Plate 3.1   The Grand Canal, Venice. *Source*: Corbis

hour by car or train there are more than 62,000 rooms. In addition to hotels there are numerous other classes of accommodation (camp sites and houses for rent) on the northern Adriatic coast. The tourism reception area thus encompasses the entire metropolitan ring.

Looking again at various studies and research, we can delineate the following day-tripper typology:

- *commuters*: departure from and arrival back in the place of residence after having seen the city. It is the commuters of the "post-Fordist" city, however, who reproduce the spatial dynamics of the "Fordist" city: the organized mass tourist or the individual mass tourist, coordinated by the tourist industry, moves around according to synchronized rhythms but at the same time uses various infrastructures to gain access to the magnet;
- "*rebounders*": they leave from and return to their main holiday destination which is not Venice but a seaside resort. Venice is a secondary excursion. Their main motivation is to sunbathe on a resort beach and have a swim in the sea. Therefore, they cannot *not* take a "look" at the romantic city. Venice is a stop on a circuit of excursions with a hotel or rented house as its center.
- *multi-trippers*: they are visitors passing through who stay overnight after their visit in a different place from the previous night. Venice makes up part of an itinerary, of a journey planned by tour operators or by themselves.

Within each group we can distinguish between "voluntary" and "forced." The former plan to stay on the "terra firma" before the trip. The latter are forced there by lack of vacancies in the historic center or to save money.

Venice becomes all the more "hypertourist" not only because more and more often the visitors outnumber the residents on various days of the year, but also because visitors travel around the metropolitan ring with the aim of "experiencing" the city's atmosphere as they would go to an amusement park to experience the atmosphere invented by the company that created it. The visitors are not cultural tourists, they do not belong to the "new" middle class to which sustainable tourism refers, but "hypertourists" who absorb images through mental maps created by the mass media and by urban "interpretations" created by tour operators.

Urry's (1990) distinction between the "romantic gaze," based on nostalgia for heritage rescued from contemporary urbanism, and the "collective gaze," based on the four "S"s (sea, sand, sun and sex) and on entertainment, is not observable in Venice. Visitors go to Venice to participate in an urban spectacle, unique and unrepeatable, as if the city were a game for the eyes of an adult, but planted in the mind of a child – a game of images called atmosphere. Consequently, the tourist gaze is both romantic and collective.

Several urban marketing choices confirm the intertwining of images and games. During the 1980s, local administrators made a deliberate effort to revitalize the Carnival, which did not seem to be "felt" anymore by the local population, with the aim of attracting tourists in February which was considered a low tourist season. A neighboring community called Iesolo, whose economy was based on seaside tourism, advertises the sea and Venice casino with the aim of attracting visitors to the town during winter when the hotels are empty, thus feeding the number of "rebound" day-trippers.

The negative consequences that the day-trippers cause to the Venetians are the following: increase in public costs of flow management (e.g., refuse disposal, which costs the council 10 million euro a year), local transport congestion, increases in the property values leading to the displacement of residents, services favoring tourists rather than residents.

Responding to the threat of deterritorialization, the local council decided to apply the ethic of sustainable tourism. On March 23, 2002, the mayor, an economist and expert on the carrying capacity of tourism, introduced a measure to regulate flows: he set up a limited traffic zone for tourist buses. Coaches with a carrying capacity of more than 16 now have to obtain a pass in order to enter the city. There are four check-in areas where it is possible to obtain a pass, and prices range from 30 to 150 euros per day. Coaches can park in three areas where there is space for up to 300 vehicles. In peak season Venice is able to receive, assuming that each coach can carry a maximum of 54 people, 48,600 "atmosphere" seekers, spread all over the city.

The "booking" of the pass (booking is an essential concept of tourist marketing) thus shifts, conceptually speaking, from the tourism agency to the whole city, to which a macro technique of "pay-for show" is applied. Booking to see an urban spectacle becomes like booking a theater ticket. Moreover, with the "new" perspective, we are not selling a single hotel but an entire city. At the same time, the external big players' domination of city space is shifting in favor of the local community. In fact, the booking of the pass is used to reduce the impact of the coaches on the roads to better distribute the flows during the day and to charge tour operators part of the cost of providing public services throughout the city.

The ticket has been criticized by local entrepreneurs (hoteliers, bus operators), who constitute the final stage of the Fordist line of mass tourism and depend on the big international players. They fear that it does not affect the commuters, rebounders and multi-trippers but instead discourages hotel clients who find out they have to pay twice. In reality, the economic problem does not exist: the measure weighs entirely on tour operators who will see an increase in costs of 3–4 euros per person; after having earned huge amounts on the "atmosphere" of Venice, they will certainly not be ruined by such a meager increase.

The conflict between tourist operators and local councils is cultural. Regarding the gradual shift from a multifunctional city with a prevalent tourist function (subjected to little local governmental regulation but regulated by a Fordist hospitality industry) to a hypertourist city governed by sustainable tourism procedures, one should start by considering it from a community approach. This shift, as we will see in the next paragraph, can be monitored if "collaboration theory" is applied. From a "punitive" response towards mass tourism, we pass to a local development project centered on a post-Fordist hospitality industry.

Collaboration Theory as a Regulation Theory of Tourism

A new perspective is "collaboration theory," recognized as a "new" version of sustainable local development. It avoids the snobbish repudiation of mass tourism and favors a post-Fordist hospitality industry. The collaboration is a process of joint decision-making among autonomous, key stakeholders of an inter-organizational community tourism domain so as to resolve planning problems and/or to manage issues related to local development (Gray 1989; Jamal and Getz 1995).

The politics of particularity and of local economic development is the focus of the "collaboration theory" for community-based tourism planning. The connections with some sociological theories of tourism are evident. The principal ideas are derived from the "best practices" of sustainable tourism; from scientific and professional activities of intellectuals as interpreters of culture or intercultural brokers; from relational marketing for flexible service industries. These ideas can be applied to attract the responsible tourists and city users. Collaboration theory avoids dismissing mass tourism but rather considers its regulation as an important factor for local development. It therefore raises the issue of how to manage localities as "bordering shopping communities," where the exchange of goods and services can favor a more authentic meeting between hosts and guests.

Critical to the understanding of collaboration is the concept of the inter-organizational domain. Rather than concerning itself only with turbo-capitalism, which regulation theorists seek to control, collaboration theory also considers local institutions and firms. Trust among local stakeholders is critical. It follows that the local public authorities have a highly responsible task: to be "meta-managers" in planning the local system as an interactive system and facilitating the collaboration among locals and between locals and municipalities. After that stage, the local tourist industry is in a position to compete in the global tourist market.

In Venice the regulatory regime is very contradictory, because the locally based tourist businesses are fragmented and do not collaborate within the local tourist system. Venice is unlikely to become a "collective business," i.e., an industrial district like the "Third Italy"(Costa 2002), nor is it probable that it will be dominated by the so-called post-modern industries that mix visual culture, commerce, tourism, and advanced technology.

The future of the "lagoon city" is already that of "sustainable mass tourism." Nevertheless, the restraints on environmental exploitation are not enough if they do not contribute to a policy for local development. The case of Venice demonstrates that the macro and micro management techniques regarding the environmental impact of tourism are efficient if they start from the bottom, if the stakeholders mediate the diverging points of view and apply principles of participation, information and negotiation, if therefore "collaboration theory" is applied. Since you learn as you go, it is likely that the local population will accept restraint if it gives rise to effective benefits, in particular if it stimulates the creation of new jobs within tourism services and cultural facilities. In fact, relational theory can greatly aid local planners in developing entrepreneurial ideas that renew the attraction of widely consumed goods (think of artistic handicrafts), for example, by combining the purchase of goods with the booking of an internal visit to an urban market and with a more general cultural exchange between hosts and guests.

Conclusion

The simultaneous use as applied to competitive and collaborative strategies in tourism planning and destination management by organizational stakeholders merits greater examination in the field of regulation theory of tourism. We are beginning to see experiments with an interorganizational management strategy that points toward a sustainable mass tourism. Times and spaces of urban fruition are being modified to function with a kind of tourism which is more responsible, paying careful attention to the needs of the local community, recognized as an integral and reterritorialized part of the local tourist system. Social scientists can have an active role as interpreters, who, after having set the goals and characteristics of sustainable tourism, become supporters and integrators of local scale processes. They can contribute to solving conflicts through management of the environmental images of the various social groups, so that no single idea dominates. The sustainable tourist thus forms the matrix of a specific theory of local development – collaboration theory.

NOTES

1   Theories of international tourism are summarized in Apostolopoulos, Leivadi, and Yannakis (1996); Nash (1995); Graburn and Jafari (1991); Crick (1989); Cohen (1984, 1988).

2   Thus, for example, Roche (1992), dealing with mega-events and micro-modernization, proposes to initiate a sociology of "new" urban tourism.
3   See Boorstein (1961); Cohen and Taylor (1976); Turner and Ash (1975); Adler (1989).
4   Baudrillard (1988; 1991); Augé (1992; 1997); MacCannell (1992); Webber (1964).
5   Graburn (1983); Costa (1989); Shields (1991).
6   MacCannell (1976); Cohen (1992, 1995).
7   For a synthesis, Mathieson and Wall (1982); Costa (1989; 1991); Hunter and Green (1995); Mowforth and Munt (1998); and the *Journal of Sustainable Tourism*, which began publication in 1993 and provides a wide range of articles on the argument.
8   The first-generation metropolis is the industrial city inhabited by residents who abandon it for the summer vacation and commuters who use it mainly as a workplace.
9   The need for new diagnostic instruments is recognized by the World Tourism Organization (WTO) and by the Statistical Office of the European Union, Eurostat (WTO-Eurostat 1995).

REFERENCES

Adler, J, 1989a: Travel as a performed art. *American Journal of Sociology* 96: 1366–91.
—— 1989b: Origins of sightseeing. *Annals of Tourism Research* 16: 7–29.
Apostolopoulos, Y., Leivadi, S., and Yannakis, A. (eds.) 1996: *The Sociology of Tourism: Theoretical and Empirical Investigations*. London: Routledge.
Augé, M. 1992: *Non-lieux*. Paris: Seuil.
—— 1997: *L'impossible voyage: Le tourisme et ses images*. Paris: Tayot & Rivages.
Baudrillard, J. 1988: *America*. London: Verso.
—— 1991: L'Amerique, ou la pensée de l'espace. In J. Baudrillard et al., *Citoyenneté et urbanité*. Paris: Esprit, 155–64.
Bauman, Z. 1987: *Legislators and Interpreters*. Cambridge: Polity Press.
Boorstin, D. 1961: *The Image: A Guide to Pseudo Events in America*. New York: Atheneum.
Boyer, R. 1990: *The Regulation School: A Critical Introduction*. New York: Columbia University Press.
Brosio, G. and Santagata, W. 1992: *Rapporto sull'economia delle arti e dello spettacolo in Italia*. Turin: Fondazione Giovanni Agnelli.
Brundtland, G. (ed) 1987: *Our Common Future: The World Commission on Environment and Development*. Oxford: Oxford University Press.
Cohen, E. 1984: The sociology of tourism: approaches, issues and findings. *Annual Review of Sociology* 10: 373–92.
—— 1988: Tradition in the qualitative sociology of tourism. *Annals of Tourism Research* 15: 29–46.
—— 1995: Contemporary tourism – trends and challenges: sustainable authenticity or contrived post-modernity? In R. Butler and D. Pearce (eds.), *Change in Tourism: People, Places, Processes*. London: Routledge, 12–29.

Cohen, S. and Taylor, L. 1976: *Escape Attempts*. London: Routledge.

Costa, N. 1989: *Sociologia del turismo*. Milan: Iulm.

——1995: *La città dell'iperturismo*, Milan: Cuesp.

——2002: Verso la progettazione e gestione dei sistemi turistici locali. In F. Sangalli, *Le organizzazioni del turismo*. Milan: Apogeo.

Crick, M. 1989: Representations of international tourism in the social sciences: sun, sex, sights, savings and servility. *Annual Review of Anthropology* 18: 307–44.

Di Maria, E. 2000: *Cambiamenti e innovazioni nelle città d'arte: il caso di Venezia*, in E. Rullani, S. Micelli and E. Di Maria (eds.), *Città e cultura nell'economia delle reti*. Bologna: Il Mulino.

Ellsworth, J. H. and Ellsworth, M. V. 1995: *Marketing on the Internet*. New York: Wiley.

Falassi, A. 1987: *Time out of Time*. Albuquerque: University of New Mexico Press.

Giddens, A. 1990: *The Consequences of Modernity*. Cambridge: Polity Press.

Graburn, N. H. H. and Barthel-Bouchier, D. 2001: Relocating the tourist. *International Sociology* 16: 147–72.

——and Jafari, J. 1991: Introduction: tourism and social science. *Annals of Tourism Research* 18: 1–11.

Gray, B. 1989: *Collaborating: Finding Common Ground for Multiparty Problems*. San Francisco: Jossey-Bass.

Hannigan, J. 1998: *Fantasy City*. London: Routledge.

Hunter, C. and Green, H. 1995: *Tourism and the Environment: A Sustainable Relationship?* London: Routledge.

Jamal, T. B. and Getz, D. 1995: Collaboration theory and community tourism planning. *Annals of Tourism Research* 22: 186–204.

Jansen-Verbeke, M. 2000: Urban tourism. In J. Jafari (ed.), *Encyclopedia of Tourism*. London: Routledge, 615–17.

Judd, D. R. 1999: Constructing the tourist bubble. In D. R. Judd and S. S. Fainstein (eds.), *The Tourist City*. New Haven, CT: Yale University Press.

Krippendorf, J. 1987: *The Holiday People. Towards a New Understanding of Leisure and Travel*. London: William Heinemann.

Lauria, M. (ed.) 1997: *Reconstructing Urban Regime Theory*. London: Sage.

Law, C. M. 1993: *Urban Tourism*. London: Mansell.

MacCannell, D. 1976: *The Tourist*. New York: Schocken.

——1992: *Empty Meeting Grounds*. London: Routledge.

Martinotti, G. 1993: *Metropoli*. Bologna: Il Mulino.

Mathieson, A. and Wall, G. 1982: *Tourism: Economic, Physical and Social Impacts*. London: Longman.

Mowforth, M. and Munt, I. 1998: *Tourism and Sustainability: New Tourism in the Third World*. London: Routledge.

Munt, I. 1994: The other postmodern tourism: travel, culture and the new middle class. *Theory, Culture and Society* 11: 101–24.

——1995: The travel virtuosos. *Contours* 7 (2): 29–34.

Murphy, P. E. 1985: *Tourism: A Community Approach*. New York: Methuen.

Nash, D. 1995: *The Anthropology of Tourism*. Oxford: Pergamon.

Oggiano, M. 1992: *Venezia: un modello di polo turistico*. Venice: Cafoscarina.

Pearce P. L., Moscardo, G. M., and Ross, G. F. 1991: Tourism impact and community perception: an equity social representational perspective *Australian Psychologist* 26:147–52.

Poon, A. 1994: The "new" tourism revolution. *Tourism Management* 22: 91–2.

Ritzer, G. 1996: *The McDonaldization of Society*. Thousand Oaks, CA: Pine Forge Press.

Roche, M. 1992: Mega-events and micro-modernization. *British Journal of Sociology* 43: 563–600.

Ryel, R. and Grasse, T. 1991: Marketing ecotourism: attracting the elusive ecotourism. In T. Whelan (ed.), *Nature Tourism: Managing for the Environment*. Washington, DC: Island Press.

Shaw, G. and Williams, A. M. 1994: *Critical Issues in Tourism*. Oxford: Blackwell.

Shields, R. 1991: *Places on the Margin*. London: Routledge.

Turner, L. and Ash, J. 1975: *The Golden Hordes: International Tourism and the Pleasure Periphery*. London: Constable.

Urry, J. 1990: *The Tourist Gaze*. London: Sage.

Webber, M. 1964: The urban place and the non-place urban realm. In M. Webber (ed.), *Explorations in Urban Structures*. Philadelphia: University of Pennsylvania Press, 79–153.

WTO-Eurostat 1995: *Notes on Statistics of Tourism*. Brussels: Eurostat morfologia sociale della città (Bologna, 1995).

Part II

Regulating City Space

4   Amsterdam: It's All in the Mix
    Pieter Terhorst, Jacques van de Ven and Leon Deben

5   Revalorizing the Inner City: Tourism and Regulation in Harlem
    Lily M. Hoffman

6   Barcelona: Governing Coalitions, Visitors, and the Changing City
    Center
    Marisol García and Núria Claver

7   The Evolution of Australian Tourism Urbanization
    Patrick Mullins

4

Amsterdam: It's All in the Mix

Pieter Terhorst, Jacques van de Ven, and Leon Deben

Amsterdam has achieved a style of tourism that accommodates the concerns of both residents and a diverse group of visitors whose activity and spending patterns are extremely varied. What explains its appeal to such a broad spectrum? One answer is that Amsterdam offers a mix of unique and standard attractions in a monumental setting (Student Research Group 1999). Tourists and day-trippers visit the historic city center to enjoy its monuments and canals; make use of its varied opportunities (shopping, cultural and leisure facilities, offices and residential neighborhoods); and experience its unparalleled libertarian atmosphere as witnessed by "coffee shops" where one can freely buy hash and marijuana, a red-light district with sex shops and a sex museum, and a well-developed gay scene. Moreover, Amsterdam attracts visitors to a growing number of festivals and events that are held throughout the year.

This means that visitors regard Amsterdam's historic city center as "a place to let it all hang out" as well as a cultural mecca. But people do not travel to other locales only to experience that which is unique; they also want to experience much of what they enjoy in their everyday life (Ritzer and Liska 1997: 134–50). In Amsterdam's historic center, low-income housing intermingles with gentrification and its associated amenities. These amenities, found in all cities characterized by large-scale gentrification, attract middle- and upper-class tourists and day-trippers, many of whom are themselves living in gentrified areas elsewhere. And like any other big city, Amsterdam's historic center offers many ordinary shopping streets, dominated by international chain stores, cinemas, and leisure services, used by visitors and residents alike.

Apart from drugs, sex, and fun, Amsterdam is also an archetypal tourist-historical city like Prague, Boston, and Jerusalem (Judd and Fainstein 1999). It has no well-demarcated spaces that have been converted from previous activities to tourism uses. Instead, tourist sites and uses are built into the architectural and cultural fabric of the city. Tourists mix with the residents and workers, so that it is hardly possible to distinguish between Amsterdam's historic city center as a leisure, shopping, and cultural center for the local population, and as a tourist venue. As is the case with other tourist-historic cities, tourism did not originate from a carefully planned strategy by local government officials and business leaders. Amsterdam's success is rather the unintended consequence of the interaction of activities and processes that were undertaken deliberately, but for quite other reasons than to promote tourism. Attracting tourists did not play a role in "producing" monuments, or the highly varied land-use mix in the historic city center, or a libertarian atmosphere, and tourism promotion has been of only minor importance in reproducing them. The growth of Amsterdam's tourism and leisure industry has been dependent on a series of political, social, and cultural supports that are only contingently co-present.

The aim of this chapter is threefold. First, to analyze the processes that have created what are now referred to as the key assets of Amsterdam's tourism: monuments, a highly varied land use in the historic city center, and a libertarian atmosphere. Second, to shed light on the wave-like growth pattern of Amsterdam's tourism. We argue that it is in part the outcome of global, national, and local processes. Third, to discuss the political struggle over Amsterdam's dual image as a tourist city: sex, drugs, and fun on the one hand, and history, architecture and the arts on the other. We stress the economic importance of Amsterdam's historic center as a "cannabis district" and argue that Amsterdam's tourism market is much less segmented in terms of visitors and activities than is commonly assumed by policy makers.

Creating the Assets of Amsterdam's Tourism

Amsterdam's historic city center, which dates from the Netherlands' Golden Age of the seventeenth century when the city was the leading commercial and financial capital in the world, has largely survived the pressures of modernization during the nineteenth and twentieth centuries. What accounts for the contemporary character of Amsterdam's historic city center, with its mixed land use and libertarian atmosphere?

Plate 4.1 Legalized prostitution in Amsterdam. *Source:* Corbis

Having taken the dead-end path of mercantile capitalism, Amsterdam failed to make the transition to industrialization until about 1870. Consequently, for much of the nineteenth century its land uses remained relatively fixed. Since that time, the city center has undergone two distinct rounds of restructuring. The first round, which ended in the early 1970s, transformed the historic center into a classic central business district (CBD). The *second* round, beginning in 1974 and continuing through the present, has supported the growth of the tourism and leisure industry and its specialized shops and population. In both eras, the restructuring of Amsterdam's historic city was the outcome of an integral process that included economic as well extra-economic forces, shaped and mediated by successive local regimes. A local institutional regime is made up of institutional spaces constituted at various scales: international, national and local. These institutional spaces are nested, which means that their combination, interaction, and mode of articulation vary from place to place and from period to period. Thus, as we move from one area or period to another, not only do the specifics of institutional nestedness change, but so too may the interactions within that ensemble. This is why local institutional regimes are historically and geographically specific (see Boyer and Hollingsworth 1997; Martin 2000).

The first round of urban restructuring and the restructuring generated crisis,
1870–1974

The first round of restructuring of Amsterdam's historic core is very similar to that of most other Western cities. It involved a gradual decline of population, manufacturing industries, crafts, wholesale and storage, and the growth of the producer and consumer services that are associated with a classic CBD, e.g. department stores, shops, banks, business services, public administration, and hotels. In Amsterdam, this came about partly within the existing building stock, with limited restructuring of the built environment (Wagenaar 1990). There was little pressure on the inner city land market because Dutch economic growth was diffused rather than concentrated in a few cities, and during the Great Depression and World War II, Amsterdam's economy stagnated altogether. Moreover, because of its status as a world city in an earlier capitalist era, the size of the historic center was relatively large for a medium-sized city, too large to be completely filled up by a modern CBD. Thus residents were not completely displaced by offices and shops.

After World War II pressure on the historic core increased and property prices rose sharply. But even then, property values varied substantially. Buildings on the main arteries and along the main canals were much more expensive than on side streets and alleys (Kruijt 1974). This suggests that despite growing pressure on the inner-city property market, the classic CBD was not able to "colonize" the historic city center in the post-war period. Consequently there was already a highly varied land-use mix at the onset of the second round of restructuring (Heinemeijer 1968).

Although capital appeared to have ample room to maneuver in the historic city center and the first round of restructuring appeared to be the outcome of "pure," self-regulating market forces, this was not the case. The movement of population and goods-processing industries out of the historic center to surrounding areas was a highly regulated process. The city has always controlled the urban land market, and from the mid-1930s on, capital's freedom to maneuver was part of a local capital–labor accord on the future development of the city as a whole. The accord gave large-scale social housing to workers while providing industrial sites, port areas, and infrastructure to goods-processing firms. These aims could be realized simultaneously because Amsterdam's territory was large enough and because after the fiscal centralization of 1929, the city was no longer vulnerable to suburban competition.

After World War II, capital's freedom in the central core was further limited by regulation at the *national* level through a nationwide capital–labor accord. Labor unions agreed to refrain from strong wage demands in exchange for the expansion of the welfare state. To keep wages low, the central state pursued a policy of tight rent control accompanied by subsidies for new social housing construction as well as an extended system of rent protection and allocation of dwellings according to need ("queuing"). Renters in the historic city center as well as elsewhere could not be evicted from their homes and the conversion of dwellings into offices or shops was, for the most part, not permitted.

In the 1960s, both national and local capital–labor accords were undermined and the deconcentration of population and goods-processing industries could no longer be prevented. During this period, the city launched a comprehensive plan for the whole metropolitan region which would transform large parts of the historic city center into an American-style CBD and move a good part of Amsterdam's population to new towns. The CBD would become the major node of a metropolitan subway network. This plan – strongly supported by the Chamber of Commerce, the automobile lobby, and a majority of the city council including a substantial part of the Labor party – led to a "restructuring generated crisis" (Soja 2000) in the early 1970s, characterized by mass protests and violent riots. The driving force behind these protests was the baby-boom generation aligned with the urban social movements struggling for a "livable" city on a "human scale." Joining forces with residents of older central-city neighborhoods who faced "deportation" to more expensive dwellings in satellite towns, the urban social movements won the intense political struggle over Amsterdam's historic city center, which marked the end of the first round of restructuring. Reconstruction plans were withdrawn and replaced by a social policy of urban renewal. After the construction of one metro line, further extension of the network was cancelled.

The second round of restructuring, 1974 to the present

The second and ongoing round of restructuring has, for the most part, taken place in a physically stable built environment which nonetheless sustains changing uses. While the majority of producer services have declined, the tourism and leisure industries have grown, and the population has increased. The rise in population is partly the result of urban renewal-related public-housing construction in the 1980s and partly of the conversion of offices, lofts, and warehouses into condominiums for gentrifiers. Today about 35 percent of the housing stock in the historic center is made up of social-rental housing, 45 percent is private-rental housing, and owners occupy the remaining 20 percent. With the exception of financial services, universities, public administration, and culture, the scale of all firms has declined. Research shows that the latter trend indicates a growing diversification. Thus Amsterdam's historic center has not only become a place for consuming, but also of more diversified production (Van Duren 1995).

Preservation of the built environment has shaped the development of Amsterdam's historic center and has been of crucial importance in its emergence as a leisure and tourism center. Amsterdam now has 7,600 listed "monuments," i.e. buildings that are not allowed to be demolished and that are subject to government control regarding physical changes as well as use. Monuments make up more than 10 percent of all buildings in Amsterdam's historic city center, but the impact of these monuments on the built environment is greater than the figure itself reveals. Because monuments are scattered throughout the historic city center and on nearly every block, land-use plans and zoning ordinances have been very conservative regarding the overall appearance of the historic urban landscape, including non-listed buildings and street patterns. Recently, Amsterdam's historic center has been listed as a historic preservation district. That means that non-listed buildings and public spaces have become subject to even stricter forms of political control.

As a result of these preservation policies, the built environment of Amsterdam's historic center – including streets and canals – is more or less frozen. We say "more or less" because the city has often been flexible in making compromises on adaptations of monuments as long as original appearance of the façades is maintained (and new structures have been built behind many façades). Regulation maintaining the frozen built environment has had a major impact on the area's land-use, and consequently economic, mix. First, historic buildings are too small for large offices and shops, and the fragmented ownership structure makes it hard to combine two or more buildings. In addition, historic street patterns make them nearly inaccessible by car. This has made Amsterdam's historic center an attractive place for activities that are small scale and insensitive to time pressure, like leisure and "fun" shopping. Second, the fact that the buildings in the historic city center vary widely as regards size, quality, and location (main streets versus side streets and alleys) prevents a homogenized land use and has provoked variety. Third, the historic city landscape offers many opportunities for upper-class households to distinguish themselves by accumulating "cultural capital" (Bourdieu 1979). The same applies to specialized firms like antique shops, second-hand bookshops, *haute cuisine* restaurants and other niche-market firms that are very sensitive to an exclusive built environment. Fourth, because functional segregation of land uses may conflict with the preservation of monuments, most types of land use have been accepted in the historic city center on the condition that the outside of the building is respected. In this fashion, Amsterdam has combined strict controls on the appearance of the built environment with

considerable flexibility in its uses. As a result, regulation of the built environment has unintentionally provoked a market-led land-use change and
has unwittingly stimulated the rise of a flexible leisure economy in the historic city center.

One zoning ordinance from the 1980s deserves to be mentioned here
because of its substantial impact. Due to housing shortages, buildings in
the historic city center can be converted into housing units, but not the
other way around. Consequently, the booming housing market has dominated all other real estate sub-markets for the past 20 years. Ever since the
1980s, lofts and offices have been displaced by owner-occupied apartments,
and in some exceptional cases, by private rental and public-housing apartments (the Entrepôtdok is an example of the latter).

Owner-occupiers have been able to outbid offices for several reasons.
Office-based companies are less attracted to the historic but frozen inner
city. The city's housing policy has also played a role. Between 1945 and
1985, 90 percent of all new construction was public rental housing. As a
result, aspiring homeowners had little choice: they could either move to
suburbia or resort to loft or office conversion within the historic city center
– among the few locations in Amsterdam available to them. The fact that
owner-occupiers receive generous tax credits in the Netherlands has also
contributed to the outbidding of offices and lofts by apartments. The use
of tax relief has been particularly strong in the city center, because historic
dwellings are "positional goods" with an elasticity of supply of zero.

Some gentrification has taken place through incumbent upgrading, but
most gentrifiers live in converted lofts or offices. As a result, widespread
gentrification has not produced large-scale displacement. Gentrification
and the policy of constructing new social-rental housing went hand in
hand, and more remarkably, were often carried out on the same street or
block.

Amsterdam's social movements and quality of life issues

How did the urban social movements succeed in blocking the first round
of restructuring and enforce a switch to the second round? This is a crucial
question because their political victory unintentionally stimulated the later
growth of gentrification and tourism. Well-educated young baby-boomers
were the driving force behind the struggle for a more livable city, and urban
social movements were the pioneers of a post-materialist culture. The
struggle over the character of the city was intimately interwoven with the
battle against authoritarianism, with women's liberation, the environmental movement, and the call for more flexible attitudes towards sex and
drugs. Although this cultural shift was going on in all Western countries, it

was particularly strong in the Netherlands (see Inglehart 1977), and involved fierce intergenerational conflict.

The power of urban social movements was, first and foremost, the unintended outcome of pillarization and depillarization. Historically, Dutch Protestants and Catholics (alongside social democrats and liberals) were organized in "pillars," i.e. self-contained *non-territorial* communities. Each had its own political parties, unions, mass media, and sport clubs, and each also controlled its "own" semi-private organizations (schools, hospitals, public housing corporations) that provided public goods, financed by the central state. In the 1960s, however, a process of depillarization had set in: religious attendance and voting declined; Catholic and Protestant associations and parties disappeared or merged; the ties between interest groups and parties loosened; and elite control over society lessened. Depillarization fuelled a further expansion of the welfare state, because it made the formerly cooperative relationship between the leaders of the pillars more competitive and undermined the ability of these leaders to withstand pressures from below for radical democratization of industrial relations and more welfare state services. All this was grist for the mill of urban social movements. And although they took the lead in breaking up the old system of pillarization, their power was paradoxically based on a new form of pillarization. Like the religious groups before them, the baby boomers claimed the right to live their own lives and have "their own" public goods and services, financed by the central state (Zahn 1989). Thus, the move to the second form of spatial restructuring resulted from a movement inspired by a transformation in the mode of regulation which partially caused, and then interacted with, a shift in the regime of accumulation to a new structure of production.

These processes were felt more strongly in Amsterdam than in the country as a whole. A growing number of baby boomers moved to the city. As the largest center for higher education in the Netherlands, Amsterdam became the main battleground for a young intellectual avant-garde who claimed the right to experiment socially on a wide range of issues. Drug policy is a case in point. Pressured by this generation, a semi-legal compromise on the use and sale of soft drugs was negotiated in the mid-1970s.

The growth of a young population stimulated the rise of a flourishing youth culture marked by music centers, cafés and "coffee shops" that stocked hash and marijuana. As suburbanization proceeded, Amsterdam's older housing stock – composed of small, cheap dwelling units – opened up to young households, and when inner-city renewal began, a new type of subsidized social-rental housing was created for young single households.

The political power of urban social movements was strengthened by the structure of the Dutch state, territorially consolidated and fiscally centralized (Terhorst and van de Ven 1997). During the heyday of Dutch fiscal centralization in the 1980s, local taxes made up only 6 percent of the revenues of Dutch municipalities, and general and specific grants 32 percent and 62 percent respectively. This structure allowed urban social movements and leftist politicians to forge a non-growth alliance for the historic center. First of all, a more livable city center coupled with social housing would hardly affect the local tax base. Furthermore, the fact that offices were *de facto* excluded from Amsterdam's historic city center was not a major problem for the growth of the city's service sector. Thanks to its territorial size, the city offered excellent alternative locations for office development along its ring road.

The prioritizing of a *local* distributional policy over an urban growth policy was helped by the fact that the post-war *national* capital-labor accord was over by the late 1960s/early 1970s. Dutch corporatism had become "immobile" in the face of the economic crisis of the 1970s, and at the national level redistribution was favored over a pro-growth policy (Visser and Hemerijck 1997). This benefited a big city like Amsterdam because general and specific grants (and tax deductions for renovating monuments) dramatically increased in the 1970s. In addition, the organization of Dutch capital at the national level along sectoral (neo-corporatist) rather than territorial lines meant that local businesses were too weak to obstruct the switch to the second round of restructuring. There are no American-style urban growth coalitions in the Netherlands (Terhorst and van de Ven 1995).

Crisis-Generated Restructuring of the City Center

Tourism in Amsterdam has fluctuated sharply in the past 30 years due to factors such as the cyclical growth of world trade, floating exchange rates, and events like Chernobyl (1986) and the Gulf War (1991). Along with these short-term fluctuations, a long-wave-like growth pattern can be discerned: fast growth in the 1960s, stagnation in the 1970s and 1980s, and a strong recovery in the late 1980s and 1990s.

Apart from its reputation as a tourist-historical city, the growth of tourism in Amsterdam in the 1960s was largely based on a booming global economy and Amsterdam's transformation into a "hippie" center like Copenhagen and San Francisco. Growing numbers of backpackers traveled to Amsterdam to stay in cheap hostels or even the open air (the "magic" Vondelpark). After the "legalization" of soft drugs, the stream of drug tourists increased, a fact which partly explains why the tourism industry began stagnating in the 1970s. Most youth tourists were low-budget travelers whose demand for cheap services and drugs was crowding out middle- and upper-class tourists.

However, the growing number of low-budget tourists was not the "real" cause of Amsterdam's tourism stagnation. From the mid-1970s to the late 1980s, well-to-do tourists no longer visited Amsterdam because it was a city in crisis. Its population was declining, unemployment was very high (over 25 percent), the number of people on welfare was skyrocketing, and crime rates related to drug trafficking were on the increase. The privately owned buildings along the main canals were poorly maintained, graffiti were omnipresent, and dirty streets were the rule rather than the exception. Moreover, the high level of Dutch taxes and social charges worked to the disadvantage of a labor-intensive industry like tourism. In short, high prices for services in an increasingly dirty and unsafe city made Amsterdam less attractive to tourists. No wonder that the Amsterdam Tourist Organization (VVV), a cooperative of 1,200 Amsterdam tourist firms, complained loudly about the city's bad image.

The economic crisis of the late 1970s and early 1980s hit the Netherlands more severely than other European countries and was a catalyst for change at the local as well as the national level. In Soja's terms (2000), it provoked a "crisis-generated restructuring" of Amsterdam's historic center. Attempts to make Dutch corporatism more responsive (Visser and Hemerijck 1997) resulted in the "Wassenaar Accord" in which labor unions agreed to keep wages low in exchange for redistributing jobs by reducing the work week. This, in turn, allowed the national government to regain control over public sector finance by cutting state expenditures, reforming the welfare state, and deregulating and/or privatizing many public services. In turn, these policies have been beneficial for labor-intensive service industries such as tourism.

National spending cuts, however, adversely affected local finances and forced Dutch cities to switch from a redistributive approach to a pro-growth policy. Amsterdam sought to reverse its population decline and attract middle- and upper-class households, by rejecting the national new-towns policy in favor of a "compact city policy," as Rotterdam had done somewhat earlier. The Netherlands national government later adopted a country-wide urban pro-growth policy (Terhorst and van de Ven 1995). Amsterdam reduced social-housing production to make way for the construction of expensive private-rental and owner-occupied housing and sought to attract foreign companies by making the city safer and cleaner. Although not primarily intended to stimulate tourism, the tourist industry has certainly benefited from these policies. Accompanying these changes were phenomena new to Dutch society: local "boosterism" and "city marketing strategies." Amsterdam, for example, lobbied for the Olympic Games of 1992, initiated publicity campaigns directed at countering its negative image as an unsafe and dirty city, and began to support private initiatives for organizing festivals.

In the late 1980s, the economy recovered slowly, with unemployment remaining high. The rapid influx of well-educated, double-income households coupled with the freezing of welfare benefits produced a more "dual city" with gentrification gaining full speed in the historic city center, while some of the newer neighborhoods were growing poorer. Since gentrification in the historic city center happened mainly through the conversion of lofts and offices, the population in the center not only became more affluent on average but increased in size. This led to a rapid rise in the services associated with gentrification, i.e. restaurants, trendy bars, antique shops, and art galleries. It also stimulated large-scale renovation of the building stock. As a result, these areas have become more attractive to day-trippers and tourists, particularly those who are themselves gentrifiers in their home country. The process of large-scale gentrification, with the accompanying changes in size and quality of consumer services, has played an important role in improving Amsterdam's image. The rise of consumer services in the historic city center is also related to national policies of wage moderation and labor-market flexibility, which are estimated to account for two-thirds of Dutch job growth (CPB 1997). The large student population of Amsterdam not only functions as a reservoir of cheap, flexible labor but also as a workforce at ease with "demanding" foreign tourists.

Nowadays, although many tourists come to Amsterdam as part of a standard (often low-budget) package, and backpackers still arrive in great numbers, more and more people travel on an individual basis. Since the late 1980s, middle-class tourists have rediscovered the city, stimulating a further expansion of cultural and leisure facilities, which in turn has made the historic city center an even more attractive place to live. This process of cumulative attraction has been further reinforced by the growing number of foreign firms that have established their regional headquarters in Amsterdam.

Although the national and local economy began sliding into a recession in the summer of 2001, September 11 has hardly proved to be a negative factor. Despite a decline of visitors after September 11, the total number of visitors in 2001 was equal to that of 2000. Thus, according to the Amsterdam Tourism Board, "the development of Amsterdam's tourism in 2001 was not so bad after all" (*Trouw*, July 10, 2002: 3).

Amsterdam's Contested Image

Amsterdam's attractiveness as a tourist destination for extremely diverse groups arises from its dual image. The "city of culture" is also the place "to let it all hang out." Drugs, sex, and fun are offered next to Rembrandt, Van Gogh, Golden-Age architecture, and cultural events. In the past 25 years, politicians and interest groups have argued about Amsterdam's image as a tourist destination. Right-wing politicians and the Amsterdam Tourist Board have tried to change Amsterdam's image from "city of soft drugs" to city of "high culture." Their main argument is that a city of "high culture" will attract the well-to-do tourists who spend more money than the backpackers. They downplay the economic importance of Amsterdam's historic city center as a "cannabis district" and implicitly assume that backpackers and middle- and upper-class tourists represent segmented markets: that backpackers only come to Amsterdam for its "coffee shops," and middle-class tourists for its "high culture." Both assumptions, however, need further examination.

Soft drugs as big business in the historic center

Since the 1960s, soft drugs have been widely used and sold in Amsterdam. This practice was semi-legalized in 1975, when "coffee-shops" selling soft drugs in small quantities were no longer prosecuted. This led to a wave of new openings, with street peddling replaced by a more regulated distribution system.

Dutch soft-drugs policy has given the country a "comparative advantage" in relation to its neighbors. More than 50 percent of all soft drugs are sold to foreign clients. As in all new product markets, a growing competition has provoked specialization in the geographic origin of drug "brands," the geographic origin of clients, and the selling of seeds for home growing. Although not officially allowed to advertise, many "coffee shops" distribute full color catalogues and function as mail order companies that sell seeds and equipment via the Internet all over the world. Every year a "best weed festival" is organized, including "nominations" and "awards." Since 1990, a new variety of "coffee shop" has appeared on the scene – the "smart shop," which sells all kinds of "natural" products that are supposed to have a stimulating influence on the mind. Related industries have taken off in proximity to the "coffee shops," such as tattoo and body-piercing studios that deliver their services to the same clientele. Taken together, there are now a few hundred of these shops and studios in the historic city center.

The "soft drugs complex" is an important part of Amsterdam's inner city economy. "Coffee shops" are lucrative businesses that sell for hundreds of millions of euros and employ thousands of young people who "learn by doing." The labor force is highly skilled, very mobile and international in its recruitment. There is probably no other place in the world where the knowledge of soft drugs is as localized as in Amsterdam's historic city center. Due to its uniqueness, the Amsterdam "soft drug complex" has become an international tourist attraction.

However, the rise of the "cannabis district" is not unchallenged. Neighboring countries have complained about the Dutch soft drugs policy, and recently the rules regarding "coffee shops" have tightened somewhat. But a further containment of the "soft drugs complex" is extremely unlikely, because the soft-drugs policy is widely supported in the Netherlands, particularly in Amsterdam. And even if other European countries relax their legislation (as recently happened in Belgian Flanders), it would be hard to compete with Amsterdam. Therefore, the city will probably remain the "world capital of soft drugs.'

Amsterdam's tourism market – segmented or mixed?

Due to the growing number of tourists and their differentiation, the tourist sector itself has become more diversified. We find the specialized, flexible and small-scale tourism that typifies post-Fordism, as well as the completely standardized and mass-organized Fordist style, and everything in between. Although both formulas have grown in Amsterdam, the more specialized and small-scale tourist services have increased the most.

The activity patterns of Amsterdam's visitors are also much less segmented than one might expect. Our research shows that it is very difficult to tie types of visitors to tourism modes. Many visitors arrive as part of a complete package, but the number of travelers who organize their own travel is increasing. That makes the latter less dependent on big, standardized tourist operators. But more often than not, visitors switch between both extremes. Backpackers use low-budget offers by large travel agencies, stay in small hotels and frequent extremely diversified niche markets during the daytime. Many middle-class tourists more or less do the same. They arrive with a budget flight, sleep in a four-star hotel, have lunch at McDonald's, frequent small art galleries, do some luxury shopping, have a standard boat trip through the canals and have dinner in a moderately priced Korean or Ethiopian family restaurant (Student Research Group 1999).

Although the majority of young tourists visit a "coffee shop," only a minority say that using soft drugs is the exclusive reason to travel to the city. The backpackers who frequent the "coffee shops" also visit the Van Gogh Museum, and many well-educated middle-class tourists walk through the red-light district and visit the "coffee shops." Moreover, not all backpackers are low-budget tourists as was the case in the 1960s and 1970s. Many are affluent tourists for whom a backpack is merely a life-style symbol (Student Research Group 1999). Overall, the activity patterns of

Amsterdam's visitors intermingle and intertwine. It may even be that the variety of tourists and locals adds to Amsterdam's attraction and benefits all, because the net result is an exotic and varied street life.

At present, the activity patterns of Amsterdam visitors and the highly varied mix of small-scale facilities reinforce each other. Nonetheless, we predict that a further growth of tourism will threaten this mix of small-scale activities which is one of Amsterdam's key assets. Activities that depend on large numbers of visitors are displacing more marginal economic activities in the booming real-estate market of Amsterdam's historic city center. For example, a hairdresser in a traditional residential neighborhood, confronted with a 500 percent rise in rents, will eventually make way for another ice-cream chain store. In the long run, this may disturb the delicate mix of small-scale activities. The increasing dominance of the tourist economy may even lead to less tolerance, since public space has first and foremost to be clean and safe. In short, key assets of Amsterdam's tourism – the variety of activities, the liberal outlook – may ultimately be undermined by the exponential growth of tourism.

Another danger is that the synergy between tourism and gentrification is coming undone as friction between visitors and residents grows. Local policy-makers may have to reconcile the increasingly conflicting demands of the ever more powerful tourist industry with those of the new residential elite.

Conclusion

This chapter has shown that the emergence of Amsterdam as a tourist city is only partially the intended outcome of a planned strategy by tourist business leaders and local government officials. The foundations of a flourishing tourist economy were laid earlier in the successful struggles against the reconstruction of the historic city center, the social policy of inner-city renewal without displacement, and the avant-garde role of the Dutch baby-boom generation that used Amsterdam as the main stage for social experiments. All these factors – which draw upon a mix of cultural, political, and economic institutions and actors, articulating at differing levels of society and government – unintentionally created ideal preconditions for the gentrification and incumbent upgrading that started in the late 1980s. The local regime, by opting to only lightly regulate activities which elsewhere have been subjected to zero-tolerance policies, made possible Amsterdam's particular blend. Interestingly many of these activities are perceived as threatening in other cities but here retain broad appeal. This seemingly odd state of affairs is largely attributable to the urban social movements that contested the mode of state regulation and caused the municipality to retreat from its massive urban renewal program in the early 1970s.

Formal and informal rules arising from national government programs, Amsterdam's own policies, and the social norms of a highly tolerant local culture thus combined to create the framework supporting the tourism regime. The balance among the elements of that regime, however, is becoming increasingly unstable. During the 1990s, the tourist sector has gained dominance in the central-city economy, raising questions as to the sustainability of the balance between the claims of residents and visitors and threatening to undermine key assets of Amsterdam's tourism – its varied mix of small-scale activities and its dual image. How these evolving tensions are resolved is central to the fate of Amsterdam's historic core and to Amsterdam's tourism.

REFERENCES

Bourdieu, P. 1979: *La Distinction: critique sociale du jugement.* Paris: Editions de Minuit.

Boyer, R. and Hollingsworth, J. 1997: From national embeddedness to spatial and institutional nestedness. In J. R. Hollingsworth and R. Boyer (eds.), *Contemporary Capitalism, the Embeddedness of Institutions.* Cambridge: Cambridge University Press, 433–84.

CPB 1997: *Macro-Economische Verkenningen.* The Hague: Centraal Planbureau.

Heinemeijer, W. F. 1968: De Amsterdamse Binnenstad als Centrum van Attractie. In W. F. Heinemeijer, M. van Hulten, and H. D. de Vries Reilingh (eds.), *Het Centrum van Amsterdam. Een Sociografische Studie.* Amsterdam: Polak & Van Gennep.

Inglehart, R. 1977: *The Silent Revolution: Changing Values and Political Styles among Western Publics.* Princeton, NJ: Princeton University Press.

Judd, D. R. and Fainstein, S. S. (eds.) 1999: *The Tourist City.* New Haven, CT: Yale University Press.

Kruijt, B. 1974: *De Prijsontwikkeling op de Tweedehands Gebouwenmarkt.* Deventer: Kluwer.

Martin, R. 2000: Institutional approaches in economic geography. In E. Sheppard and T. Barnes (eds.), *A Companion to Economic Geography.* Oxford: Blackwell, 77–94.

Ritzer, G. and Liska, A. 1997: "McDisneyization" and "post-tourism": complementary perspectives on contemporary tourism. In C. Rojek and J. Urry (eds.), *Touring Cultures, Transformations of Travel and Theory.* London: Routledge, 96–109.

Soja, E. W. 2000: *Postmetropolis: Critical Studies of Cities and Regions.* Oxford: Blackwell.

Student Research Group 1999: *Toerisme in Amsterdam.* Faculteit Maatschappij en Gedragswetenschappen, Afdeling Geografie en Planologie, Universiteit van Amsterdam.

Terhorst, P. and van de Ven, J. 1995: The National Urban Growth Coalition in the Netherlands. *Political Geography* 14: 343–61.

—— 1997: *Consolidated Brussels and Consolidated Amsterdam: A Comparative Study of the Spatial Organization of Property Rights* (*Netherlands Geographical Studies* 223). Amsterdam: Netherlands Geographical Society/Department of Geography, Faculty of Environmental Sciences, University of Amsterdam.

Van Duren, A. J. 1995: *De Dynamiek van het Constante: Over de Flexibiliteit van de Amsterdamse Binnenstad als Economische Plaats.* Utrecht: Jan van Arkel.

Visser, J. and Hemerijck, A. 1997: "*A Dutch Miracle*": *Job Growth, Welfare Reform and Corporatism in the Netherlands.* Amsterdam: Amsterdam University Press.

Wagenaar, M. 1990: *Amsterdam 1876–1914: Economisch Herstel, Ruimtelijke Expansie en Veranderende Ordening van het Stedelijk Grondgebied.* Amsterdam: Amsterdamse Historische Reeks No. 16, Historisch Seminarium van de Universiteit van Amsterdam.

Zahn, E. 1989: *Regenten, Rebellen en Reformatoren: een Visie op Nederland en de Nederlanders.* Amsterdam: Contact.

5

Revalorizing the Inner City: Tourism and Regulation in Harlem

Lily M. Hoffman

This chapter brings regulation theory and the broader post-Fordist debate together with an empirical study of the emergence and consequences of tourism in the disadvantaged, racially segregated, inner city community of central Harlem, New York.[1] It asks what a restructuring economy and accompanying institutional change mean for this beleaguered area and its residents. How will they fare socially, spatially, and economically in the post-Fordist city, and what is the role of tourism in this process?

A regulation framework allows us to address the relation between large-scale external forces and local conditions – the issue of scale. Its focus on institutional structure also helps clarify the complex web of cultural, political, and economic factors which are central to this case study and to tourism in general. Harlem has been chosen on methodological as well as substantive grounds. First, analyzing intra-urban difference leads us to disaggregate areas within cities in relation to tourism, thereby making for a more complex analysis. Second, Harlem is a critical site because its rapid transformation allows us to look more closely at the interplay of consumption and production at the heart of the new economy. Tourism – in this context – embodies the relationship between the economic development of ghettos and the marketing of diversity.

Social/Spatial Inequality in the Post-Fordist City

Regulation theory, broadly conceived, assumes two partially autonomous systems: the macro economy or regime of accumulation and a comprehensive mode of "regulation" – an institutional system that stabilizes a given regime of accumulation (Amin 1994). Despite numerous debates, a consensus has developed as to the elements of the emerging macro economy: changing market trends, flexible specialization for niche markets, globalized industries and processes, and information technology. In contrast to the Fordist paradigm of mass production for mass markets, the restructuring of production, marketing and consumption has been characterized as post-Fordist.

However, the institutional framework or mode of regulation is less clearly delineated and there is much less agreement about its basic elements. This has given rise to differing and conflicting views of the post-Fordist future, due partly to neo-institutionalist expectations of social/cultural variation but also to the belief that outcomes are not determined but a matter of political contest. Drawing on Ash Amin's synthesis of the regulation/post-Fordist discussion, I identify several debates with implications for social and spatial inequality and reframe them in terms of the marginalized inner city.

Local/global effects of economic restructuring

One issue is the spatial impact of economic restructuring. Will flexible specialization make for greater or lesser localization and with it, more or less opportunity for revitalizing localities and integrating them into regional and/or global networks (see *inter alia* Storper and Scott 1989; Amin and Malmberg 1994; Sabel 1994; Storper 1994)? As noted above, to study a marginalized inner city area which is demographically and economically distinct, we need to disaggregate – to look closely at how the aspects of economic restructuring play out on specific areas and their populations.

Culture and social/spatial polarization

Does the increasing importance of culture and consumption to cities exacerbate existing forms of social and spatial inequality (Harvey 1994) or provide new opportunities for marginalized areas and populations? The differentiation of formerly standardized markets has valorized multiculturalism and diversity, giving rise to new forms of cultural capital and creating interest in formerly unattractive places. This cultural capital may translate into social, economic, and/or political clout for formerly disadvantaged groups, or become a new form of commodification, controlled by old elites.

The geography of the cultural sector also seems to be shifting. Studies of nonprofit arts and cultural organizations have found that they concentrate in economically and ethnically diverse neighborhoods (Stern 1997, 1999). Urban planning initiatives such as cultural districts promote this trend. The studies also show agglomeration effects related to cultural production as cultural organizations draw related businesses and jobs and enhance commercial and residential real estate.

Politics and policy

The question here is whether politics and policy are becoming more democratic and inclusive as they become more market driven (Hirst and Zeitlin 1991; Lipietz 1994; Mayer 1994), or more exclusive, restrictive, and unaccountable (Esser and Hirsch 1994). Trends include: greater involvement of localities in economic regeneration (Jessop 1994; Mayer 1994); new types of social and political alliances (Hirst and Zeitlin 1991); and new actors and methods of decision-making.

A related issue is the role of social capital. A mostly progressive literature has tied social capital to community development and political inclusion by means of bonding within communities and linkage to outside resources (Putnam 2000; Gittell and Vidal 1998; Body-Gendrot and Gittell 2003). Programs like as the Empowerment Zone[2] exemplify this approach, requiring the participation of differing levels of government as well as public and private sectors, to make for new working relationships (Gittell and Vidal 1998). But these approaches are susceptible to accusations of cooptation and ineffectiveness.

This analysis, based on an ongoing case study of the emergence and consequences of tourism in Harlem, argues that:

- Changes in Harlem's political economy and culture are a response to the restructuring macro economy, although not determined by it.
- As development occurs, the nature of regulation pertaining to Harlem also begins to change, so as to stabilize and support the restructuring economy.
- Tourism-based development has the potential to be an equalizing force, helping to rebalance the uneven social/spatial development symbolized by places like Harlem in the past (Fordist) era.

Global Forces/Local Conditions: Tourism and Development in Harlem

Demand by foreign visitors stimulated tourism to Harlem beginning in the late 1980s (Hoffman 1997, 2000). Although they came to see New York City, which was enjoying a tourism boom, many had Harlem on their itinerary and the Harlem tour was paid for and organized abroad. Over the next decade tourism to Harlem increased exponentially so that by 2000, over 800,000 people were coming annually, including an increasing number of domestic visitors (Audience Research and Analysis 2000). This growth *preceded* both the development of a tourism infrastructure and the decline in the crime rate (New York City Economic Development Corporation 1997). Initially there were no jazz clubs, only a few restaurants that could handle a busload of visitors, and few places to shop. Security was an issue, and guidebooks warned against traveling Uptown alone.

For visitors, Harlem represented Black America and its music and entertainment traditions. Their interest was fueled by trends in the music and pop culture industries such as the resurgence of classic jazz, the revival of soul and funk, and the interest in gospel music. US movies and TV also disseminated an image of the inner city as a source of cultural innovation – from clothes to music to graffiti. Visitor demand, in turn, jump-started a fledgling tourism industry, giving rise to Harlem-based tours and activities initiated by local (Harlem) entrepreneurs as well as city-wide tour bus operators. At first, Harlem did not capture many tourism dollars as visitors only got off the bus in a few designated places. By the latter half of the 1990s, however, an economic revival was underway which made tourism development more possible.

To understand the interplay of external and internal forces that bring tourism and development to Harlem, we need to look more closely at trends in the tourism and entertainment industries and at their "fit" with a ghetto economy and culture. For although Harlem is a unique community with global name recognition, it shares social and demographic characteristics with other disadvantaged urban areas – namely a distinctive political economy and cultural diversity. During a period of economic restructuring, marked by a shift to flexible production for targeted markets, these same social/demographic characteristics acted as a *draw* for industries including tourism and entertainment and brought into play public and private actors at city, state, and local level.

The political economy of the inner city

Urban economists have noted that declining inner-city neighborhoods take on distinctive patterns in regard to economic activities. Modeling ghetto economies according to type and size of enterprise, Bingham and Zhang (1997) found that changes in the pattern of economic activity occur early in the poverty cycle. When the poverty rate reaches 20 percent, there is "economic ghettoization." Most activities associated with a middle-income neighborhood (supermarkets, commercial banks, legal and accounting services) disappear, replaced by used merchandise outlets, check cashing operations, liquor stores, job training and family services – the hallmarks of a transfer economy based upon government-funded services and informal activity.

Harlem fits this profile. The 1996 data for Upper Manhattan – an area larger than Harlem – show it to be densely populated (520,000 residents) and characterized by the small-scale retail and service establishments of a ghetto economy. The net result is that residents make most of their purchases elsewhere (Schaffer 1996). Unmet shopping demand in Harlem is over twice that of the average inner city – 60 to 70 percent as compared to the average of 25 percent (ICIC 1998).

Market demand. In a seminal article that served to redirect policy to the inner city, Michael Porter put a different spin on these figures (1995). Reinterpreting the statistics from a marketing perspective, Porter argued that local market demand is one of the "true" competitive advantages of economically disadvantaged inner-city areas. Compared to suburbs and other urban areas, they are under-serviced and under-retailed. Although average household income is low, the dense residential population has an aggregate buying power comparable to that in other parts of the city. But few businesses entered these markets by themselves. Porter's "economic" model, disseminated by his non-profit organization – the Initiative for a Competitive Inner City (ICIC) – played an important role in encouraging investment by providing convincing analytic support for the inner city as a new economic frontier. The ICIC influenced such Harlem-based organizations as the Abyssinian Development Corporation[3] and the Upper Manhattan Empowerment Zone (UMEZ). The organization begun in 1996, which administered the largest of the six federal urban empowerment zones.[4] UMEZ commissioned a study of Upper Manhattan and used the findings to target four high-growth industries, one of which was tourism and entertainment. The plan was to recruit leading companies, stimulate small businesses, and develop the local workforce. Entertainment and heritage tourism would build on Harlem's well-known connections to music and performance and on its unique cultural and historical attractions.

Building social capital, providing political reassurance. Red tape and political conflict between city and state (which provided matching funds) delayed the start of the program for a year, then stalled the grants process for another year. Although critics claimed that UMEZ had done too little too late, the empowerment zone made Harlem appear to be a safe place for investors and visitors. New and emerging markets require support and reassurance. UMEZ's importance, aside from projects, was as a "bridge" to the downtown business community. The initial UMEZ Board formed in 1996 – composed of public officials and chaired by Richard D. Parsons, then CEO of Time Warner – was key to this process, reaching out to relevant institutions and actors to expand Harlem's social capital and capacity and to attract national and international publicity.

The 1990s marked the ascendance of a new generation of leaders. To revive Harlem, they believed that Harlem had to be open to investment, albeit with watchdogs in place to make certain that there were local stakeholders and that Harlem was not "given away." A symbolic marker of Harlem's success in building bridges was the Abyssinian Development Corporation's first fundraiser – a black-tie affair held in an Uptown venue and attended by a large cross-section of the city's business, social and political elite.

Marketing diversity

Multiculturalism and diversity have recently become a positive demographic characteristic for business and tourism. Contributing to this sea change is the move toward "niche" or targeted production and marketing, an aspect of flexible specialization which coincides with the saturation of traditional markets, heightened global competition, and the search for new economic frontiers (i.e. non-traditional markets/populations).

Local entrepreneurs potentially can take advantage of this shift. However, given the inner city's lack of access to loans, financial know-how, and adequate technology, exploiting these opportunities has required concerted, politically inspired efforts typically related to federal policy initiatives. Commercial banks have not willingly entered the inner city despite evidence of profit, unless required to do so under the fair banking/fair lending provisions of the 1977 Community Reinvestment Act (Grogan and Proscio 2000). UMEZ's small business lending arm targeted restaurants and tourism-related activities for start-up and expansion along with ethnically based retail or service providers (e.g. cosmetics, clothing). It has had some success, mainly with established businesses such as a well-known Harlem soul food restaurant. Overall, small business start-ups and expansions struggle, particularly in economically depressed areas.

Branding and place. The logic of niche marketing becomes a form of "branding" that has also brought new productive activities and jobs to Harlem. Pushed by rising commercial rents in lower Manhattan, a number of businesses and organizations have opted to move to Harlem to take on its place-based identity.

Although some ventures have become victims of economic recession and the post-9/11 environment, published interviews with businesses relocating Uptown give some insight into this process: Edison Schools, the country's largest school management company, together with the Museum for African Art, proposed in 2000 to build a combined corporate headquarters, school and museum at 110th Street and Fifth Avenue, the gateway to Harlem. Edison Chairman Benno C. Schmidt, Jr. said: "That particular location stands as a crossroads between the Latino and the African-American communities, which made it a perfect location in terms of representing the communities that are our partners around the country." The Museum of African Art, which originally moved from Washington, DC, to Soho to be in the art scene, said in 2000: "We want to be located in a community with a significant population of African-Americans" (Wyatt 2000). The best-known example of place-branding belongs to former President Clinton, who established his offices on Harlem's main commercial thoroughfare.

The pursuit of ethnic and cultural branding reflects the fact that minorities are the fastest growing (new) consumer population. Discussing their "aggressive targeting of minorities," Time Warner executive Derek Johnson stated: "Both the US and world populations are becoming less homogenous and we want to reach out and touch the entire population base" (Block 2000).

Trend-setting and innovation. The trend-setting sensibility of the inner city is another potential attraction for tourism and entertainment. This quality made Harlem great during the Harlem Renaissance of the 1920s, but has been a concern during the present revival. When international tourism began, there was no live music scene in Harlem; cutting-edge music and performance had long since moved to downtown clubs and the annual jazz festivals, which spread out to a number of locations in Manhattan, did not even have an Uptown venue. Although response to demand prompted jazz nights with old "greats" at a few local clubs, this was nostalgia rather than an authentic jazz scene.

Beginning in the late 1990s, Harlem began to attract talented and committed leadership to the cultural as well as the economic development arena. African-American curators have left downtown institutions to build Harlem's many cultural institutions. Harlem has begun to have an active arts scene with galleries, openings, new clubs, theater, and boutiques (Soccar 2002; Lee 2002). Under the auspices of UMEZ's first tourism director, an umbrella organization of Uptown cultural institutions has emerged and made concerted efforts to enhance their position within the

NYC cultural scene. UMEZ also proposed a $25 million grant and loan fund to "stabilize and expand" uptown cultural institutions. Although opponents contended the initiative did not constitute "economic development," the program was finally approved, and the first grants totaling $5 million were awarded in spring 2001. This coincided with a citywide effort by arts organizations to lobby for city and state support by presenting "culture as infrastructure" much as any other source of economic growth (Soccar 2001). In the aftermath of 9/11, which triggered a sharp downturn in visitors to the city, this point has become widely recognized: tourism and culture are potent economic generators.

Tourism and the revalorization of Harlem

Reinforcing the move toward niche marketing, several other trends accentuate the tourism industry's post-Fordist characteristics and have relevance for Harlem. Cultural tourism has emerged as the fastest growing market segment; differentiated tourism products aim for targeted markets; and information technology has been applied to marketing and sales.

Cultural tourism. In a relatively short time, the concept of cultural tourism has broadened beyond the traditional focus on museums and theaters to include an anthropological concern with people and place. Ethnicity and diversity are central to this perception. As tourism officials and organizations in the city and state began to position themselves competitively by promoting cultural sites and building on the theme of diversity, Harlem has taken on special importance. This has increased the flow of resources to Harlem and has had political as well as economic significance. Several examples illustrate these processes:

Over the past decade, historic preservation and heritage tourism – key forces in building bridges between cultural tourism and the development community – have begun to celebrate the ethnic heritage of minority and ethnic working-class communities (Barthel 1996). During 1998–99, Harlem was spotlighted at several conferences bringing together developers, community leaders, professionals, and commercial interests to link development to preservation and cultural tourism. Speakers emphasized the benefits of getting on the heritage/preservation bandwagon for low-income, minority communities; the message was – there is something here for everyone.

New York's business community has also become pro-active on the part of cultural tourism. New York's convention and visitor's bureau (NYC & Co.) is a case in point. Funded by members and driven by political as well as financial realities, its fundamental mission had been to market the city by drawing overnight visitors to midtown hotels. At a 1998 conference spotlighting Harlem, however, the director did the equivalent of a U-turn and outlined a strategy to turn New York's diversity from disadvantage to unique advantage, calling on each community to define itself so the CVB could actively market *all* boroughs and uptown as well as downtown Manhattan (Reiter 1998). This vision is gradually taking shape. In 2001, The Conference Board, a business and research organization, began a pilot community tourism project "to promote tourism in areas of NYC off Manhattan's beaten tourist paths" by working with community groups at sites in each borough including the Mount Morris neighborhood of Harlem (Fried 2001). The objectives include community economic benefits, civic engagement, and earned income (Dykstra 2001). As of 2002, all of New York City's boroughs sponsor cultural and tourism initiatives funded by a variety of public and private sector organizations.

The New York State Division of Tourism's about-face in response to this fast-growing market is no less remarkable. Its first advertising venture – the well known "I love NY" campaign in 1977 – was decidedly anti-urban and featured commercials depicting upstate parks and waterfalls. In 2001, the tourism division added a director of cultural tourism whose first project was an "I love NY" travel guide and related website entitled "Explore New York State's Diversity." The theme was "cultural connections" with tourist attractions color-coded on a map *by ethnicity* (African-American, European, Hispanic, multicultural, and Native American). Harlem accounted for six of the 27 NYC attractions and this popular guide received 58,000 requests in the first few months.

In spring 2001, New York State Governor George Pataki told a luncheon of Harlem business leaders that the Fall 2001 "Isle of NY" tourism campaign would feature Harlem. NY State's development agency (Empire State Development Corporation) has committed funding to Harlem's tourism/entertainment infrastructure (the Victoria and Apollo Theaters) as well as to gospel production. In the words of a senior state official: "We need to take a neighborhood view of economic development. In Upper Manhattan it is tourism and small business – not just the Pathmarks [supermarkets]" (personal communication, n.d.).

Information technology and the marketing of place. The Internet has both facilitated tourism to Harlem and enabled Harlem-based businesses to enter the tourism market. Low-budgeted city and state agencies whose mandate includes tourism promotion have turned to websites to promote events and attractions, including those in Harlem. Overall this technology allows small places and small business to compete for visitors with big places and big business by increasing local independence from tourism industry networks.

For the many local restaurants, clubs, tour operators, and bed and break-
fasts which operate on the margin, booking events electronically enables
them to plan ahead, expanding the local tourism industry and keeping
more tourism dollars in the community.

Global forces: the entertainment industry moves uptown

The entertainment/media conglomerates need global cities like New York
not only as command centers but as sites for mass national and international consumption, and tourism has encouraged this function. To reach
this market, the industry is investing in the urban equivalent of theme parks
– urban entertainment destinations. These complexes include high-tech
and live entertainment, theme restaurants, cinema multiplexes, sports
venues, retail outlets, and production studios that allow media conglomerates to cross-market their brands and products (Braun 1995; Roost 1998).
Although most urban entertainment destinations are in central locations,
the entertainment giants have begun to reach out to diverse urban sites in
their marketing plans. Harlem provides examples of two different types of
projects: Harlem USA and the projected Apollo Performing Arts Center.

Harlem USA, a new retail and entertainment complex on Harlem's
main commercial thoroughfare, 125th Street, is the first such project in
the community. It has a 6,000-square-foot Disney Store, a Magic
Johnson/Sony 9-screen multiplex theater, and the outlets of several
national retail chains. Harlem was a logical choice for Disney which had
been expanding its retail stores to the commercial centers of NYC's outer
boroughs. So far, Magic Johnson Theaters is the only existing multiplex in
Harlem and its first-run movies and amenities make it a potent symbol of
change for the community.

In contrast to the multiplex, the proposed Apollo Performing Arts
Center will be a major cultural institution involved in production as well
as consumption. The plan is to link the legendary Apollo Theater to a
nearby theater to create a complex with performance space, rehearsal
studios, a television facility, and gift shops. Many believe the Apollo is a key
element in the economic development of Harlem and expect it to lead
Harlem's cultural rebirth.

Time Warner (now AOL Time Warner) was involved with the Apollo
Theater and Harlem's revitalization from the start. Richard D. Parsons,
current president of AOL Time Warner, chaired the UMEZ Board from
its inception (January 1996) and became board chairman of the restructured Apollo Theater Foundation in Spring 2001. The first president of
the restructured Apollo Foundation was a former AOL Time Warner exec-

Plate 5.1   The Apollo Theater, Harlem's cultural icon. *Source*: Lily M. Hoffman

utive, and a nationally prominent board of directors has been recruited for prestige and fundraising.

What led Time Warner to Harlem? Like other industries over the past decade, the entertainment/movie industry has become increasingly concentrated, diversified, and dependent upon global marketing for profits. Like many corporations, Time Warner was pursuing an intensive multicultural strategy, purchasing black businesses – magazines, digital media units, book publishers (Block 2000). Given this objective, identification with the Apollo Theater – a highly symbolic black cultural institution – was branding that advertising alone could not buy. Moreover, in a highly concentrated industry with a small number of companies offering everything from movies to theme parks, Time Warner lacked identification with a live performance site such as Disney's successful New Amsterdam Theater on 42nd Street. Indeed, initial reports spoke about the Apollo as the Uptown equivalent of 42nd Street. However, community criticism led to re-envisioning the Apollo along more community-oriented lines (Block 2001). With corporations such as AOL Time Warner, Harlem would have global players interested in initiating business and products related to minorities. At the same time, multinational corporations would be under pressure to remain on good terms with a wary Harlem community regarding issues of authenticity, control, and local participation. In the aftermath of economic recession and 9/11, however, the proposed expansion of the Apollo and other NYC cultural institutions has been scaled back (Pogrebin 2002).

These different projects illustrate some of the tensions and pitfalls in these ongoing processes and in the relation between tourism and development. There is synergy, but up to a point. Too many multiplexes can degrade the cultural attractiveness of 125th Street. Yet too few will mean that the community fails to capture visitor and residential spending related to entertainment and tourism. The Apollo project also raises questions as to the relation between use and exchange value. How would the proposed performance center respond to the needs and claims of residents, visitors, producers, and consumers?

Emerging Issues: The View from Harlem

Although consensus is hard to reach in the politicized central Harlem community, tourism-based development gained support from a diverse group of local leaders. Tourism was not viewed as a strategy foisted on Harlem by the outside development community, but one with a history within Harlem that drew upon Harlem's unique assets.

The late Ron Brown, a native Harlemite and former Secretary of Commerce, was a force behind the first White House Conference on Travel and Tourism to which he invited a delegation from Harlem (October 29–31, 1995). They joined with others to express minority concerns, using the concept of multicultural or ethnic tourism to focus attention on the cultural heritage of minority communities and the need for economic development. The idea was to "get into our own neighborhoods and develop the local and ethnic products we have overlooked" (*Harlem Week* 1996). Tourism fit the emergent thrust of African-American politics toward cultural empowerment and entrepreneurialism. For local actors, tourism has many advantages as a development strategy, particularly because it combines cultural and economic objectives.

As tourism has grown, however, a number of concerns have emerged related to development in general and tourism development in particular. First and foremost is the question – whose Harlem? In the face of rapid change, the interest of outside developers in Harlem has made residents uneasy and stimulated opposition. Although the entertainment and retail establishments being planned for 125th Street will benefit both residents and visitors, rising rents have forced out small businesses and black ownership has generally declined.[5] For Harlem, development resonates with a long, bitter history of resentment over perceived economic colonization by white outsiders. Consumer boycotts and civic disturbance have undercut efforts at economic revitalization. Historic experience has engendered an anti-market, anti-business attitude, and some might opt to give up development if the outcome is a further "sharing" of Harlem.

Debates about competing models of development reflect a struggle over political control between generations with differing experience and outlooks. An "old guard" emphasizes black ownership and control but is accused of having nothing to show for millions of dollars in federal, state and city funds – "not a single brick" (Horowitz 1997; Hernandez 2002). Many of the new leaders, now running the development engines, are Ivy League-trained professionals who have left corporate careers to rebuild their community. They want capitalism to enter the inner city and support a Porter-style model which stresses integrating Harlem's economy with the larger city by means of partnerships. Harlem has been cut off from the market by poverty and by an economy based upon government transfers. They argue that the issue is not just available funds, but know-how and networks.

Commercial gentrification is also an issue. Some residents believe that 125th Street is being transformed from an "economic and cultural icon for blacks" to a "center of mainstream youth-culture and merchandising . . . in which black culture will be only part of the marketing package" (Kirk Johnson 1998). Others argue just as forcefully for upscale shopping in their community. This debate has a strong economic basis with middle-income, long-term residents opting for better retail and commercial services and poorer residents fearing their ultimate displacement. The interests of residents and visitors may also diverge along these lines. From the standpoint of the tourism industry, Harlem's attraction is its ethnicity. The removal of eye-catching, car-stopping street vendors along 125th Street cost the street much of its tourist appeal.[6] But many residents (and merchants) want an upscale shopping street with quality services and stores rather than an Afro-centric street market.

To add to the complexity, much of what visitors hear and see is already a tourism product – a reconstruction of the historical past, while some tourist "discoveries" like the many professional gospel choirs in Harlem, have become the basis of new productive activity – recording and touring. Cultural tourism projects like the renewed Apollo Theater encourage innovation and production. Economic development, which has accompanied tourism, stimulates creative activity. Niche production and marketing may play an interesting role in this process. By revalorizing that which is ethnic, cultural tourism and related activities may strengthen cultural difference.

Development pressures have also begun to clash with the nascent Harlem preservation movement, and landmark status has gained opponents among community leaders. The Abyssinian Development Corporation, a leader in community development, is now cited among the worst offenders, a case in point being the Renaissance Ballroom on 138th Street. It argues that landmark status would raise the cost and time needed to return the building to active commercial use (Kemba Johnson 1998). Having courted low-income, minority communities, preservationists now find that the perspectives and objectives of these groups do not always mesh.

Community resentment of visitors is a significant issue. As tourism has grown, so has general antagonism towards tour buses, tourists in local churches and on residential streets. Members of Harlem's hard-pressed minority community feel wary of what they experience as racial voyeurism – "whites on safari." According to heritage tourism guidelines, only the active involvement of local residents in the tourism project can help negate this problem. The Empowerment Zone has held focus groups to explore these concerns and to plan how to control the flow into tourist areas with input from local residents. The Conference Board's Community Tourism project is directed at just this issue. Although tourism and development create similar problems elsewhere, these issues take on important symbolic as well as social/political dimensions given the history of race relations in US cities in general, and Harlem in particular.

Tourism and Changing Social/Political Realities

There is a tendency within the regulation perspective to view Fordism as the "golden age" of capitalism – the age of the affluent worker – a period when steady work and rising wages gave workers access to middle-class

Table 5.1 Repositioning of the US inner-city minority community

Fordism	Post-Fordism
1 Distinct "ghetto" economy	Increased integration into mainstream urban economy
2 Social/spatial isolation and exclusion	Social capital and contact
3 Negatively perceived culture	Revalorized culture
4 Political patronage	Political player
5 Social policy	Economic policy

consumption patterns (Elam 1994). However, Fordism was not a golden age for all workers. Minorities (and women) were, for the most part, left out of this equation. In the US cities of the Midwest, minorities held only a small proportion of the well-paid unionized jobs in heavy manufacturing; in northeastern cities like New York, jobs in industries like clothing manufacture were less well paid and much less secure.

Overall, inner city minority communities in the US did not do well under Fordism (Florida and Jonas 1991; Painter 1995).[7] They were marginalized economically, socially, spatially, and politically[8] and isolated by the resulting differences in economy, society, and culture (see Table 5.1). Social/spatial isolation along with economic exclusion from the American Dream (based on mass consumption), gave rise to a variety of distinct innovative cultural patterns such as street-culture, black English, graffiti, and rap.

At present, economic restructuring is making for a new fit between the larger political economy and the inner city. Revalorized by a shifting economy, increasingly integrated through tourism into a leading edge of the NYC/NYS economy, and linked by development to an entrepreneurial urban regime, Harlem is at an interesting political moment. Less dependent upon NYC, Harlem finds itself being wooed by NYS for reasons that range from electoral politics to economic development.

One possibility is that tourism may act as an equalizing force; in part because of the redistribution of public and private resources; in part because of the ability of multinational capital to influence local sites. Tourism development may help to rebalance the type of uneven urban spatial development characteristic of Fordism and symbolized by the social isolation and concentrated poverty of the racial ghetto. Using a conventional non-scaled urban framework, we might conclude that Harlem is being increasingly integrated (and co-opted) into the wider urban entrepreneurial regime. The strength of a regulation framework in mapping the larger forces at work is that it makes us balance this view with Harlem's propensity for "stepping out" of the city map.

A weakness of the regulation/post-Fordist literature is the failure to link the elements of the restructuring economy to outcomes for specific areas of the city and their residents – for places like Harlem. One result is an overly pessimistic view of the post-Fordist future for inner city minority communities – increasing marginalization and exclusion, or gentrification and displacement. As shown above, economic restructuring can create new opportunities for Harlem and its residents. Although there will always be winners and losers, they are not necessarily the same areas or populations.

Tourism, economic development, and difference

The study of tourism illuminates the interplay of production and consumption in the new economy. In Harlem, cultural capital is the engine of growth, fueling the development of Harlem with multiplier effects for residential and commercial development as well as retail and services. We see the synergy between cultural capital and economic development at work with real estate development, preservation, heritage tourism, entertainment, and retail. Both residents and visitors use facilities such as movies, shopping centers, and restaurants, and the power of tourism derives, in part, from the fact that we cannot disentangle the two groups of users (Hoffman and Musil 1999). The recognition of this cross-promotional quality is illustrated by the tendency among economic development actors such as the Empire State Development Corporation and the UMEZ to broaden and redefine economic development so as to include cultural and tourism activities. This reality calls into question the tendency to dichotomize production and consumption – the city of work and the city of play.

The role of culture in the revitalization of Harlem has meant that revitalization promotes cultural differentiation along with standardization. The need to produce differentiated products for targeted markets – to mine culture for commodity – means more, not less ethnic production. Thus, Harlem USA, the retail/entertainment center noted for its mainstream retail outlets like Disney and Old Navy, also houses a 4,000-square-foot bookstore which specializes in African-American subjects, stocks at least 10,000 titles, and features a busy schedule of readings by African American authors (Dunlap 2002).

Tourism as a mode of regulation

The increased importance of urban tourism and related development has led to changing urban policies for inner-city Harlem, ranging from land use, housing, transportation and security to economic development. Overall, tourism gives political and economic actors new incentives and resources with which to reach out to this hitherto neglected area as well as providing the means – a consensus-building agenda (Dowding 2001). However, there are some constraints.

The requirements of cultural tourism are complex. Cultural tourism requires substantial *civic* as well as public/private participation. Cultural experience must be codified, scripted, and presented. Community groups must agree on what to preserve and how to mark it. To go after funding, they must work collaboratively with other groups and with the public sector. Based on ethnicity and place, cultural tourism also gives rise to claims of legitimacy that require a degree of compliance. Tourism to Harlem is a case in point. Negative interactions with visitors walking through neighborhoods – in the words of a proponent of heritage tourism – "ruin the experience for visitor and resident" (Heritage Trails Conference 1998). Like eco-tourism, the goal is sustainability. In fact, Heritage Trails advises that to work well, the community must give the tours as well as prepare the sites.

For the Harlem community, tourism has stimulated group formation and networking. Social contact has brought new resources for upgrading and defending place as well as the tools (historic preservation, heritage tourism) used by others to control development and shape it towards their own interests. For the urban regime, tourism development serves broad political functions of inclusion and political stabilization and helps to extend a development agenda into areas of the city formerly perceived as no-man's land.

Civic engagement is a two-way street. It gives the community control, but at the same time, disciplines and stabilizes. Community pride and collaboration also instill civic values. Support for Harlem's rich cultural assets also creates cultural capital (tourist sites) for city, state, and the general business community. Many benefits for visitors (improved streets, security) are also benefits for residents. We can see the interactive, synergistic qualities of cultural tourism at work in the social and political sphere as well as in the economic, promoting grass-roots along with regime objectives – something for everyone. Thus *urban tourism incorporates a new mode of regulation*, making for greater social/political and economic inclusion, but with the associated costs as well as the benefits.

Looking Forward, Looking Back

The events of 9/11, which underlined both the economic importance and vulnerability of the tourism industry, offer a postscript to tourism development in Harlem. The failure of international visitors to return to New

York City after 9/11 has posed a particular threat to Harlem. Foreign visitors started the tourist boom in the late 1980s and have accounted for the greater majority of its tourists. In addition, tourism is seen as a linchpin of Harlem's revival, linked to plans for entertainment, retail, offices and hotels. Although the city as a whole picked up some of its slack with regional and national visitors, Harlem is differently perceived within the US than abroad, and given the ever-increasing number of international visitors, until recently had not cultivated a regional and national market to the same extent.

At the seven-month mark (April 2002) and the beginning of the summer tourist season, tourism was dramatically down and the absence of foreign visitors was felt at the Harlem churches visited for gospel singing, by tour operators, and local restaurants. The general economic downturn and the plight of the technology sector, which preceded and accompanied 9/11, softened the commercial real estate market downtown. This put less pressure on businesses to relocate Uptown, undermining the synergy that helped sustain new restaurants, shops, and galleries. City and state are strapped for public funds, and private investment is down in general and in NYC in particular.

Although still uncertain – several large projects such as the Edison corporate headquarters and the relocation of Black Entertainment Television have collapsed – there seem to be enough major projects already in the pipeline to assure Harlem's transformation. The major real-estate developers working Uptown take a long-range view of their investments, and Harlem's many cultural institutions see themselves as national repositories and resources. Paradoxically, although there is less money in the immediate present, there is *more support* by officials for tourism and cultural development, and this will eventually turn into funding.

The slowing-down of the rapid pace of development/gentrification offers a breathing space, which may be used to advantage by the small local businesses who have criticized rising commercial rents. It may also offer new opportunities for planning. Manhattan's 42nd Street was first planned as an office complex with entertainment demoted to peripheral importance; only after an economic recession characterized by a glut of office space did the present revitalized theater district take shape. The fall-off in tourism has also softened the anti-tourism/anti-development sentiment and given rise to a new appreciation of visitors and their contribution to the local economy (Blair 2002).

Harlem – in many respects a world unto itself over the past 60 years – is being re-woven into the urban fabric with a capitalist agenda. The entry of multinational capital accompanied by public/private partnership programs that stress entrepreneurial skills presages a move away from a "transfer" economy based upon publicly funded services. Economic integration will most likely polarize winners and losers in Harlem, just as it has in the former state socialist societies in East Central Europe, undermining a solidarity based upon a relatively flat opportunity structure. During the Harlem Renaissance of the 1920s, the dominant strategy was to advance the race through cultural achievement, but lacking an economic base, the movement faltered with the end of Prohibition and the beginnings of the Great Depression.

Tourism's strength as a development strategy for Harlem (and other similar communities) stems from the fact that it *combines* economic with cultural and political objectives. In this context the present downturn invokes the concern, voiced by community leaders over the past decade, that an economic recession would undercut Harlem's revitalization mid-stream. Although there are obvious costs to development, without a viable economy Harlem will remain marginalized.

NOTES

This chapter is a version of Lily M. Hoffman, "The marketing of diversity in the inner city: tourism and regulation in Harlem," *International Journal of Urban and Regional Research*, June 2003. Earlier versions have been presented at the Eastern Sociological Association Annual Meetings, Albany, 1998 and the Urban Affairs Association Annual Meetings, 1999. A PSC-CUNY Research Grant provided initial support (1996–8).

1 Central Harlem is bounded on the south by Central Park, to the north, by the Harlem River, and runs east to west, from Fifth Avenue to Morningside Avenue.
2 The federal program grants tax credits over a ten-year period to stimulate economic development in depressed areas.
3 The Abyssinian Development Corporation (ADC), begun by the Abyssinian Baptist Church in 1989, has engaged in housing and large scale commercial developments such as the Pathmark supermarket on 125th Street. ADC has received national recognition for its community development activities.
4 In New York, city and state matched the federal grant for a total of $300 million. UMEZ, which administers the project for Harlem and Washington Heights, manages 83 percent of the $300 million NYEZ budget.
5 According to the 125th Street Business Improvement District, between 1996 and 1998, rents rose from $10–$35 to $40–$65 per square foot, and black ownership declined from nearly half to one-fifth of the storefronts.
6 Businesses on 125th Street wanted them out, and their removal fit Mayor Giuliani's "quality of life" campaign.
7 Florida and Jonas (1991) link federal urban policy to Fordism, citing the subsidization of suburban growth and the greater polarization of city and suburb.

Along similar lines, one could argue that the Great Society programs helped consolidate the inner city's social/spatial marginality as well as creating new tensions with local government.

8 Theorists in the "development of underdevelopment" tradition rightly point out that these asymmetric relationships serve a variety of economic and political functions.

REFERENCES

Amin, A. 1994: Post-Fordism: models, fantasies and phantoms of transition. In A. Amin (ed.), *Post-Fordism: A Reader*. Oxford: Blackwell, 1–40.

——and Malmberg, A. 1994: Competing structural and institutional influences on the geography of production in Europe. In A. Amin (ed.), *Post-Fordism: A Reader*. Oxford: Blackwell, 227–48.

Audience Research and Analysis 2000: Upper Manhattan tourism market study. Unpublished report.

Barthel, D. 1996: *Historic Preservation: Collective Memory and Historical Identity*. New Brunswick, NJ: Rutgers University Press.

Bingham, R. D. and Zhang, Z. 1997: Poverty and economic morphology of Ohio central city neighborhoods. *Urban Affairs Review* 32 (July): 766–96.

Blair, J. 2002: For the crossroads of the world, far less traffic. *New York Times*, April 14.

Block, V. 2000: Time heads media majority in targeting minorities. *Crain's New York Business*, October 16: 4.

Body-Gendrot, S. and Gittell, M. (eds). 2003: Social capital and social citizenship. Lexington, MA: Lexington Books.

Braun, R. E. 1995: Exploring the urban entertainment center universe. *Urban Land* 54 (8): 11–17.

Dowding, K. 2001: Explaining urban regimes. *International Journal of Urban and Regional Research* 25 (1): 7–19.

Dunlap, D. W. 2002: The changing look of the new Harlem. *New York Times*, February 12.

Dykstra, G. 2001: I love New York . . . neighborhoods: community tourism emerges in New York. Unpublished report (April).

Elam, M. 1994: Puzzling out the post-Fordist debate: technology, markets and institutions. In A. Amin (ed.), *Post-Fordism: A Reader*. Oxford: Blackwell, 43–71.

Esser, J. and Hirsch, J. 1994: The crisis of Fordism and the dimensions of a "Post-Fordist" regional and urban structure. In A. Amin (ed.), *Post-Fordism: A Reader*. Oxford: Blackwell, 71–98.

Florida, R. and Jonas, A. 1991: US urban policy: the postwar state and capitalist regulation. *Antipode* 23 (4): 349–84.

Fried, J. P. 2001: Harlem sites to be pitched in campaign for tourists. *New York Times*, February 15.

Gittell, R. and Vidal, A. 1998: *Community Organizing, Building Social Capital as a Development Strategy*. Thousand Oaks, CA: Sage Publications.

Grogan, P. S. and Proscio, T. 2000: *Comeback Cities: A Blueprint for Urban Neighborhood Revival*. Boulder, CO: Westview Press.

Harlem Week 1996: Anonymous panel speaker. The economic development conference and exposition, A tribute to Ron Brown Seminars. New York.

Harvey, D. 1994: Flexible accumulation through urbanization: reflections on "postmodernism" in the American city. In A. Amin (ed.), *Post-Fordism: A Reader*. Oxford: Blackwell, 361–86 (reprinted from *Antipode*, 1987).

Heritage Trails Conference 1998: Celebrating our heritage: New York's new tourism market. J. M. Kaplan Center, The New School. *New York*, February 25.

Hernandez, R. 2002: Rangel's star grows dim as democrats lose ground. *New York Times*, November 30.

Hirst, P. and Zeitlin, J. 1991: Flexible specialisation versus post-Fordism: theory, evidence and policy implications. *Economy and Society* 20 (1): 1–55.

Hoffman, L. M. 1997: Antecedents of "ghetto" tourism in a global city: The case of international tourism to Harlem. Paper presented at meetings of Research Committee 21, International Sociological Association, Berlin, July.

——2000: Tourism and the revitalization of Harlem. *Research in Urban Sociology* 5: 207–23.

——and Musil, J. 1999: Culture meets commerce: tourism in postcommunist Prague. In D. R. Judd and S. S. Fainstein (eds.), *The Tourist City*. New Haven, CT: Yale University Press, 179–97.

Horowitz, C. 1997: The battle for the soul of Harlem. *New York Magazine*, 30 (3) (January 27): 22–31.

Initiative for a Competitive Inner City (ICIC) and Management Horizons 1998: The inner-city shopper, preliminary findings. Boston: Boston Consulting Group, June.

Jessop, R. 1994: Post-Fordism and the state. In A. Amin (ed.), *Post-Fordism: A Reader*. Oxford: Blackwell, 251–79.

Johnson, Kemba 1998: Landmarks omission. *City Limits* 23 (7) (September/October): 19–22.

Johnson, Kirk 1998: Uneasy renaissance on Harlem's street of dreams. *New York Times*, March 1.

Lee, D. 2002: Exeunt Omnes, neighbors say to theater seeking new home. *New York Times*, November 17.

Lipietz, A. 1994: Post-Fordism and democracy. In A. Amin (ed.), *Post-Fordism: A Reader*. Oxford: Blackwell, 338–58.

Mayer, M. 1994: Post-Fordist city politics. In A. Amin (ed.), *Post-Fordism: A Reader*. Oxford: Blackwell, 316–37.

New York City Economic Development Corporation 1997: Economic revitalization in NYC's poorest neighborhoods: executive summary. New York: New York City Economic Development Corporation.

Painter, J. 1995: Regulation theory, post-Fordism and urban politics. In D. Judge, G. Stoker, and H. Wolman (eds.), *Theories of Urban Politics*. Thousand Oaks, CA: Sage, 276–95.

Pogrebin, R. 2002: Apollo Theater postpones expansion; foundation's chief resigns. *New York Times*, September 10.

Porter, M. E. 1995: The competitive advantage of the inner city. *Harvard Business Review*, May–June: 55–71.

Putnam, R. D. 2000: *Bowling Alone: The Collapse and Revival of American Community*. New York: Simon and Schuster.

Reiter, F. 1998: Celebrating our heritage: New York's new tourism market. Lecture at the New School University. New York February 25.

Roost, F. 1998: Recreating the city as entertainment center: the media industry's role in transforming Potsdamer Platz and Times Square. *Journal of Urban Technology*, 5 (3): 1–21.

Sabel, C. F. 1994: Flexible specialisation and the re-emergence of regional economies. In A. Amin (ed.), *Post-Fordism: A Reader*. Oxford: Blackwell, 101–56.

Schaffer, R. 1996: *Report on Economic Base of Upper Manhattan*. Columbia University Empowerment Zone Monitoring and Assistance Project, February 8.

Soccar, M. K. 2001: A change of art. *Crain's New York Business*, June 4: 3.

—— 2002: Uptown Bohemia. *Crain's New York Business*, July 1: 3.

Stern, M. J. 1997: *Representing the City: Arts, Culture and Diversity in Philadelphia*. Working Paper #3. Philadelphia: University of Pennsylvania School of Social Work.

—— 1999: *Is All the World Philadelphia? A Multi-City Study of Arts and Cultural Organizations, Diversity and Urban Revitalization*. Working Paper #9. Philadelphia: University of Pennsylvania School of Social Work.

Storper, M. 1994: The transition to flexible specialisation in the US film industry: External economies, the division of labour and the crossing of industrial divides. In A. Amin (ed.), *Post-Fordism: A Reader*. Oxford: Blackwell, 195–226.

—— and Scott, A. 1989: The geographical foundations and social regulation of flexible production complexes. In J. Wolch and M. Dear (eds.), *The Power of Geography: How Territory Shapes Social Life*. Winchester, MA: Unwin Hyman.

Wyatt, E. 2000: School-managing company and museum plan Harlem headquarters. *New York Times*, July 7.

6

Barcelona:
Governing Coalitions, Visitors,
and the Changing City Center

Marisol García and Núria Claver

With the celebration of the Olympic Games in 1992 Barcelona became an international tourist city. Since then, the number of visitors has grown annually, making Barcelona one of the most popular European cities for urban tourism. Barcelona's special appeal is related to its particular combination of historic and modern, in which architecture, accessible public space, and sociability are the elements of attraction. In 1990 Barcelona was awarded the Prince of Wales Prize by Harvard University for its urban reconstruction and in 1999, the Royal Institute of British Architects gave it the Royal Gold Medal for Architecture. This was the first time the prize had been awarded to a place rather than to a particular architect. Like Berlin, Barcelona has become a landmark for urban architecture and visitors count architecture as one of its major attractions (Turisme de Barcelona 2001).[1] As with other elements of Barcelona's appeal, this did not happen by chance, but took concerted planning.

In this chapter we highlight the importance of local regulation and governance in the expansion of Barcelona as an international tourist city. By local regulation and governance, we mean the capacity of local actors to coordinate agents so as to allocate national, local, and international resources directed at modernizing the city. Some regulation theorists overemphasize industrial restructuring and economic agents to the neglect of other factors, such as infrastructure and services, and other actors, such as local political and business leaders (Preteceille 1994). Only by examining the complex interplay of the many actors involved in the city's transformation is it possible to interpret the social forces that promote or inhibit the broad restructuring of a particular city and its degree of internationalization.

Local growth coalitions are a significant feature of urban governance in US cities and increasingly in the European context, although this statement needs to be qualified. In European as in US cities, competitive pressures have brought about an entrepreneurial style of governance. But in the European case, urban governance is also defined as the capacity to integrate and give form to local interests – both public and private – and to reinforce local identity. In Barcelona, as in other European cities, the public sector has played a significant role in urban policy and urban life in general (Musterd and Ostendorf 1998). In discussing the capacity of local governing coalitions, we will therefore include the ability to construct compromises between political entities and local civil society.

Barcelona's modernization has taken place in three periods or stages, characterized by different local growth and governance coalitions: (1) the late Francoist period (1960–78); (2) the period of the democratic transition (1979–94); and (3) the period from 1995 to the present. What is referred to as the "Barcelona model" – the successful co-ordination of economic and political with general civic interests – was strongest during the second period, when local leadership was strongest. In the first period, the non-democratic Spanish government indirectly determined the character of Barcelona, and during the third, the market was increasingly influential in determining the course of urban redevelopment. Nevertheless, local planning is still important.

Stage One: The Planning Freeze under Franco

The tourism industry in Spain began to develop during the late Francoist regime from 1960 until the re-establishment of local democracy in 1979.[2] During that period Barcelona was the industrial step-sister of the favored city, Madrid.[3] Barcelona's infrastructure was neglected by the central government and urban planning was relegated to the periphery, leaving a "frozen" city center. Despite the neglect by the national government, however, in the 1980s Barcelona's metropolitan area received almost 60 percent of the total investment in Catalonia.

In the late 1950s, Spain began a process of economic growth and liberalization, which included opening its borders to foreign tourists. Cities also began to benefit from the liberalizing political climate. The "Municipal Charter" (1960) allowed the Barcelona City Council to increase its planning authority, leading to development on the periphery of the city.

This took the form of poorly constructed housing developments, lacking infrastructure and communal facilities, for migrants from other regions in Spain. Similar developments can be found on the outskirts of Paris (Castells 1983; Leal 1994). These projects, which generated high profits for developers, reflected a political atmosphere of clientelism and a general lack of accountability that led to land speculation and to the neglect of infrastructure and collective services. Civic participation during this period was severely limited by the climate of political repression. The Old Town, with the oldest housing stock in Barcelona, experienced a "rent gap" which further hindered inner city investment, since profits could be realized more immediately on the outskirts of the city. The net result was a city center in decay and a new periphery which became home to low-income groups.

The regime's ability to control sectors of the population seeking social and cultural change gradually weakened, in part because of the economic growth that it stimulated. The Franco regime assisted tourism by a *laissez-faire* attitude regarding land speculation and the private development of tourist resources. Low prices and the guarantee of "sun and sand" led to a spectacular growth of tourism in Spain during the 1960s. In turn, tourism became a catalyst for change; tourists introduced new ways of life and liberal views, which made local residents chafe under the restrictions of Franco's regime.

In Catalonia, tourism took hold on the Girona coast, the Costa Brava, and on the Costa Dorada in Tarragona. In the summer of 1964, 78 percent of the tourists staying on the Costa Brava were foreigners and only 22 percent were Spanish (Duocastella 1969: 128–9). This model of mass tourism, so characteristic of the Fordist era, responded to demand from other countries, particularly from Europe and the United States. There were no policies aimed at diversifying the tourist product by making the cities more attractive to tourists. Within Catalonia, tourists visited Barcelona as another stop on a programmed tour, but overnight hotel stays were few. Although there is little data on the subject, sources indicate that overnight stays were mostly related to business travel. In fact, it was not until the 1990s that the numbers of overnight stays in Barcelona by visitors on holiday overtook those of business travelers.

Stage Two: Modernization under Strong Local Leadership

In the second period of its development (1979–94), Barcelona's restructuring was achieved with relative consensus by a strong local governing coalition which involved the local citizenry through the processes of representative democracy, community planning, and the cooptation of urban social movements. The concerted search for new directions was prompted, in part, by the crisis in the industrial sector. The democratic transition that restored local governance played a major role in the rise of a new leadership to undertake the transition. The new municipal authorities placed a high priority on modernizing the city. The issue was how to finance a major reconstruction when neither the previous highly centralized Spanish taxation system nor the newly decentralized system benefited Barcelona or any other Spanish city.

Fiscal decentralization to the autonomous regional governments was not extended to the city councils and this meant that municipal autonomy was undermined by the lack of resources. The share of overall public spending by city governments was lower in Spain than elsewhere in Europe, and only increased slowly, from 10 percent in 1970 to 15 percent in 2001. In contrast, regional administrations rapidly increased their share of public spending, from less than 1 percent in 1980 to 35 percent in 2001. Negotiations between local leaders and national and regional governments, to finance special projects, such as the Olympic Games and the Cultural Forum in 2004, became a major strategy of urban modernization.[4]

Barcelona's winning bid for the 1992 Olympic Games became the motor for its transformation. Major infrastructure projects were undertaken in a political climate of "hegemonic consensus"[5] guided by the local government, which had successfully negotiated national and regional (Catalan) financial support for the infrastructure and construction related to the Olympic Games. A dual process was involved: amendments to the 1978 Constitution devolved power from central to regional governments, while local grassroots movements simultaneously applied social and political pressure upwards. The 1992 Olympic Games prompted an exceptional planning process (Bosquets 1992) in which neighborhood associations together with planning professionals pressured the local government to improve the historic center and the peripheral neighborhoods. The result – the so-called Barcelona model based upon social cohesion – achieved urban restructuring with a degree of redistributive justice; specifically, public space was improved and housing was upgraded.

The role played by urban social movements in the processes of decentralization, democratization and urban transformation was quite modest and has been over-emphasized by scholars and by the movements themselves (Castells 1983). Social cohesion was important, in part because it fit within an overall framework of urban development embraced by politicians and planners. The Olympic Games proved an excellent means to address issues associated with the Francoist period. These ranged from long-awaited transportation infrastructure and urban renewal, to new initiatives focused on developing tourism, to a reinvigoration of civil society by means of citizen participation and more public space. The festivities associated with the games – from street fairs to cultural events – strengthened local patriotism and civic pride.

At the start of the democratic transition, Barcelona's city center was run down and dismal due to the lack of prior investment. The city council became a major city booster, encouraging inner-city investment and stimulating urban renewal, while, it was argued, preventing extensive gentrification. The council's overall strategy was to coordinate public and private actions so as to leverage public resources. What started as small, isolated projects quickly became major infrastructure works and shifted from a public to a partnership mode of intervention. The real estate sector became involved at first in direct response to public initiatives, but soon investment flowed more freely. These efforts were marked by a close relationship between the regeneration of the city center and its development as a tourist destination through the creation of a new image. Marketing stressed the city's architectural significance and social cohesion. Attracting tourism was an important objective in both the First and Second Strategic Plans, ratified in 1990 and 1994 respectively, by a coalition of public and private sector actors. The growth of public and private investment and the rising property values of the mid-1990s are signs of a much broader process of urban "unfreezing" in which the city's new image, based mainly on its historical and architectural heritage, plays an important role.

Tourism has been an essential element in the revitalization of Barcelona's Old Town district. In the 1980s, the Old Town was characterized by a high density of small family-owned businesses – small shops, workshops for crafts, textiles, graphic arts, restoration, and catering. Old Town also had the highest concentration of bars and restaurants, hotels and guesthouses. The district is divided into four neighborhoods, each with a distinctive identity: *La Barceloneta*, geographically bounded by the sea and the city's Old Port, was already a combination of a traditional working-class community and tourist area. *El Gòtic* combines a local community with the distinctive historical buildings around the Cathedral, while *El Raval* and *Casc Antic* are more insular, working-class neighborhoods.

Beginning with urban renewal in 1988, direct public investment was allocated to collective services, public spaces, housing, and infrastructure projects and was concentrated in the two neighborhoods less oriented to tourism. Private investment flowed towards the more commercial/tourist neighborhoods and into small shops and service companies. By 1998, approximately 100,000 jobs had been created in the district, but due to the relatively low skill and education levels of *Ciutat Vella*'s population, only 2,000 of these were taken by district residents. Moreover, housing prices have increased at a higher rate here than in the city as a whole due to gentrification.[6]

Plate 6.1 Doing business in Barcelona's medieval center. *Source*: Corbis

In Barcelona's Old Town, the non-systematic block-by-block basis of regeneration has meant that varied functional values have been preserved. Traditional shops – although fewer in number – have not yet entirely disappeared. Public administrative functions are interwoven with commercial functions. Adding to these elements, the power of design – both historical and modern – has created a dynamic urban landscape that combines fast-paced inhabitants going about their daily business with the more leisurely pace of tourists. The types of public space much praised by Jane Jacobs (1961) for enhancing tolerance, urbanity, and cosmopolitanism have expanded. However, tourism has also attracted crime, and there has been an increase in petty crime.

Barcelona became a major tourist destination following the publicity it received hosting the Olympic Games, with tourism increasing by about 10 percent each year since 1994. The regenerated city center both parallels and reflects this trend. The tourism industry has expanded along with related services; educational and cultural institutions have located and relocated there; and existing hotels, restaurants, and bars have gone up-scale. Planning regulations have played a role in this process. To control prostitution and drug trafficking (mainly in the *Raval* and *Casc Antic* areas), planners implemented a "Plan of Uses" in 1992 to regulate and limit the number of guesthouses and bars in the Old Town.

Investors have been attracted to both the pre-modern and the "modernista" areas of Barcelona, as noted by David Harvey. According to him these areas offer a "monopoly rent,"[7] as they constitute a unique value in the international urban market. There have been two forms of development. In areas with historical and symbolic significance, investment and the making of a new image have proceeded with only *ad hoc* guidance from planners. But Barcelona has also promoted a more standardized waterfront development similar to those found in many European and American cities. In those areas, investment has been coordinated with a high level of intentional urban planning. The result is a mix of spaces and uses that gives Barcelona its new image as a city attractive to visitors.

Stage Three: Consolidating the City of Visitors

The third period of Barcelona's development (1995 to the present) has been marked by an ongoing economic recession, a new mayor, and a new local governing coalition in which market and private sector actors have gained ground relative to political leadership and formal planning processes. The service sector has become increasingly important to the urban economy, and a national program of economic regulation has made the formerly rigid urban labor market flexible. During this period, Barcelona's city government made tourism a priority within a broader economic model that emphasizes attracting foreign investment, developing new "high tech" companies, and maintaining a high quality of life. The new emphasis favors private investment over communal life and weakens the general consensus over redevelopment. Increasingly, the Barcelona model is a thing of the past. At the same time, tourism has continued to grow.

As Barcelona has become a leading tourist destination and tourism has become a leading sector of the urban economy, more attention is being paid to maximizing tourism potential by attracting the visitors who spend the most. In 2001, Barcelona's hotels recorded nearly 7.9 million overnight stays. Of these, almost 3.3 million corresponded to leisure tourists; the others came for business, conferences, and professional networking. It is this latter type of visitor whom Barcelona's Tourism Agency wishes to attract.[8]

As noted above, tourism policy was previously directed towards promoting mass tourism at seaside resorts on the Catalan coast with the occasional day trip to Barcelona. In sharp contrast, the new business, conference, and holiday visitors are interested in more varied and urbane activities. More than one-quarter of visitors to Catalonia in recent years made Barcelona their destination. These tourists share public spaces and cultural activities with the city's residents. As a result, galleries and craft shops share space with the bars, coffee shops, and restaurants in tourist areas. The preservation of cultural heritage has become a key strategy of the new tourist policies. A campaign begun in the 1980s to protect and improve late nineteenth-century modernist palaces and early twentieth-century buildings has been extended to more recent construction. The key actors in these preservation efforts are the City Council, savings banks, and the owners of real-estate.

Barcelona has become a post-Fordist tourist city made up of local residents and visitors who use city services and amenities, both public and private (Martinotti 1993). Among those who use city services, visitors are proportionally on the increase. Residents may even lose the central status they previously enjoyed, as new services are directed towards tourists, commuters, and shoppers. In the case of the Old Town, for example, the needs of the aged for senior citizens' residences receive lower priority than commercial centers directed at other city users.[9]

An ongoing series of projects are transforming both the landscape and the socio-economic dynamics of some centrally located neighborhoods. Projects under construction to enhance the waterfront are likely to extend the gentrification that followed the construction of the Olympic Village. Barcelona is also preparing to host another large-scale event, the Universal Forum of Cultures in 2004, which is expected to increase international tourism. But unlike the redevelopment during and after the Olympics, there has been almost no consultation with neighborhood associations. An amendment to the Metropolitan General Plan which allows individual housing blocks to propose their own plans opens up the possibility of a deregulated urban transformation with the decisions made by holders of private capital replacing planning decisions.

These new directions may bring many problems that will require a new round of public intervention. The environmental impact of the growing number of visitors on limited space is a question that has not been addressed. Tourism also raises security issues because of the increase in crime in tourist areas. The official position of local government is that Barcelona is backing "quality" tourism as its strategy for sustainability. This includes encouraging the docking of cruise ships in the city's port, business tourism, conventions and scientific/university-based visits. But these kinds of visitors will insist that a very high level of urban experience be maintained.

Tourism and the Flexible Labor Market: An Example of National Regulation

The tourism industry has been aided by changes in national legislation. Beginning in the mid-1990s, working hours and employment contracts have become considerably more flexible, with little resistance from trade unions. Labor market deregulation has gone hand in hand with the needs of the booming service sector, particularly shops, bars, restaurants and hotels. As a percentage of the wages for the entire workforce, service sector wages increased from 63.1 percent in 1990 to 74.5 percent in 1996 to 78.6 percent in 2000.[10] Income opportunities have expanded, particularly in the tourist sector. Between 1993 and 1996, the number of bars increased by 25 percent with higher increases in other services such as shops, cultural activities, insurance, show business, and real estate. Between 1990 and 2001, the number of hotels in the city increased from 118 to 203 (as shown in table 6.1), and the average number of overnight stays per person increased from two to three. Unlike cities in which international hotel chains operate in significant numbers, Spanish companies have, with the exception of two five-star hotels, virtually monopolized the industry in Barcelona and most hotels are nationally or locally owned.[11]

Despite the marked rise in international tourism and the entry of foreign capital into two of the city's largest hotels subsequent to the Olympics, local companies still control the lion's share of the market in Barcelona. In January 1999, the market share of hotel chains in Barcelona stood at 74 percent, but the majority of the chains were owned by small and medium-sized local companies. The high proportion of local ownership probably accounts for the fact that the number of five-star hotels in the city has fallen from nine to six from 1990 to 2001, while the number of one- and two-star hotels has grown as fast as hotels in the upper categories (see table 6.1). The weak penetration of foreign capital in the hotel sector can be explained by the lack of interest shown by Spanish hotel owners in franchising and management systems, a crisis in the hotel industry at the

Table 6.1 Number of hotels by category, Barcelona, 1999–2001

	1990	1992	1994	1996	1998	2000	2001
Five star	9	9	6	6	6	6	6
Four star	30	43	46	48	49	56	64
Three star	45	56	60	60	61	70	73
Two star	14	16	22	21	24	28	31
One star	20	24	24	26	26	27	27
Total	118	148	158	162	166	187	203

Source: *Turisme de Barcelona*. Tourism statistics for 2001.

beginning of the 1990s, and the industry's influence on local policy. Considerable resistance comes from local owners and chains against the increasing pressure from tour operators to build more hotels. On this issue, hotel owners are backed by workers' unions, which are suspicious of international ownership.

The hotel operators also are quietly supported by local and regional governments. Barcelona's hotel structure is regulated by a Hotel Plan drawn up by the City Council in 1988, with the aim of modernizing existing establishments and increasing availability, especially in top categories. The plan, which controls the location, construction, and to some extent, the ownership of hotels, requires that profits must be re-invested in the city and not appropriated for speculative purposes (Ajuntament de Barcelona 1988). These regulations have been strongly criticized by many elements of the city's hotel industry, and recent legislation deregulating it will probably be adopted. In the face of varying and conflicting demands from different interest groups, local authorities are likely to opt for letting the private market take the initiative in land redevelopment.

Deregulation has already occurred in other service businesses related to tourism. Workers in hotels have trade union representation and collective wage negotiations. This is not the case with bars and restaurants. The tourist industry typically employs workers under the age of 40 and, increasingly under 30 years of age. Although wages are regulated as in other economic sectors, workers formally employed for a 40-hour working week often work many more hours. This overtime is non-regulated and usually off the books. New labor regulations allow employers to sign contracts with workers who may be called to work irregularly and on short notice, but who must be available every day. Since most workers in the service sector are not unionized and the small size of companies would make industrial action virtually impossible anyway, it is no surprise that an increasing number of these jobs are taken by immigrants, mainly from Latin America.

Conclusion

Over time, there has been a marked shift from national to local regulation of Barcelona's tourism industry. Especially during the period when Barcelona needed to transform itself into a city favored by visitors, a local governing coalition capable of coordinating and mobilizing players and resources at different scales was essential. More recently, market forces have begun to eclipse planning and intentional development. Barcelona's experience shows that in the context of limited financial resources, an international event, in this case the 1992 Olympic Games, was crucial in bringing national and regional resources to the city. It also shows that mega-events like the Olympic Games can be used to the benefit of local residents as well as visitors.

At the same time, it is clear that the "Barcelona model" of restructuring is historically contingent. One of its much-heralded features, its focus on social cohesion, was related to the task of creating local democratic institutions in the years following the demise of an authoritarian regime. The Barcelona model appears to have set the context for the present style of urban development, which emphasizes private market forces. However, tourism development may lead to problems that require, once again, a stronger public role. The recent mode of development reduces citizen participation to a minimum, and the needs of users are prioritized over those of local residents. Moreover, the rising cost of housing is dispersing new households towards other towns in the metropolitan region, where there is no tourism. As a result, the city of Barcelona is becoming a home for the upper and middle classes, and its Old Town is developing some of the classic inner-city problems associated with immigration and slow-paced gentrification.

The increasing reliance on tourism may make Barcelona overly dependent on a fluctuating international tourist market. Security has become an important and costly issue as growing numbers of tourists and immigrants flow into the city. Although the events of September 11 have not deterred tourism to Barcelona, and visitors from Europe and other regions of Spain have compensated for the declining numbers from the United States, Japan and Latin America, the tourist market has recently fluctuated more than in the past, with a sharp decrease in the summer of 2002. Moreover, security measures have been strengthened in the aftermath of September 11, with an accompanying increase in taxes and fares for airport and railway infrastructure. Clearly, Barcelona must continue to rely on state regulations and direction for tourism development.

NOTES

1 According to periodical opinion polls conducted by *Turisme de Barcelona*, 2001.
2 The Francoist dictatorship is characterized by an autarkic period from 1940 to 1959 followed by a "desarrollista" period from 1960 to 1979.
3 The period was characterized by a limited Fordist mode of production and by organized mass consumption. To understand the impact of Fordism, we need to know that the industrial sector in Barcelona had a strong traditional character with a large proportion of small and medium-sized companies and that this model held for the rest of the Catalan region.
4 In terms of the role of the state and the finance system, the reader can contrast Barcelona to Amsterdam. In the Dutch case the highly centralized taxation system has benefited the largest cities.
5 Hegemonic consensus – made possible by a combination of strong leadership and the co-optation of urban movement leaders into local government – previously enabled several unpopular urban projects to be implemented (García 1993).
6 *Barcelona Economia*, nos. 37 and 42.
7 Harvey used this term in a public talk given in Barcelona, May 2000, at the Barcelona Museum of Contemporary Art.
8 *Turisme de Barcelona*, a consortium created by the City Council, the Chamber of Commerce and Industry and the Foundation for the International Promotion of Barcelona in 1993, has the mission of promoting the city worldwide.
9 Two excellent PhD theses illustrate this point. See Sergi Martínez, "El retorn al centre de la ciutat. La reestructuració del Raval entre la renovació i la gentrificació," University of Barcelona, 2000. Also Monica Degen, "Regenerating public life?", University of Lancaster, 2001.
10 *Barcelona Economia*, no. 43, June 2000, Ajuntament de Barcelona. In comparison, industrial sector wages dropped from 29.3 percent in 1990 to 18.5 percent in 1996. See *Ajuntament de Barcelona* 1990, 1996 and 2001.
11 Barcelona has also been promoted as a cruise center. The number of international cruise passengers increased by an estimated 20 percent between 1998 and 1999.

REFERENCES

Ajuntament de Barcelona 1988: *Plan de Hoteles de Barcelona. Document de treball.* Barcelona.
—— 1990: *Anuari Estadistic de la Ciutat de Barcelona.* Barcelona.

——1996: *Anuari Estadistic de la Ciutat de Barcelona*. Barcelona.

——2001: *Anuari Estadistic de la Ciutat de Barcelona*. Barcelona.

Barcelona Economia: nos. 37, 42. Barcelona.

Bosquets, J. 1992: *Barcelona: evolución urbanística de una capital compacta*. Barcelona: Mafre.

Castells, M. 1983: *The City and the Grassroots*. London: Edward Arnold.

Degen, M. 2001: Regenerating public life? A sensuous comparison of Barcelona and Manchester. PhD thesis, Lancaster University.

Duocastella, R. 1969: *Sociología y pastoral del turismo en la costa Brava y Maresme*. Madrid: Confederación Española de Cajas de Ahorro.

García, S. 1993: Barcelona und die Olympischen Spiele. In: H. Hausserman and W. Siebel (eds.), *Festivalisierung der Stadtpolitik*. Opladen: Westdeutscher Verlag, 251–77.

Jacobs, J. 1961: *The Death and Life of Great American Cities: The Failure of Town Planning*. Harmondsworth: Penguin.

Leal, J. 1994: Transformaciones sociales y política urbana de las ciudades españolas: El caso de Madrid. In A. Alabart, S. García, and S. Giner (eds.), *Clase, poder y ciudadanía*. Madrid: Siglo XXI, 187–203.

Martinez, S. 2001: El retorn al centre de la ciutat: la reestructuració del Raval, entre la renovaciió i la gentrificació. PhD thesis, University of Barcelona.

Martinotti, G. 1993: *Metropoli, la nuova morfologia sociale della città*. Bologna: Il Mulino.

Preteceille, E. 1994: Paradojas políticas de las reestructuraciones urbanas, globalización de la economia y localización de los político. In A. Alabart, S. García, and S. Giner (eds.), *Clase, poder y ciudadanía*. Madrid: Siglo XXI, 61–96.

Turisme de Barcelona *Estadístiques de turisme / Tourism Statistics* 2001: Barcelona.

7

The Evolution of Australian Tourism Urbanization

Patrick Mullins

Introduction

This chapter examines the regulation regimes that have brought about and sustained Australian tourism urbanization. Tourism urbanization is the process by which cities and towns are built or redeveloped explicitly for tourists. People visit these resort centers for a few days or a few weeks so that they can become full-time consumers and thus be in a position to have as good a time as possible. This urbanization is new both because it comprises cities and towns devoted almost exclusively to leisure and pleasure, and because it has evolved mainly over the latter half of the twentieth century (Mullins 1991, 1999).

Three of Australia's 14 largest metropolitan areas – the Gold Coast, the Sunshine Coast, and Cairns – are resort centers, thus suggesting a high rate of tourism urbanization, with these three locations accounting for 4 percent of the country's population (see table 7.1). What is happening in Australia is also happening elsewhere. Tourism urbanization is evident, for example, along the northern Mediterranean coastline, around the Gulf of Thailand, in Latin America (e.g. Cancun), and in the US, notably around the Florida coastline, and in Nevada, with Las Vegas and Reno (Judd and Fainstein 1999).

Australia's high rate of tourism urbanization and the development trajectory of individual resort areas like the Gold Coast, have essentially

Table 7.1 Australia's 14 largest urban areas at the 2001 Census (ranked) and population change, 1991–2001

		Population at 2001 Census	% Change 1991–2001
1.	Sydney (NSW)	3 997 321	13.0
2.	Melbourne (Vict)	3 366 542	11.4
3.	Brisbane (Qld)	1 627 535	22.0
4.	Perth (WA)	1 339 993	17.2
5.	Adelaide (SA)	1 072 585	4.9
6.	Newcastle (NSW)	470 610	9.3
7.	Gold Coast (Qld/NSW)	444 077	53.1
8.	Canberra (ACT/NSW)	353 149	23.6
9.	Wollongong (NSW)	257 510	6.3
10.	Sunshine Coast (Qld)	192 397	47.7
11.	Hobart (Tas)	191 169	6.1
12.	Geelong (Vict)	151 851	1.7
13.	Townsville (Qld)	135 142	12.5
14.	Cairns (Qld)	126 364	38.9

Source: Australian Bureau of Statistics 1991, 2001.

been governed by a mode of regulation that focuses on the exploitation of the natural environment. This system evolved in the nineteenth century to govern Australia's traditional land-based economy, an economy that exploited soils, grasslands, and minerals for agriculture, pastoralism, and mining. Australian tourism also exploits nature, but in this case it is the oceans, rainforests, beaches, wildlife, and deserts (cf. Perkins and Thorns 2001). Thus, the easy transference of this nineteenth-century mode of regulation to a new, but parallel, economic activity explains Australia's high rate of tourism urbanization and why this urbanization is located in areas such as the Gold Coast with exploitable natural resources. Of course, the contemporary, global age has brought a diversity of tourism experiences, mainly in the form of consumption spaces, like theme parks, to complement these natural advantages.

Tourism Urbanization

As a process, tourism urbanization parallels other forms of urbanization. Industrial urbanization, for example, emerged in the nineteenth and early twentieth centuries, when manufacturing was the ascendant economic sector, and then declined in the 1970s and 1980s with de-industrialization (see Gordon 1978). In contrast, tourism urbanization is part of an emergent, globally oriented, postindustrial age whereby cities and towns are built or redeveloped exclusively for tourists, meaning that their economies, politics, residential life, and built environments are different. Where industrial urbanization, for example, was accompanied by an infrastructure of production, such as factories, canals, and railways, tourism urbanization is supported by an infrastructure of consumption made up of theme parks, casinos, hotels, convention centers, condominiums, golf courses, and so forth.

Tourism urbanization is not identical to and does not necessarily arise from urban tourism–defined as the process by which tourism becomes a major urban industry, but one that is subordinate to other industries (Mullins 1991, 1999). London, for example, has a highly developed tourism industry, even receiving more visitors than many resort cities, but its economy is dominated by producer services, and tourism is merely one key industry. By contrast, tourism is the major economic activity of resort centers.

Urban tourism is most clearly identified by consumption spaces; geographic areas specially built, redeveloped, or repackaged to attract tourists and residents engaging in recreational and leisure activities (Hannigan 1998; Mullins et al. 1999; Ritzer 1999). These include historical precincts (e.g. the Tower of London), theme parks (e.g. Disney World), waterfront developments (e.g. Sydney's Darling Harbour), and cultural centers (e.g. New York's Lincoln Center). Whereas consumption spaces constitute only part of the socio-spatial structures of non-resort urban centers, they virtually define the social and spatial structures of resort cities and towns.

Tourism urbanization and urban tourism have, together, produced a new socio-spatial system for organizing consumption. Entire cities and towns, on the one hand, and major precincts of other cities, on the other hand, have been built as specialized spaces that provide an array of goods and services focusing on fun. In the history of urbanization, this is new (see Griffiths 1995; Hannigan 1998; Judd and Fainstein 1999; Eisinger 2000).

Australian Tourism Urbanization

The Gold Coast, the Sunshine Coast, and Cairns form the core of Australian tourism urbanization, all three being located in coastal locations in subtropical/tropical Queensland. The Gold Coast and Sunshine Coast are located in the state's southeast corner, immediately south and north, respectively, of Brisbane, the Queensland capital and the state's largest city, with the Gold Coast overlapping into northern New South Wales (see Mullins 1984, 1991, 1992a, 1992b, 1994, 1995, 1999) (see figure 7.1). Both cities evolved from the middle of the twentieth century and, together with Brisbane, they dominate the South East Queensland (SEQ) urban region

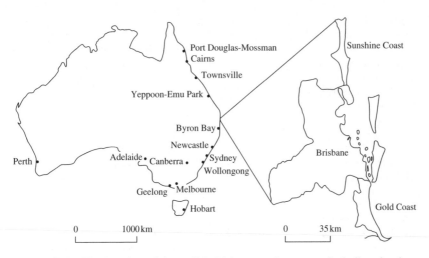

Figure 7.1 The location of Australia's 14 largest urban areas, including the three major tourist centers, and other selected tourist centers

(Baum et al. 1999, 2002). Cairns is located in far north Queensland and has historically been a service center for primary producers, but it evolved into a tourist city in the 1980s, initially to serve Japanese visitors. There are, of course, many smaller resort centers, mostly in coastal locations, and they include Port Douglas-Mossman, Yeppoon-Emu Park, and Byron Bay (Baum et al. 1999) (see figure 7.1).

All resort centers have grown very rapidly. The Gold Coast and the Sunshine Coast doubled their populations every ten years for much of the past 50 years, although their growth rates have slowed somewhat over the last decade (table 7.1). In the early 1970s the Gold Coast was Australia's fourteenth largest urban area, but it is now the seventh largest, while the Sunshine Coast is the eleventh largest. Cairns, in contrast, increased its population by an extraordinary 25 percent over the last half of the 1980s and it is now Australia's fourteenth largest urban area.

Table 7.2 identifies the importance of the Gold Coast, the Sunshine Coast, and Cairns as Australian tourist destinations. The first two centers are important as international and domestic destinations, while Cairns is significant only as an international destination. Its low ranking (nineteenth) as a domestic tourism destination is a consequence of its geographic isolation from the main concentrations of population.

The significance of the Gold Coast, the Sunshine Coast, and Cairns as Australian resort cities, relative to three other Australian cities – the federal capital (Canberra), the largest city (Sydney), and Brisbane, the largest city

Table 7.2 Australia's top ten tourism destinations for international and domestic tourists (percentage of overnight visitors)

International Tourists (Mean number of visitors, 1996-99) (% of total international tourists)*		Domestic Tourists (Mean number of visitors, 1998–99) (% of total domestic tourists)**	
1. Sydney	57.8	1. Sydney	11.1
2. Melbourne	23.7	2. Melbourne	8.0
3. Gold Coast	23.6	3. Brisbane	5.8
4. Cairns/Far North Queensland	18.4	4. Gold Coast	4.5
5. Brisbane	17.6	5. Wollongong/South Coast	3.5
6. Perth	12.4	6. Sunshine Coast	3.3
7. Adelaide	7.0	6. Newcastle/Hunter Valley	3.3
8. Uluru/Ayers Rock	6.7	8. Adelaide	3.2
9. Sunshine Coast	4.3	9. Perth	3.1
10. Whitsunday, Qld	4.3	10. Mid North Coast, NSW	2.9

Note
Cairns/Far North Queensland covers the Cairns urban area and its surrounding region. Whitsunday Region encompasses Mackay, Bowen, and Proserpine.
Wollongong/South Coast covers the Wollongong urban area and urban centers immediately south, such as Bateman's Bay.
Newcastle/Hunter Valley covers the Newcastle urban area and the Hunter Valley, an important wine growing area.
Mid-North Coast of NSW covers a number of urban centers, including Byron Bay and Coffs Harbour.
* Covers visits to more than one place.
** Covers the distribution of domestic tourists around Australia at specific periods in 1998 and 1999.
Source: For international tourism data, Bureau of Tourism Research, 2001a; for domestic tourism data, Bureau of Tourism Research, 2001b.

in Queensland – is apparent when these six cities' labor forces are contrasted. As the data in table 7.3 reveal, the three resort cities have much larger shares of their workforces in tourism-related industries than more economically complex cities like Sydney and many other Australian cities. In Sydney, 4.3 percent of the workforce is engaged in accommodation, cafés, and restaurants, compared to 9.9 percent in the Gold Coast, 8 percent in the Sunshine Coast, and 10.9 percent in Cairns. Cultural and recreational services account for 2.4 percent of Sydney's economy, but 10 percent of the Sunshine Coast's and 4.9 percent of the Gold Coast's economy.

The events of September 11, 2001, brought a temporary decline in international tourist flows to Australia, including to the Gold Coast,

Table 7.3 Employment in tourism industries: Gold Coast, Sunshine Coast, and Cairns compared (1996) (percentages)

INDUSTRY	Gold Coast	Sunshine Coast	Cairns	Canberra	Brisbane	Sydney	Australia
Retail trade	17.9	18.7	16.4	12.0	14.4	13.1	14.0
Accommodation, cafes and restaurants	9.9	8.9	10.9	5.0	4.3	4.6	4.8
Cultural and recreational services	4.9	10.1	3.3	8.1	2.4	2.8	2.4
Personal and other services	4.0	2.8	4.1	3.4	4.1	3.7	3.8
TOTAL	36.7	40.5	34.7	28.5	25.2	24.2	25.0

Source: Australian Bureau of Statistics 1996.

although this decline was also a consequence of the collapse of Ansett Airlines (the country's second carrier) in 2001 and the inevitable decline in numbers following the 2000 Sydney Olympics. But the impact of September 11 appears to have substituted one set of tourists for another. The Gold Coast had a record 2001–2 summer season because many Australians who would have traveled internationally decided to holiday at home. Moreover, there is also little to suggest that the World Trade Center attack has had any effect on high-rise construction on the Gold Coast. In November 2001, the Gold Coast City Council (GCCC) approved plans for the world's tallest (80-story) residential tower, to be completed in 2005. This is hardly the action of a city fearful of aerial terrorist attacks.

The Land Economy and Australian Tourism Urbanization

The long-established regulatory framework for the exploitation of natural resources by primary producers, which evolved in the nineteenth century, provided the framework for the initial development – and ultimately the high rate – of Australian tourism urbanization. Australian tourism urbanization's natural resources focus contrasts sharply with that of other countries' tourism urbanization. Culture and history, for example, define Venice's tourism (van der Borg 1998), while gambling defines Las Vegas (see Foglesong 1999; Parker 1999). Therefore, although Australian resort cities may partly fit Judd's classification of resort centers as "cities as theme parks" or "tourist bubbles" (Judd 1999), they must also be classified as places that sell nature, albeit in a highly controlled and stylized way.

The "natural resources mode of regulation" was institutionalized over the years 1860 to 1920, and notably at the turn of the twentieth century through "colonial socialism," a private–public "partnership" providing the ideological and institutional structures for twentieth-century Australian capitalism (Butlin 1976; Castles 1985; Buckley and Wheelwright 1988). The key focus was on the exploitation of land for both rural industries and urban development. Banks, real estate, and land development interests worked closely with the state to develop these resources, with banks providing loans on favorable terms to primary producers, urban land developers, households, and real estate interests. The state controlled the land – and even today owns an extraordinary 84 percent of the country (Powell 1988) – and it introduced a market system enabling the easy buying and selling of land (cf. Massey and Catalano 1978). In this way, resort centers sprung from adaptations to the regulatory system guiding primary production, meaning that the more dominant role played by primary production in Queensland explains why tourism urbanization is more extensive here than in other states. Therefore, Australia, and Queensland specifically, had a regulatory framework highly suited to the easy and rapid exploitation of land for tourism.

The Gold Coast

The Gold Coast evolved in the middle of the twentieth century from three small service towns and a number of hamlets scattered along 30 km of coastline. In the late 1940s, the city's population of 13,000 people was thinly spread along this littoral, but it now extends some 50 km from the southern outskirts of Brisbane to northern New South Wales. Tourist precincts and residential areas are clearly segregated, with the tourist strip abutting the beach and residents living beyond the littoral. There is also no dominant central business district. Instead, a number of commercial centers are scattered along the coast, the largest concentration being in the north, around and near Surfers Paradise.

Post-Fordism, the regulation regime of the contemporary (post-1970) global age, is said to be characterized by transnational corporations, a service-oriented flexible workforce, weak trade unions, enterprise bargaining, a fragile or declining welfare state, growing social polarization, high rates of unemployment, high levels of geographic mobility, public–private partnerships, and increasing household diversity (Eiser and Hirsch 1989; Boyer 1990; Dunford 1990; Jessop 1990; Goodwin et al. 1993; Amin 1994; Low 1994, 1995). When we examine the pattern of Gold Coast development, post-Fordism is seen to have substantially structured the city from its beginnings and long before globalization exerted its dominant impact (see Mullins 1984, 1991, 1992a, 1992b, 1994, 1995).

Regulation regimes and Gold Coast development, 1945–80

The Gold Coast's economy has always been service-based, with a flexible workforce marked by part-time or casual employment, high rates of unemployment, and low levels of worker security, unionization, job skills, labor force participation, and household income. Moreover, the city has a distinctive class structure. A large *petite bourgeoisie* (self-employed and small employers) drove the city's early development and although this class remains strong today, large corporations now have a far more determining effect. The Gold Coast is also a migrant city – albeit from internal migration – and has greater household diversity than other major Australian cities.

The natural resources mode of regulation profoundly shaped the Gold Coast tourism industry over this early period for the benefit of land developers, builders, building workers, real estate interests, and banks. The two local governments at the time (the GCCC and the Albert Shire Council [ASC]), whose politics were populist in style (Mullins 1984, 1986), provided the conditions for easy and speedy development. Bruce Small, a Gold Coast mayor for a significant part of this period – whose family company was involved in land development – was the most important of the coalition leaders. The alliance Small led brought a rapid change, most strikingly with canal estates and beachfront condominiums, although this development was also accompanied by land and real estate scandals.

While this land-oriented regime dominated the 1945–80 period, a system of regulation also focused on attracting tourists, a process presided over by the GCCC in cooperation with local tourism interests. The goal was to promote the city as a domestic tourism destination (although New Zealanders were also targeted) and to guard against perceived threats to the city's small-business-based tourism. Apart from the free pleasures offered by the natural environment, accommodation was largely self-catering, with tourists renting apartments and self-servicing their needs. There was only one theme park, a few nightclubs, and a limited number of restaurants, with other entertainment being confined to the beach and to pubs.

The two parties involved in this dual system of regulation were in constant conflict, this being most apparent in actions taken over shopping center development. Although shopping centers were built and promoted by landed interests, tourism operators saw their proliferation as undermining the livelihood of established shopkeepers. The tourism industry also felt that the more powerful land development and real estate interests received unfair advantages from local government, a claim leading to conflicts that were played out within the GCCC. So serious were these conflicts that the Queensland government sacked the GCCC in 1978 and installed an administrator until new elections were called 12 months later. However, tensions still remain between the two groups.

In these early years, a system developed for responding to the negative impact of the city's development on residents. Perceived deficiencies in residential facilities, such as drainage and public transport, provoked resident action during the 1940s–60s, with many urban movements over this period being led by neighborhood organizations. These "progress associations" also successfully sponsored candidates at local government elections, in order to effect change from the inside. However, when the city's residential infrastructure was substantially provided (by the late 1960s), progress associations essentially disappeared; their reason for existence had vanished (Mullins 1995; Mullins and Shaw 1999).

Regulation regimes and Gold Coast development after 1980

From the early 1980s, Gold Coast tourism became increasingly international, with visitors coming mainly from Japan; a trend shared with Australia as a whole. A third of Gold Coast visitors are now from overseas. Although Japan remains the largest market, Japanese tourists have declined in importance over recent years as new international tourism markets have opened up and because of the 1990s' downturn in the Japanese economy.

This more recent stage of development was accompanied by a wider set of changes, the most notable being federal government deregulation of the Australian labor market, the airline industry, and the finance sector, all of which had important consequences for the Gold Coast. The deregulation of the labor market ensured that the city's tourism and construction/real estate industries remained "flexible." The deregulation of the finance industry enabled easier access to investment funds, including foreign capital, thus ensuring an even more rapid rate of development. The deregulation of the airline industry removed the "two airline agreement," which had given Qantas and Ansett a monopoly and opened up the market to new carriers. However, with the exception of Richard Branson's Virgin Blue, all the new carriers have ceased operation, a demise compounded by Ansett's collapse in 2001.

The system of regulation dominating Gold Coast development over this post-1980 period focused primarily on the city's natural resources and built environment, and this was for the benefit of visitors, land development/real estate interests, and the tourism industry. As in the earlier period, considerable attention was directed at tourism infrastructure, but in this case it focused particularly on Japanese tourists.

Japanese tourists encouraged the rapid expansion of golf resorts (in response to a growing demand for golfing holidays), international hotels (for a clientele little interested in self-catering holidays, the most common form of accommodation in the city), luxury shops (in response to affluent visitors seeking an array of sophisticated gifts), condominiums, apartments, and a private university (Rimmer 1992; Hajdu 1999, 2000). These developments also promoted a wider transformation of the city's hospitality industry. There was an increasing number and diversity of goods and services available, and the entry of large operators, such as major hotel chains, heralded the beginning of the end of an overwhelmingly domestic tourism industry, a tourism produced by an army of small operators.

The new infrastructure was built by public–private partnerships and involved Japanese investment companies, the Japanese government, the Australian government, local developers, local real estate interests, the GCCC, and the Queensland government. Yet, these alliances disintegrated in the 1990s following a Gold Coast property crash and because of continuing difficulties in the Japanese economy. The proposed, but now defunct, multi-function polis (MFP) well illustrates the rise and fall of Japanese property interests. Developed as an Australian government–Japanese government initiative, it was to have been a high-technology tourist/recreation city built in the northern Gold Coast. When the Queensland government refused to annex necessary land, the venture relocated to Adelaide. Japanese interests withdrew shortly thereafter, and the project was scrapped (Stilwell 1991).

Domestic capital was also switching from Australia's declining manufacturing sector into tourism (Berry and Huxley 1992). Several theme parks opened during the 1980s and 1990s, notably Dreamworld, an Australian venture, and Warner Bros Movie World, a US venture involving a theme park and Australia's largest movie studio. Sanctuary Cove, a large gated community that includes a golf resort and marina, opened in the early 1990s. Built by Australian and international capital, it is infamous for the special zoning its developers obtained from the Queensland government, an action that provoked a public outcry.

Negative impacts arising from many projects initiated a regulatory system that aimed at protecting the city and its residents from unacceptable outcomes. Although most tourism infrastructure was built with little difficulty, vociferous attacks were directed at a number of projects. The most significant included the 1980s' proposal to develop the Southport Broadwater (a large lagoon) and, more recently, a planned cable car that was to run from the city's western edge into the rainforest-clad hinterland. Following vigorous public opposition, the Queensland government blocked both proposals. Indeed, much of the grassroots political action of the 1980s and 1990s focused on similar environmental issues. Developers' attempts at accessing the most profitable sites – the beachfront, the rainforest, and the city's unique system of waterways and maritime environments – provoked residents' ire (Mullins 1995; Mullins and Shaw 1999).

Public anger forced the GCCC and the Queensland government to implement environmental and social regulations to block projects perceived to have negative impacts on residents, the environment, and the city as a whole. Governments and a number of pro-growth interests have become increasingly aware of the way environmental degradation threatens the city. They now acknowledge the ultimate conundrum: that the Gold Coast exists to enable tourists to exploit its natural environment, but this exploitation may, if it is not managed, destroy the tourist base.

Refining the system of regulation

Improvements in transport infrastructure reflect the presence of a regulatory system emphasizing the importance of tourists' easy access to and from the city. The Australian government, the Queensland government, the GCCC, and private sector interests came together in the 1980s and 1990s to transform air, rail, and road transport within southeast Queensland.

Although the Gold Coast has a domestic airport, Brisbane Airport is the region's international gateway, being one hour from the Gold Coast by freeway or train. A new Brisbane airport was built in the late 1980s on the old site, with a domestic terminal opening in the early 1990s and an international terminal in the late 1990s. The federal government sold the airport in the mid-1990s to a public–private consortium involving the Brisbane City Council, the Dutch company Schiphol International, which runs the airport, and a number of other Australian private and public sector interests. Brisbane now has Australia's second busiest international airport (after Sydney), having surpassed Melbourne, and the airport is about to undergo major expansion.

Attention has also been directed at rail development. In 1996, the Queensland government opened a rail link between Brisbane and the Gold Coast, replacing a line that it had removed in 1964 following a prolonged downturn in passenger numbers and a belief that private motor vehicles would dominate trips between the cities. The line not only links the two cities but caters to those living in the Brisbane–Gold Coast corridor, an area of very rapid population growth.

A privately built and operated 5-km railway line linking the Brisbane Airport with the state-owned rail system opened in 2001. This enables tourists to travel directly by train from the airport to the Gold Coast (and the Sunshine Coast). The company that built the system will operate it until 2031, when it will be handed over to the Queensland government.

Road transport has also been revolutionized. In 2000, a new Pacific Highway was opened, the M1, between Brisbane and the Gold Coast. Built by the Queensland government, this six- to eight-lane system replaces a four- to six-lane freeway. This link is particularly important because 40 percent of the Gold Coast's domestic tourists are from Brisbane, and Brisbane residents contribute the bulk of day-trippers. Yet, the M1's capacity will be reached within a few years, as the population living along the Brisbane–Gold Coast corridor grows, meaning a new freeway is likely within the decade. As with other new Southeast Queensland freeways, this will probably be built and operated as a toll road by the private sector.

In the past, the GCCC and the local tourism industry were largely responsible for tourism promotion, but this changed radically from about 1980. The Queensland government established the Queensland Tourist and Travel Corporation (QTTC) – now Tourism Queensland – in 1980 to promote the state's tourism, and this includes, for example, chasing major events. At the same time, the federal government, through the Australian Tourism Commission (ATC), became more involved in promoting Australian tourism. Although the ATC was established in 1967, funded equally by the Australian government and the tourism industry, it had little promotional impact until the 1980s when international tourists began to arrive in large numbers.

Whereas tourism promotion received most attention from Gold Coast tourism interests in the past, the maintenance of social order has now become increasingly important, thus signaling a shift towards policies that regulate visitors so as to protect residents. Like all resort centers, the Gold Coast sells illegal pleasures, notably drugs, as well as goods and services that raise moral indignation, such as casino gambling and prostitution. Still, the city has managed to project an image as a good city for all tourists. This view is stated implicitly for those wishing to engage in illegal or morally questionable activities and explicitly for those searching for a safe, happy, and desirable place to visit. Such managed outcomes emanate from actions taken by a loose coalition of interests, notably the GCCC, the Queensland government (particularly police and welfare departments), tourism interests, and non-government welfare organizations.

"Schoolies week" reflects well the city's relative success at managing social order. Schoolies are graduating high school students, mainly from Queensland and New South Wales, who have a week of fun on the Gold Coast at the end of each academic year. Beginning in the early 1980s, tens of thousands of students have descended on the city each November.

Whereas early schoolies weeks resulted in mayhem, both for the city and for the students themselves, particularly following drug overdoses and sexual assaults, the city guardians have managed to protect the city from the schoolies and the schoolies from themselves, and from predators. This has been achieved through advisory groups and street-based welfare organizations.

If we accept Castells's (1998) claim that a global criminal economy run by an international mafia is attracted, for speculative purposes, to the economies of booming centers like resort cities, then we can presuppose that this criminal economy is present on the Gold Coast. Land and real estate opportunities, plus the sale of morally questionable pleasures, provide ideal opportunities for these people to launder money. Yet the mafia's presence is not obvious, at least if judged by criminal activity and, at present, it has not intruded into the city's day-to-day tourism activities in a way that would deter tourists. By implication, a system of regulation is in place to protect visitors, residents, and the city more generally from these effects.

Responsibility for the overall physical planning and management of Gold Coast development rests with the GCCC. In the mid-1990s, the GCCC amalgamated with its neighboring council, ASC, to form a new GCCC, whose area of jurisdiction extends from Brisbane to the Queensland/New South Wales border. This decision had been taken to enable a more coordinated approach to the city's development.

The GCCC plays its most important role in the city's development through zoning. However, in collecting less that 10 percent of total government revenue, Australian local governments – like the GCCC – have limited economic power, meaning they can never control all planning decisions made within their borders. State governments play the pivotal, though indirect, role because they are responsible for major services and planning decisions, from education to main roads.

With a regulatory system disproportionately focusing on the exploitation of natural resources, those who have benefited most from Gold Coast development have been landed interests, although the negative effects of regular property crashes have brought frequent bankruptcies to these people and organizations. Those providing tourism services have also benefited from the city's development, although they too have felt the negative effects of economic downturns. Some stability in the tourism industry has followed the arrival of large operators during the 1980s and 1990s, their size enabling them to ride out downturns in the economy. Yet, of all the players involved in the city's development, residents appear relatively disadvantaged, for they still receive low incomes, have low job skills, and are subject to high rates of unemployment.

Plate 7.1   Beachfront property on Australia's Gold Coast. *Source*: Corbis

Conclusion

Australia's high rate of tourism urbanization, and the development trajectory taken by individual resort cities like the Gold Coast, have been governed by a mode of regulation that focuses on the exploitation of the natural environment for purposes of tourism. This regulatory system was easily transferable from an economy focusing on the exploitation of nature for agriculture, pastoralism, and mining to an economy focusing on the exploitation of natural resources for tourism. The Gold Coast was especially favored because of its natural amenities – the ocean, the beaches, the waterways, and the rainforest hinterland. Yet, to make it a fully-fledged tourist space, an infrastructure of consumption spaces was also required (e.g. golf courses and theme parks), and this was effected by the global age. Although Australian tourism urbanization was well under way before globalization, it gained considerable momentum with the arrival of globalization and associated increased flows of travelers.

With more and more people around the world being able to satisfy the global cultural demand to consume an increasing array of goods and services, we can expect many more Australian cities and towns to be built, or transformed, for tourists. Yet, if Australian tourism continues to focus disproportionately on the exploitation of nature, negative environmental consequences are likely to bring economic, social, and political crises to a number of tourist centers. These, in turn, will inevitably bring about increasingly elaborate regulatory structures, and these are likely to reflect, as in the past, an adaptation to inherited institutional structures and political traditions.

REFERENCES

Amin, A. 1994: Post-Fordism: models, fantasies and phantoms of transition. In A. Amin (ed.), *Post-Fordism: A Reader*. Oxford: Blackwell, 1–40.

Australian Bureau of Statistics, 1991: *Australian Census of Population and Housing*. Canberra, Australian Bureau of Statistics.

—— 1996: *Australian Census of Population and Housing*. Canberra, Australian Bureau of Statistics.

—— 2001: *Australian Census of Population and Housing*. Canberra, Australian Bureau of Statistics.

Baum, S., Mullins, P., Stimson, R., and O'Connor, K. 2002: Communities of the postindustrial city. *Urban Affairs Review* 37 (3): 322–57.

——, Stimson, R., O'Connor, K., Mullins, P., and Davis, R. 1999: *Community Opportunity and Vulnerability in Australia's Cities and Towns*. St. Lucia: University of Queensland Press.

Berry, M. and Huxley, M. 1992: Big build: property, capital, the state, and urban change in Australia. *International Journal of Urban and Regional Research* 16 (1): 35–59.

Boyer, R. 1990: *The Regulation School*. New York: Columbia University Press.

Buckley, K. and Wheelwright, T. 1988: *No Paradise for Workers*. Melbourne: Oxford University Press.

Bureau of Tourism Research 2001a: *Top 20 Regions Visited in Australia by International Tourists, 1996, 1997, 1998, 1999*. Sydney: Bureau of Tourism Research (http://www.btr.gov.au/statistics/Datacard/dc_top_20.html).

——2001b: *Travel by Australians: Annual Results of the National Visitor Survey, 1999*. Sydney: Bureau of Tourism Research.

Butlin, N. 1976: *Investment in Australian Economic Development*. Canberra: Australian National University.

Castells, M. 1998: *End of Millennium*. Oxford: Blackwell.

Castles, F. 1985: *The Working Class and Welfare*. Wellington: Allen and Unwin.

Dunford, M. 1990: Theories of regulation. *Society and Space* 8: 297–321.

Eiser, J. and Hirsch, J. 1989: The crisis of Fordism and the dimensions of a "postfordist" regional and urban structure. *International Journal of Urban and Regional Research* 13: 417–37.

Eisinger, P. 2000: The politics of bread and circuses: building the city for the visitor class. *Urban Affairs Review* 35 (3): 316–33.

Foglesong, R. 1999: Walt Disney and Orlando: deregulation as a strategy for tourism. In D. R. Judd and S. S. Fainstein (eds.), *The Tourist City*. New Haven, CT: Yale University Press, 89–106.

Goodwin, M., Duncan, S., and Halford, S. 1993: Regulation theory, the local state, and the transition of urban politics. *Society and Space* 11: 67–88.

Gordon, D. 1978: Capitalist development and the histories of American cities. In W. Tabb and L. Sawers (eds.), *Marxism and the Metropolis*. New York: Oxford University Press, 25–63.

Griffiths, R. 1995: Cultural strategies and new modes of urban intervention. *Cities* 12 (4): 253–65.

Hajdu, J. 1999: Japanese capital on Australia's Gold Coast as a catalyst of a localist-globalist conflict on national identity. *Global Society* 13 (3): 327–47.

——2000: Japanese investment on the Gold Coast. Unpublished PhD thesis, Deakin University, Victoria, Australia.

Hannigan, J. 1998: *Fantasy City*. London: Routledge.

Jessop, B. 1990: Regulation theories in retrospect and prospect. *Economy and Society* 19 (2): 153–215.

Judd, D. 1999: Constructing the tourist bubble. In D. R. Judd and S. S. Fainstein (eds.), *The Tourist City*. New Haven, CT: Yale University Press, 35–53.

——and Fainstein, S. (eds.) 1999: *The Tourist City*. New Haven, CT: Yale University Press.

Low, N. 1994: Growth machines and regulation theory. *International Journal of Urban and Regional Research* 18 (3): 451–68.

——1995: Regulation theory, global competition among cities, and capital embeddedness. *Urban Policy and Research* 13 (4): 205–21.

Massey, D. and Catalano, A. 1978: *Capital and Land*. London: Edward Arnold.

Mullins, P. 1984: Hedonism and real estate: resort tourism and Gold Coast development. In P. Williams (ed.), *Conflict and Development*. Sydney: George Allen and Unwin, 31–50.

——1986: Queensland: populist politics and development. In B. Head (ed.), *The Politics of the Australian States*. Sydney: George Allen and Unwin, 138–62.

——1991: Tourism urbanization. *International Journal of Urban and Regional Research* 15 (3): 326–42.

——1992a: Do industrial cities have the highest rates of urban unemployment? *Urban Policy and Research* 10 (1): 24–32.

——1992b: Cities for pleasure. *Built Environment* 18 (3): 187–98.

——1994: Class relations and tourism urbanization: the regeneration of the petite bourgeoisie and the emergence of a new urban form. *International Journal of Urban and Regional Research* 18 (4): 591–608.

——1995: Progress associations and urban development: the Gold Coast, 1945–79. *Urban Policy and Research* 13 (2): 6–19.

——1999: International tourism and the cities of South East Asia. In D. R. Judd and S. S. Fainstein (eds.), *The Tourist City*. New Haven, CT: Yale University Press, 245–60.

——, Natalier, K., Smith, P., and Smeaton, B. 1999: Cities and consumption spaces. *Urban Affairs Review* 35 (1): 44–71.

——and Shaw, K. 1999: Households, urban movements, and the evolution of a city of the global age: Australia's Gold Coast, 1945–94. Paper presented at the *Future of Chinese Cities* Conference, Shanghai Academy of Social Science, Shanghai, China, July 28–31.

Parker, R. 1999: Las Vegas: casino gambling and local culture. In D. R. Judd and S. S. Fainstein (eds.), *The Tourist City*. New Haven, CT: Yale University Press.

Perkins, H. and Thorns, D. 2001: Gazing or performing? Reflections on Urry's tourist gaze in the context of contemporary experience in the Antipodes. *International Sociology* 16 (2): 185–204.

Powell, J. 1988: *An Historical Geography of Modern Australia*. Cambridge: Cambridge University Press.

Rimmer, P. 1992: Japan's "resort archipelago". *Environment and Planning A* 24 (1): 1599–625

Ritzer, G. 1999: *Enchanting a Disenchanted World*. Thousand Oaks, CA: Pine Forge Press.

Stilwell, F. 1991: An international new town down under. *International Journal of Urban and Regional Research* 15 (4): 611–18.

van der Borg, J. 1998: Tourism management in Venice, or how to deal with success. In D. Tyler, Y. Guerrier, and M. Robertson (eds.), *Managing Tourism in Cities: Policy, Process and Practice*. Chichester: John Wiley and Sons, 125–35.

Part III

Regulating Labor Markets

---

8   Regulating Hospitality: Tourism Workers in New York and Los Angeles
    David L. Gladstone and Susan S. Fainstein

9   Shaping the Tourism Labor Market in Montreal
    Marc V. Levine

8

Regulating Hospitality: Tourism Workers in New York and Los Angeles

David L. Gladstone and Susan S. Fainstein

I-Max screens, themed environments, mega-stores, theaters, museums, and sports venues have displaced marble-clad office towers and tasteful plazas as the most prominent trophies of urban revitalization efforts. The office glut at the start of the 1990s spurred urban growth coalitions to seek other sources of economic development. They have looked increasingly to the unique advantage cities possess as centers of entertainment, both low- and high-brow (Hannigan 1998). The never-ending struggle to restore the viability of urban cores has involved municipal leaders in frantic efforts to draw in tourist dollars by developing new attractions, adding hotel space, and marketing their cities (Fainstein and Judd 1999). In this, as in other arenas where cities compete against each other for development, there are winners and losers. This chapter addresses some of the implications of winning. In particular, within cities that succeed in attracting large numbers of tourists, how are the gains distributed between workers and owners?

Examination of the impact of tourism development allows the extension of certain themes that have been significant within urban scholarship. Of particular importance is the question of whether a tourism-oriented urban regime will enforce regulations that create opportunities for improved earnings among low-wage workers. Critics of economic development strategies that subsidize office construction have contended that, even where successful in promoting business investment, they have not generated employment for those who need it most (Squires 1989). Thus, unskilled workers displaced from manufacturing, inner-city residents with weak educational credentials, and immigrants find few job opportunities within the gleaming new office towers. They can, however, find work in the bedrooms, kitchens, and corridors of tourism complexes. Do these enlarged openings for low-skilled workers mean that the regimes pursuing tourism strategies are following a more redistributive course than if they focused on office development? Or, does the tourism industry depend on a high level of worker exploitation, putting it in the same category as the downgraded manufacturing that has reasserted itself within urban sweat-shops (Sassen 2001)?

In fact, the question of whether or not tourism can support a decent standard of living for unskilled workers cannot be answered categorically. Working conditions are not a simple function of industry type, and broadly defined industrial sectors like tourism or manufacturing encom-pass a variety of sub-industries with differing working conditions. Manu-facturing employment can produce high wages and job stability or a meager livelihood and extreme insecurity, depending on worker organiza-tion and industry competitiveness. Similarly, tourism employment can vary from comfortable to exploitative; wage rates, benefit levels, and job security reflect the formal and informal rules that govern the sector. The immense variety of organizational forms within the industry makes it especially susceptible to differing labor–management relations. In contrast to major manufacturing industries like steel and autos, tourism includes both very large multinational corporations and numerous mom-and-pop operations. Even within sub-industries, ranging from travel agencies to restaurants to hotels, business organization differs substantially from place to place and displays considerable variety even within a single city.

How conditions are organized by location and sub-sector depends on the mode of regulation that prevails. According to regulation theory, the method by which firms extract profit and retain economic control depends on a whole set of social relations governed by formal rules and informal norms. In the United States, in relation to the tourism sector, reg-ulation includes national labor and immigration laws as well as accepted relations between bosses and workers within particular industries and particular places, including customary differentials between men's and women's pay. As discussed in the Introduction to this volume, we can use the basic concepts of regulation theory to differentiate among and within locations and industries without assuming that at any point in time there is a single dominant regime of accumulation (Goodwin, Duncan, and Halford 1993; Goodwin and Painter 1997). At the same time, the use of regulation theory implies that under capitalism the economic system has a unity that is supported by an ensemble of regulations with some level of consistency.

The tourism industry operates within the broad parameters of global capitalism, and its character as a seasonal industry primarily offering personal services confines the variability of labor relations within it. The power bloc that governs relations within the US tourism industry includes national, state, and local governments and corporate leaders in various roles, including as members of public–private partnerships and as employers. Its influence and the forms of regulation that it enforces are mediated by trade unions, by the size and composition of tourism sub-industries, by flows of immigration (themselves an outcome of immigration law), and by pressures from community organizations. In order to understand the dynamics of development of the industry and how relationships within it are regulated, we need to look both at particular places and at tourism sub-industries. We would expect that, within a single country, labor relations within tourism-related industries would conform to national patterns but with some degree of local variation. It is the extent of that local variation that we address in this chapter.

We have chosen to perform this task in New York and Los Angeles, the two largest US metropolises. Both claim to be global cities, although New York's purchase on this title is most clear-cut. Los Angeles, while a major business center, does not have a producer-services, financial, and headquarters complex on the scale of New York's. They resemble each other, however, in important respects that make them significant places in which to study tourism: they are highly internationalized in both the composition of their workforces and their visitors; they are the country's two most prominent centers of cultural production; and the industry is absolutely and relatively large within them.

In this chapter we examine the employment effects of the New York and Los Angeles tourism industries. As background to the discussion of tourism labor markets, we first describe the broad contours of the two cities' tourism economies. Our discussion of the quantity, quality, and remuneration of tourism and tourism-related jobs both lays out the relative wage rates and job security within the industry and examines the forces that have created these outcomes. We find that the possibilities of extracting social benefits from tourism, especially where tourism workers are organized, are greater than in other industries because tourism is a place-dependent industry: almost by definition, a tourism industry is wedded to a particular place, making it difficult if not impossible for tourism firms to threaten workers or cities with relocation if their demands are not fully met.

The New York and Los Angeles Tourism Industries

The tourism market

World city status gives New York and Los Angeles an array of attractions that draw travelers with a variety of motives. New York accounts for a disproportionate share of the nation's international and business travelers because of its pre-eminence as a national and global financial and corporate center. Los Angeles is less significant as a business center but still attracts a substantial number of business travelers and conventioneers. Together these two latter groups account for one quarter of Los Angeles's tourist arrivals and one-third of New York's.

Both cities are also major centers of cultural production. Not coincidentally, one of New York's major tourist attractions, the recently redeveloped Times Square district, is also home to some of the world's largest news, media, and entertainment conglomerates, including Bertelsmann, Reuters, Viacom, and Condé Nast, and of a number of television production spaces. The studios of the movie industry have, of course, always been a major draw for Los Angeles. Other attributes that attract visitors are important higher education and associated research complexes, giant leading-edge medical facilities, superior shopping opportunities, and large numbers of newcomers from this country and abroad who have relatives elsewhere. Los Angeles has the additional attractions of beaches and a sunny climate. And, of course, sheer size means that the two cities draw huge numbers of people visiting friends and relatives.

Among American cities, New York and Los Angeles are the leading American destinations for foreign visitors. Of the 37.4 million tourists who visited New York in 2000, an estimated 6.8 million (18 percent) were international travelers (table 8.1). Los Angeles trailed only slightly, with 5.5 million international arrivals, constituting about 22 percent of its total of 24.7 million visitors (table 8.2). For the United States as a whole, the proportion was about 4 percent. Europe comprised New York's largest foreign tourism market, while visitors from Mexico were the largest proportion of LA's. International travelers are economically important because they spend more: in 1995 international tourists made up 19 percent of New York's tourist traffic yet generated nearly 40 percent of tourism revenue (table 8.1). In LA international visitors made up 25 percent of the region's total arrivals in 1995 but accounted for nearly 35 percent of the city's total revenues generated from tourism, a share that had grown to nearly 50 percent by 2000 (table 8.2). Generally tourism adds substantially to the export income of both cities. Altogether, visitors to New York City spent $17 billion in 2000. In LA visitors contributed $13.6 billion to

Table 8.1 New York City visitor arrivals and expenditures, 1991–2002

Year	Arrivals (millions of visitors)	Average annual growth in arrivals (%)	Internat. arrivals (millions of visitors)	Average annual growth in internat. arrivals (%)	Visitor spending (billions of $)	Average annual growth in visitor spending (%)	Internat. visitor spending (billions of $)
1991	29.1		5.5		10.1		n.a.
1995	28.5	−0.5	5.4	−0.5	11.7	3.7	4.7
1998	33.0	6.1	6.0	3.6	14.3	6.9	n.a.
1999	36.7	7.9	6.6	10.0	15.6	9.1	n.a.
2000	37.4	1.9	6.8	3.0	17.0	9.0	n.a.
2001	32.0	−14.4	5.7	−16.2	14.9	−12.4	n.a.

Notes: 2001 data estimated.
Source: New York City Convention and Visitors Bureau (1995, 1998a, 1998b, 1999, 2002).

Table 8.2 Los Angeles visitor arrivals and expenditures, 1991–2000

Year	Arrivals (millions of visitors)	Average annual growth in arrivals (%)	Internat. arrivals (millions of visitors)	Average annual growth in internat. arrivals (%)	Visitor spending (billions of $)	Average annual growth in visitor spending (%)	Internat. visitor spending (billions of $)
1991	23.3		n.a.		8.1		
1995	22.1	−1.3	5.0		9.7	4.6	3.3
1997	23.6	3.3	5.8	7.7	11.3	7.9	n.a.
1998	23.5	−0.4	5.4	−6.9	11.9	5.3	n.a.
1999	23.8	1.3	5.5	1.9	12.3	3.4	n.a.
2000	24.7	3.8	5.5	0.0	13.6	10.6	6.4

Source: Los Angeles Convention and Visitors Bureau (1996, 1998, 2002).

the regional economy, about 80 percent of the New York total (tables 8.1 and 8.2).

In both cities tourism dropped off during the first half of the 1990s and then again after September 11, 2001. In Los Angeles a combination of supply side (earthquakes, floods, fires, civil disturbances) and demand side (severe recessions in Mexico and Japan) factors discouraged both domestic and international tourists; even by 2000 arrivals had not reached their 1989 peak of 25.2 million (table 8.2). In New York the severe recession of the first half of the decade, from which the city's recovery lagged the nation's, combined to deter tourists along with a widespread perception that the city was not safe. In the latter half of the 1990s, a combination of prosperity and massive favorable publicity concerning a cleaner, safer New York precipitated a major jump in the number of visitors (table 8.1) and in hotel construction (Holusha 2000). Then, the attack on the World Trade Center caused visits to the city to plummet; as of this writing the extent of recovery remains somewhat unclear and available data are fragmentary. On the one hand, by the end of May 2002, hotel occupancy exceeded 80 percent, close to former highs despite substantial recent additions to the number of rooms (*Crain's New York Business*, June 3, 2002: 38). On the other, room rates had dropped substantially (ibid.), and, in particular, the proportion of more lucrative, international travelers was considerably reduced (Blair 2002). A further indication of the decline in international and business travel was a loss of 12,000 jobs in the air transport sector in the year ending April 2002 (*Crain's New York Business*, May 27, 2002: 54). The susceptibility of the hospitality industry to disruption by terrorism points to one of its weaknesses as an employment sector.

Types of tourism establishments

The production of tourism goods and services falls into a collection of discrete but related sub-industries: hotel, food and beverage, transport, entertainment, recreation, and retail.[1] Each tourism-related sub-industry derives a different share of its total receipts from the tourist trade. The Port Authority of New York and New Jersey (1994, Chart 8) estimates that the hotel industry depends for 85 percent of its revenue on tourist expenditures; eating and drinking places, 30 percent; transport and entertainment services, 10 percent; and retail, 5 percent. Within a sub-industry the extent to which a business caters to the tourist trade varies enormously according to location and style, making extrapolations to revenues and employment effects extremely problematic. For example, a midtown Manhattan "white tablecloth" restaurant may be half-filled with tourists, while a diner in the Bronx may have none. Thus, the industry-wide figures tell us little about the amount of revenue and employee earnings that are attributable to tourism in those specific establishments that cater to visitors.

The vast majority of tourism-related business establishments in the two cities are small-scale (about 90 percent in New York and 85 percent in LA), employing fewer than 20 workers (US Bureau of the Census 1995). Accordingly, the prospects for unionization of these establishments are small. Some sectors of the tourism industry, however, are characterized by above-average establishment size: hotels, airports and other air transport-related establishments, and museums. Compared to New York, a smaller share of Los Angeles hotels are large establishments (30 percent in New York versus 9 percent in LA), but because Los Angeles has nearly three times as many hotels as New York, the actual number of large establishments is nearly the same.

Growth in tourism-related businesses had been brisk until the recent downturn. In New York the total number of establishments grew by nearly 30 percent from the mid-1980s to the mid-1990s, about 50 percent higher that the average for all industries (US Bureau of the Census 1977–95). In Los Angeles growth from 1980 to 1990 averaged about 5 percent per year, although recession in the Southern California economy in the early 1990s slowed it to less than 2 percent annually through 1995. Even so, tourism compares favorably with other sectors, with growth of new tourism establishments averaging nearly twice the all-industry average (ibid.).

Employment and Labor Market Characteristics

Tourism is a significant source of employment for New Yorkers and Los Angelenos. In 1995 New York's tourism firms employed about 130,700 workers directly and about half again as many indirectly as a result of the tourism industry's links to other New York industries (NYCVB 1995). In terms of employment, tourism was the city's sixth largest industry, falling behind health services (303,900 employees), business services (227,800 employees), manufacturing/non-durable (205,200 employees), social services (152,000 employees), and security and commodity brokers (145,500 employees). Tourism employed more workers than either depository institutions (126,000 employees) or real estate and investment firms (116,800 employees) (ibid.).

Job growth in New York's tourism-related industries has been relatively strong since the mid-1970s, well above the city average, with the industry's employment base growing about 16 percent between 1977 and 1997 (table 8.3). Moreover, during recessionary periods fewer tourism-related jobs have been lost than in many other industries. Employment in the industry stagnated in the early 1980s, grew by about 11 percent during the late 1980s, declined by 5.5 percent during the recession of the early 1990s, but by 1997 had fully recovered. Moreover, New York's tourism industry has done well in comparative terms, since the general New York City economy shed about 7 percent of its jobs during the recession of the early 1990s.

Tourism is an even more significant proportion of the LA economy, despite the fact that New York attracts a larger number of visitors (table 8.4). Altogether nearly half a million people held jobs in tourism-related industries in 1997, representing an astonishing 65 percent increase since

Table 8.3 New York City Tourism-related employment, 1977–1997

Industry	Year	No. of Employees	Employment growth (%)	Share of tourism employment	Share of total city employment (%)	Average annual wage and salary income	Growth in average wage and salary income (%)
All industries	1977	2,714,385	—	—	—	$13,659	—
	1980	2,902,339	6.9	—	—	$16,904	23.8
	1985	3,017,996	4.0	—	—	$24,280	43.6
	1990	3,135,743	3.9	—	—	$32,527	34.0
	1995	2,918,994	-6.9	—	—	$41,904	28.8
	1997	3,038,719	4.1	—	—	$46,749	11.6
Average annual growth			0.6				6.3
Tourism-related industries[a]	1977	309,963	—		11.4	$10,891	—
	1980	327,623	5.7		11.3	$13,313	22.2
	1985	326,230	-0.4		10.8	$17,582	32.1
	1990	363,475	11.4		11.6	$20,436	16.2
	1995	343,522	-5.5		11.8	$24,122	18.0
	1997	366,831	6.8		12.1	$25,158	4.3
Average annual growth			0.8				4.3
Air transport	1977	45,615	—	14.7	—	$20,954	—
	1980	45,205	-0.9	13.8	1.7	$26,884	28.3
	1985	43,461	-3.9	13.3	1.6	$35,175	30.8
	1990	53,124	22.2	14.6	1.4	$33,999	-3.3
	1995	43,835	-17.5	12.8	1.7	$38,342	12.8
	1997	47,855	9.2	13.0	1.5	$38,867	1.4
Average annual growth			0.1				3.4

Eating and drinking places[a]	1977	99,380	—	32.1	3.7	$6,439	—
	1980	102,035	2.7	31.1	3.5	$7,717	19.9
	1985	112,676	10.4	34.5	3.7	$10,663	38.2
	1990	128,127	13.7	35.3	4.1	$12,530	17.5
	1995	126,549	-1.2	36.8	4.3	$14,526	15.9
	1997	141,806	12.1	38.7	4.7	$15,895	9.4
Average annual growth			1.8				4.6
Hotels and other lodging places[a]	1977	22,984	—	7.4	0.8	$10,036	—
	1980	28,957	26.0	8.8	1.0	$11,447	14.1
	1985	30,599	5.7	9.4	1.0	$17,173	50.0
	1990	35,444	15.8	9.8	1.1	$20,519	19.5
	1995	33,807	-4.6	9.8	1.2	$26,510	29.2
	1997	32,068	-5.1	8.7	1.1	$30,592	15.4
Average annual growth			1.7				5.7
Amusement and recreational services[a]	1977	21,943	—	7.1	0.8	$14,109	—
	1980	26,004	18.5	7.9	0.9	$17,044	20.8
	1985	28,068	7.9	8.6	0.9	$23,738	39.3
	1990	36,590	30.4	10.1	1.2	$30,401	28.1
	1995	39,304	7.4	11.4	1.3	$39,437	29.7
	1997	44,502	13.2	12.1	1.5	$38,555	-2.2
Average annual growth			3.6				5.2

Note: [a] Figures are for total employment in the industry, not just for employment attributable to tourism.
Source: United States Census Bureau 1977–97.

Table 8.4 Los Angeles County tourism-related employment, 1977–1997

Industry	Year	No. of Employees	Employment growth (%)	Share of tourism employment	Share of total city employment (%)	Average wage and salary income	Growth in average wage and salary income (%)
All industries	1977	2,647,263	—			$12,512	—
	1980	3,184,578	20.3			$15,594	24.6
	1985	3,345,520	5.1			$21,537	38.1
	1990	3,847,918	15.0			$26,379	22.5
	1995	3,494,193	−9.2			$30,001	13.7
	1997	3,588,831	2.7			$32,274	7.6
Average annual growth			1.5				4.9
Tourism-related industries[a]	1977	295,559	—		11.2	$8,016	—
	1980	335,681	13.6		10.5	$10,051	25.4
	1985	402,334	19.9		12.0	$12,222	21.6
	1990	480,686	19.5		12.5	$15,858	29.7
	1995	463,486	−3.6		13.3	$19,087	20.4
	1997	486,895	5.1		13.6	$20,352	6.6
Average annual growth			2.5				4.8
Air transport	1977	28,915	—	9.8	1.1	$21,208	—
	1980	34,142	18.1	10.2	1.1	$26,487	24.9
	1985	27,948	−18.1	6.9	0.8	$33,086	24.9
	1990	38,187	36.6	7.9	1.0	$35,591	7.6
	1995	37,711	−1.2	8.1	1.1	$38,964	9.5
	1997	43,688	15.8	9.0	1.2	$38,327	−1.6
Average annual growth			2.1				3.0

Category	Year	Employment	Growth (%)	% of total	%	Receipts	Growth (%)
Eating and drinking places[a]	1977	138,840	—	47.0	5.2	$5,008	—
	1980	164,175	18.2	48.9	5.2	$5,872	17.3
	1985	186,126	13.4	46.3	5.6	$7,715	31.4
	1990	223,633	20.2	46.5	5.8	$9,197	19.2
	1995	213,160	-4.7	46.0	6.1	$10,317	12.2
	1997	226,138	6.1	46.4	6.3	$10,639	3.1
Average annual growth			2.5				3.8
Hotels and other lodging places[a]	1977	n.a.	—	—	—	—	—
	1980	n.a.	—	—	—	—	—
	1985	31,688	—	7.9	0.9	$10,571	—
	1990	39,412	24.4	8.2	1.0	$13,565	28.3
	1995	38,412	-2.5	8.3	1.1	$15,891	17.1
	1997	37,928	-1.3	7.8	1.1	$17,710	11.4
Average annual growth			1.5				4.4
Amusement and recreational services[a]	1977	28,183	—	9.5	1.1	$11,863	—
	1980	31,327	11.2	9.3	1.0	$16,307	37.5
	1985	42,122	34.5	10.5	1.3	$20,008	22.7
	1990	48,797	15.8	10.2	1.3	$36,293	81.4
	1995	53,994	10.7	11.6	1.5	$46,606	28.4
	1997	65,123	20.6	13.4	1.8	$46,381	-0.5
Average annual growth			4.3				7.1

Note: [a] Figures are for total employment in the industry, not just for employment attributable to tourism.
Source: United States Census Bureau 1977–97.

1977. Of the total number of jobs in tourism-related industries, the Los Angeles Economic Development Corporation (LAEDC) attributed 253,000 to tourism revenues. The LAEDC ranks tourism as Los Angeles County's third largest industry in employment terms, with more workers than either the motion picture or financial services industries and exceeded only by business and professional management services firms (420,000 employees) and health services (276,000 employees) (LAEDC 1998).

Wages in the industry are low within the two cities, exemplifying the generally low pay characteristic of the industry nationwide. This situation substantiates the premise of regulation theory – that there is a general consistency in the organization of a national economy. In part, it reflects the relatively low productivity of this personal service-intensive sector. But the fact that the rising demand for workers and the increased profitability of the industry have not pushed up wages cannot be explained simply through market factors. Rather, it is the outcome of the organization of the industry – both of the size of its small-enterprise component and of its low level of unionization.

In 1997, the average annual wage in New York's tourism-related industries was $25,158 – 54 percent of the city average of $46,749; the comparable figure for Los Angeles was $20,352, about 63 percent of the Los Angeles County average of $32,274. The lower averages for tourism workers, however, obscure important differences among the various subindustries: whereas restaurant, hotel, and retail workers earn very low wages, workers in air transport and amusement and recreational services industries do considerably better. The restaurant industry in particular brings down the average, although the income figures may be misleading since they do not include unreported income from tips and do not take into account that tourist restaurants on average have higher salaries and tips than more typical restaurants. Other tourism-related sub-industries fall closer to the city average of wage and salary income.

Median wage data is not available, and it is possible that the relatively low average wage results from the absence of a large and extremely well-paid high end, as would be the case in finance or health services. Thus, for example, even though health services boasts a considerably higher average wage than tourism, home-care workers in Los Angeles County, a group that is predominantly low-skilled and minority, earned only $5.75 per hour or, based on a 40-hour week for 50 weeks a year, $11,500 (Greenhouse 1999). As this example shows, if we could control for educational level and English language competence, we would probably find that tourism workers did at least as well as others with comparable qualifications. Moreover, their working conditions, except for kitchen help, are generally superior to those of low-skilled manufacturing workers. By and large, tourism workers operate in air-conditioned environments, are not subject to severe

Plate 8.1 Waiter dressed as action hero at restaurant in Universal City Walk, Los Angeles. *Source*: Susan S. Fainstein

physical hazards, and in some jobs supplement their taxed income with unreported tips.

Despite the generally similar labor market structures of Los Angeles and New York, some of New York's tourism workers do considerably better than their LA counterparts. One of the major reasons for this disparity in income is the level and extent of unionization in New York's tourism-related industries (Waldinger 1992). The Hotel Employees and Restaurant Employees International Union (HERE) – through its two locals, Local 100 (restaurants and cafeterias) and Local 6 (hotels) – represents about 85 percent of New York's hotel workers and 10 percent of the city's restaurant workers. Those restaurants that have union contracts are all major Manhattan establishments with large tourist clienteles. The difference between New York and LA is clearly evident in New York's hotel workers' wage and salary income, which is nearly double the average of Los Angeles's. Unionized workers in New York also enjoy significant benefits not available to their counterparts in other cities, including excellent health insurance coverage, portable pension plans, and education programs. This geographical variation indicates some local difference in the mode of regulation. Even though the two cities have both had growth regimes (New York since the mid-1970s, Los Angeles arguably always), and even though both cities once had heavily unionized manufacturing sectors, the political culture of New York has remained more supportive of labor organization than Los Angeles's.

Although nearly all of LA's hotel workers were unionized 30 years ago, union membership plunged from 20,000 in the early 1970s to below 8,000 in 1995 (Geron 1997). Membership began to drop in the 1960s due to the inefficient administration of Local 11 and the failure of the predominantly white, male union leadership to organize the large number of immigrant and Latino workers seeking employment in the hotel industry. Most hotels built in Los Angeles in the 1980s and 1990s have opened non-union, including the Downtown New Otani and the Sheraton Grande. Hotel management has used the circumstances of a weak union and a large supply of immigrant labor to its advantage. As Geron (1997: 95) observes:

> LA has become a "Third World city" with an almost unlimited immigrant supply of Asian and Latino workers. Hotel management used the threat of firing workers and replacing them overnight with others to keep immigrant workers from organizing their hotels. Hotel management also took advantage of a situation where the union was weak and did not organize its membership.

Although the hotel workers' union has yet to show major organizing successes, its restructuring in the 1980s has resulted in a greater responsiveness to the needs of its members (and potential members) and the communities where they live. The union president, Maria Elena Durazo, has taken an activist role in local politics and has sought to reinvigorate the union and increase its membership rolls. The union has led boycotts and pickets against non-union hotels and those flouting local labor laws. Most importantly, it has sought to organize workers in the neighborhoods where they live and not only on the shop floor, a tactic that has proven effective in LA's immigrant and Latino communities. As Local 11 President Durazo (Leovy 1998: 1) notes, "If people can't afford to live based on wages they are earning, what does that do to neighborhoods?" This mode of organizing is probably more easily accomplished in LA than New York, as Los Angeles has a high concentration of tourism workers in a few neighborhoods within East and South Central Los Angeles. In particular, Lennox, a poor working-class community near downtown Los Angeles, characterized by overcrowded housing and high crime rates, is currently home to the city's largest number of hotel workers (HERE 1992).

In its neighborhood organizing activities, Local 11 has worked in coalition with other unions and with community groups to attain a "living wage" in a number of low-paying industries. The tourism industry has been a particular target of this campaign. A 1998 ordinance requires firms doing business with the city to pay their workers a minimum of $7.25 per hour with benefits or $8.50 per hour without benefits (Los Angeles Living Wage Coalition 1998).[2] The Los Angeles Alliance for a New Economy (LAANE), an organization that represents the labor-community coalition, has successfully pressured local politicians into making project approvals and subsidies for new development subject to living wage requirements as well. LA's living wage ordinance now extends to private sector firms receiving city subsidies of more than $1,000,000 per project or ongoing subsidies that exceed $100,000 annually. Much of the city-subsidized redevelopment currently underway in Los Angeles involves a strong tourism component (hotel, retail, etc.); if LAANE succeeds in extending the living wage ordinance to Community Redevelopment Agency (CRA) projects, then living wage campaigns will produce increased wages for tourism employees even in the absence of unionization.

LAANE has succeeded in getting a commitment from the developer of the billion-dollar Hollywood redevelopment project currently underway. In exchange for city subsidies totaling close to $100 million, project developer TrizecHahn has agreed to a deal whereby it will not only provide a living wage for employees in its own hotel and theatre complex but will ensure that businesses leasing space in its project do likewise. Moreover, the economic development fee to be paid by TrizecHahn (about $12.5 million) will be used for a local hiring hall and a low-cost health insurance plan (Meyerson 1998).

Community and labor rights groups in Los Angeles are also attempting to use the zoning and project approval process to pressure developers into agreeing to living wage agreements for those who will eventually work in completed developments requiring zoning variances. The Universal Studios expansion in North Hollywood is a case in point. LAANE has been instrumental in forming a coalition of over 60 community, religious, and labor groups in a bid to pressure Universal/MCA to ensure that the jobs in its amusement, theatre, and retail complex are living wage jobs. The proposed expansion of Universal Studios is expected to create 8,300 jobs. Currently none of the workers at Universal's CityWalk retail and theatre complex are unionized, but a victory by the LAANE would produce benefits for workers in small businesses who usually would be untouched by unionization.

In sum, several observations with respect to the tourism labor market in the two cities deserve mention. The first is that, even though tourism employment is growing faster than employment in other industries, tourism workers in aggregate earn significantly less than other workers. Average wage growth lags that in other industries, and the wage gap has been increasing since the mid-1970s. None of the tourism sub-industries in New York matches or exceeds the average wage and salary income for city workers as a whole, although some, such as air transport and amusement and recreation services, come close. In LA two exceed the county average: amusement and recreation workers earn average wages of $46,381 and air transport workers almost $39,000. Second, if we could control for skill level and language ability, tourism employment probably is no worse than other kinds of jobs, measured in terms of either wage levels, benefits, or job security, and possibly superior in terms of working conditions.

Third, New York and Los Angeles differ in the type of resistance displayed against exploitative working conditions within the tourism industry. Within the hotel sector, New York's workers have relied on a stable institutional framework that has succeeded in maintaining for them an adequate level of wages, benefits, and job security. This has been the case even though, as in Los Angeles, immigrants now dominate the labor force. The relative prosperity of New York's unskilled hotel workers, however, does not extend to workers in other tourism sub-industries. In contrast, in LA, where improvement in wages and benefits depends on community-based forces, any victory will extend to a much broader group. Thus, in the future we may possibly see increased divergence in the mode of regulation between the two cities.

Tourism and Local Regulation

Overall, the New York City and Los Angeles tourism industries are more alike than not in their internal structure and organization. Similar regulatory processes (e.g., urban growth regimes, declining unionization, federal disengagement) have accompanied the adoption of more flexible methods of capital accumulation in both cities. The structural parallels of the New York City and Los Angeles tourism industries, as well as similarities in how they are regulated, mirror broader homogenizing trends in US urban centers. The major difference between the two cities is the nature of working-class organization, with unions playing a larger role in New York and grass-roots movements such LAANE more important in the Los Angeles region. Both regulation theory and urban regime theory provide a conceptual framework to explain the similarities and account for the differences.

Similarities

From the perspective of regulation theory, an urban regime – in Stone's (1993) sense of the term – is part of the mode of social regulation.[3] Both cities are characterized by pro-growth, corporate-led urban regimes. In New York City the Koch, Dinkins, Giuliani, and Bloomberg administrations and in Los Angeles the Bradley, Riordan, and Hahn administrations have worked closely with property development interests, relying on real-estate development as the engine of growth (Davis 1992, 1993; Sites 1997; Fainstein 2001). In both cities, declining federal spending, increased competition for capital investment, and the incorporation of propertied interests into the governance structure have led city administrations to provide tax breaks for real estate developers. They have also relied on city hall's powers of eminent domain to earmark areas for tourism redevelopment, most notably Hollywood in Los Angeles and Times Square in Manhattan. This was particularly the case under the Giuliani administration, when the Mayor proposed using billions of dollars of public money to support construction of new sports venues and the reconstruction of Lincoln Center.[4] In Los Angeles, arts-related redevelopment and corporate sponsorship of the arts have been cornerstones of the downtown redevelopment process.

The structure of the industry in both cities, particularly with respect to income and occupational polarization, does not vary significantly from the structure of the travel and tourism industry nationally. Both within sub-industries and among them, employment is bifurcated along income and occupational lines, with a big low-end and a much smaller number of high-paying positions. As a consequence, the tourism industry contributes to the development of urban populations suffering from income polarization. This outcome, however, is not inherent to the industry but results from the type of labor organization within it.

Differences

With respect to capital–labor relations in Los Angeles and New York, the two cities differ mainly in the form that resistance to capital-friendly policies takes. In New York there is more reliance upon Fordist collective bargaining with little grass-roots mobilization. In Los Angeles, however, grass-roots mobilization, along with a resurgence of militant unionism, has led to the passage of living wage ordinances and higher wages for some tourism workers and others laboring in low-wage occupations. Los Angeles activists have also targeted the project and property approval process as a forum for making demands on the industry, with the Universal Studio expansion in North Hollywood and the TrizecHahn Hollywood redevelopment as two of the more notable examples.

Theoretical Significance

Regulation theory encompasses the relationships between the state and capital and capital and labor. Most efforts to apply the theory have focused on the national level, and to the extent that they have concerned themselves with capital–labor relations, have tended to assume national, or at least industrial, homogeneity. Indeed, aspects of the national regime of accumulation and its accompanying mode of regulation are critical to the situation of tourism workers and include, among other things, liberal US immigration law accompanied by lax or inconsistent enforcement; negative public attitudes toward labor unions; a low minimum wage; judicial interpretation of labor law that permits permanent replacement of striking workers; and delegation to the states of the right to determine whether unions can restrict hiring to union members ("right to work laws"). Particularly consequential for unions seeking to organize new groups of workers is the National Labor Relations Board's (NLRB's) weak enforcement of the right to organize.

In the US each state sets labor standards within broad limits – for example, the minimum wage can be above the federal level; union shops can be allowed (as they are in New York's unionized hotels) or forbidden; unions may be able to engage in housing development or prohibited from doing so. Custom and the extent of labor militancy further differentiate among places. Because protection by the NLRB of workers seeking to gain a union through an election process has been very weak, the hotel and restaurant workers locals seek to obtain members through having employees sign a card opting for union membership, thereby avoiding a full-fledged election campaign. This method, however, requires the consent of employers. Within New York City, HERE Local 6 has succeeded in organizing new hotels by the card-signing method because the economic culture of New York leads employers to permit it. The restaurant workers' local has not been equally successful in acquiring employer acquiescence, and there have been several bitter strikes as efforts at organizing restaurants have led to accusations of unfair labor practices. In Los Angeles a formal election is usually required.

Because the American system of labor regulation sets only very minimal national standards, we should expect local systems of regulation to vary according to local political culture and the force of oppositional elements. At the same time, however, national political culture establishes a sharp division between work and home, resulting in lack of concern for labor issues by local political officials, who are elected by residents within their communities where political alignments do not form along class lines (Katznelson 1981). Thus, while changes in urban regime may empower or disfranchise poor urban neighborhoods, they have little effect on the workplace. In other words, the local state largely is not a part of the regime that governs conditions of labor. The consequence is that the similarities we see between New York and Los Angeles arise out of a shared *modus operandi* among employers, a similar division of the industry as between large and small operators, and the general imbalance throughout the United States between the power of owners and workers. The dissimilarities come from different kinds of oppositional mobilization.

Differences in regard to the capital–labor relation and the community–labor relation between New York and Los Angeles stem from different traditions of labor organization, and different political discourses (Leo 1997). New York traditionally has been a "union city"; Los Angeles has not. The push to improve wages, benefits, and working conditions within tourism sub-industries in New York has remained the task of organized labor, and there are few links between organized labor and community groups. Rather, the emphasis of community groups is on collective consumption and resistance to development. The city government does not involve itself in private-sector capital–labor relations. There is a weak living wage ordinance, but it applies only to city contractors, is minimally enforced, and has not affected tourism enterprises.

In contrast, in Los Angeles, where unions command less support, they have worked together with community organizations in a fashion that has not occurred in New York. On the one hand, this has meant that workers in Los Angeles's hotel industry do worse than their New York counterparts; on the other, LA has the potential of extending an improved level of pay and benefits to workers in several of the tourism sub-industries (restaurants and retail as well as hotels). We thus see that differences in the mode of regulation can potentially produce different outcomes, even though, for the present, on the whole, tourism workers are generally poorly paid and lack job security in both cities.

In general, we can say that tourism is an important component of job growth in large central cities. Moreover, visitors combine synergistically with other consumers to heighten the demand for cultural and dining experiences, thereby enlarging the agglomeration of suppliers, and in turn increasing the attractiveness of the city to visitors and natives alike. The distributional consequences of tourism, however, are more debatable. Tourism workers have relatively low wages compared to workers in other sectors of the economy, but New York City's hotel workers do quite well, given their low educational and language skills. In Los Angeles the liaison between unions and community groups is creating a new political force that has the potential to extend gains broadly throughout the tourism economy. In the urban tourism sector in general, runaway firms do not threaten job security. Employers do not have the option of threatening to move to more hospitable locations when threatened by pressures from workers or broad-based living wage movements – they are place dependent. Whereas some tourist locales are interchangeable (one beach resort is usually not too different from another), major cities like these are not.

Our initial question was whether a tourism-oriented urban regime will enforce regulations that create opportunities for improved earnings among low-wage workers. The answer, based on the experience of New York and Los Angeles, is that it can be, even though so far it has not fulfilled its promise. To do so would require some important policy moves: the insertion of the local urban regime into labor management relations, along the lines demanded by the LA Living Wage Coalition, and the development of training programs to assist holders of low-level jobs in improving their skills. Since tourism does succeed in getting people into jobs who otherwise would have few options, it is a more promising employment strategy than office-led efforts for attaching marginal workers to the labor force. Thus, although the tourism workers of New York and LA have not realized the gains that workers in other economic sectors have enjoyed during the prosperity of the 1990s, the potential remains for them to change the rules that have kept them in their present situation.

NOTES

An earlier version of this chapter appeared as Tourism in US global cities, *Journal of Urban Affairs* 23(1) (2001): 23–40.

1 With the exception of hotels and air transport services, the tourism sub-industries we have identified cater mostly to residents and not to tourists. However, each industry is dependent on tourist spending, and city policies favoring tourism development will also contribute to the expansion of the sub-industries.

2 A similar ordinance was under consideration in New York at the time of this writing, but it had provoked strong business opposition and the threat of a mayoral veto. Although it commanded considerable support in the City council, it did not have the backing of a highly mobilized grass-roots constituency.

3 It is in the governance of particular places that Stone's theory of urban regimes dovetails with the more catholic regulation theory; as Stone indicates, urban regimes serve to "mediate" larger international, national, and regional politico-economic forces and thus form, in the terms of regulation theory, a part of the mode of regulation. See Stone (1989).

4 These plans are currently in abeyance due to the city's newest fiscal crisis.

REFERENCES

Blair, J. 2002: For the crossroads of the world, far less traffic from foreign tourists since September 11. *New York Times*, April 4.

Davis, M. 1992: *City of Quartz*. London: Verso.

——1993: The strange death of liberal Los Angeles. *Z Magazine*, 6 (11): 49–53.

Fainstein, S. S. 2001: *The City Builders*, revised ed. Lawrence, KS: University of Kansas Press.

——and Judd, D. R. 1999: Global forces, local strategies, and urban tourism. In D. R. Judd and S. S. Fainstein (eds.), *The Tourist City*. New Haven, CT: Yale University Press, 1–17.

Geron, K. 1997: The local/global context of the Los Angeles hotel-tourism industry. *Social Justice*, 24 (2): 84–101.

Goodwin, M., Duncan, S., and Halford, S. 1993: Regulation theory, the local state, and the transition of urban politics. *Environment and Planning D: Society and Space*, 11 (3): 67–88.

——and Painter, J. 1997: Concrete research, urban regimes, and regulation theory. In M. Lauria (ed.), *Reconstructing Urban Regime Theory: Regulating Urban Politics in a Global Economy*. Thousand Oaks, CA: Sage, 13–29.

Greenhouse, S. 1999: In biggest drive since 1937, unions gain a victory. *New York Times*, February 26, A-1, 18.

Hannigan, J. 1998: *Fantasy City*. London: Routledge.

Holusha, J. 2000: In Manhattan, a scattering of new hotels. *New York Times*, April 16, XI-1, 6.

Hotel Employees and Restaurant Employees Union Local 11 (HERE) 1992: *City on the Edge*. Video production.

Katznelson, I. 1981: *City Trenches*. New York: Pantheon.

Leo, C. 1997: City politics in an era of globalization. In M. Lauria (ed.), *Reconstructing Urban Regime Theory: Regulating Urban Politics in a Global Economy*. Thousand Oaks, CA: Sage.

Leovy, J. 1998: Unions battle over human issues. *Los Angeles Times*, June 29, A-1, 16.

Los Angeles Convention and Visitors Bureau (LACVB) 1996, 1998, 2002: *Quick Tourism Facts for Los Angeles County*. Los Angeles: LACVB.

Los Angeles Economic Development Corporation (LAEDC) 1998: *The Economic Base of the Los Angeles Five-County Area* (www.laedc.com/stat_econbase.html [July 2000]).

Los Angeles Living Wage Coalition (LALWC) 1998: *How the CRA Subsidizes Poverty and How Taxpayers End Up Paying For It*. Los Angeles: LALWC.

Meyerson, H. 1998: No justice, no growth. *Los Angeles Weekly*, July 17–23 (www.laweekly.com/ink/98/34/powerlines-meyerson.shtml [July 2000]).

New York City Convention and Visitors Bureau (NYCVB) 1995: *Tourism's Economic Impact on New York City*. New York: NYCVB.

——1998a: *1997 Domestic Travel to New York City*. New York: NYCVB.

——1998b: *1997 International Visitors to NYC Briefing Sheet*. New York: NYCVB.

——1999, 2002: *New York City Visitor Statistics*. New York: NYCVB.

Port Authority of New York and New Jersey (PANYNJ) 1994: *Destination New York-New Jersey: Tourism and Travel to the Metropolitan Region*. New York: PANYNJ.

Sassen, S. 2001: *The Global City: New York, London, Tokyo*, 2nd edn. Princeton, NJ: Princeton University Press.

Sites, W. 1997: The limits of urban regime theory: New York City under Koch, Dinkins, and Giuliani. *Urban Affairs Review*, 32 (4): 536–57.

Squires, G. D. 1989: Public private partnerships: who gets what and why. In G. Squires (ed.), *Unequal Partnerships*. New Brunswick, NJ: Rutgers University Press, 1–11.

Stone, C. N. 1989: *Regime Politics: Governing Atlanta 1946–1988*. Lawrence, KS: University of Kansas Press.

——1993: Urban regimes and the capacity to govern: a political economy approach. *Journal of Urban Affairs*, 15 (1): 1–28.

US Census Bureau 1977–97: *County Business Patterns*. Washington, DC: US Government Printing Office.

Waldinger, R. 1992: Taking care of the guests: the impact of immigrants on services – an industry case study. *International Journal of Urban and Regional Research*, 16 (1): 97–113.

9

Shaping the Tourism Labor Market in Montreal

Marc V. Levine

Political economists have fiercely debated for the past two decades how much "margin for maneuver" cities possess in regulating the local economy. As the Introduction to this volume underscores, the growth in urban tourism makes this a crucial sector in which to explore whether local policy "matters." Is tourism an industry with fairly immutable global tendencies and broadly similar outcomes in cities, or can the local regulatory regime significantly affect the outcomes of tourism development in a given city?

In particular, the tourism labor market clearly is a central arena for the interplay between "global tendencies" and "local variation." In job-hungry cities, tourism is often advocated as an important source of employment, particularly for unskilled workers whose economic opportunities have diminished with the decline of traditional, urban manufacturing (Eaton 1998: 29). However, precisely what *kinds* of jobs are created through tourism? Is tourism inherently a low-wage, low value-added sector, whose growth contributes to the social polarization of urban labor markets? To what extent can local economic policies (such as minimum wage laws) and institutions (such as unions) shape the tourism labor market?

Montreal, a city that has been at the forefront of North American metropolises pursuing tourism as the cornerstone of urban revitalization, offers an excellent case study to examine these questions. Since the late 1960s Montreal has invested over $7 billion (in current, Canadian dollars) in the full range of tourism "products," including mega-events (Expo 67 and the 1976 Summer Olympics), a convention center, a casino, historic museums, and a "récréo-touristique" district on the riverfront. By 2000, Montreal was one of the world's leading destinations for international meetings (OCTGM 1998: 37) and, according to industry officials, tourism had become a $2 billion industry in the city, attracting six million overnight visitors annually (Tourisme-Montréal 2001a).

Clearly, Montreal has succeeded in developing a "world-class" tourism industry. But, what has this success meant for the city's labor market? After a very brief overview of tourism development in Montreal since the 1960s, this chapter will focus on the labor market outcomes of tourism in the city. Compared to other North American cities, Montreal has strong unions, a labor-friendly legal framework, and a generous social wage. Under this "mode of regulation," has tourism development been compatible with social equity?

Tourism Development in Montreal since the 1960s

Tourism in Montreal has developed in two distinct phases. First, between the late 1960s and the mid-1970s, the city hosted two mega-events – the 1967 World's Fair (Expo 67) and the 1976 Summer Olympics – designed to put Montreal on the map as an international tourist destination (Morin 1998). Both events succeeded in that regard: in 1976, the city attracted almost six million tourists; Montreal experienced a hotel boom in the early 1970s; and massive public works expenditures in conjunction with both mega-events (i.e. the Métro and underground pedestrian network) helped physically remake modern Montreal (Levine 2002). However, both events carried fearsome fiscal costs. Expo 67 ran $265CDN million over budget, while the Olympics' cost overruns – and subsequent expenditures on the architecturally flawed Olympic stadium – meant that by 2006, when the Olympics and stadium debt will be paid off, the 1976 Games will have cost nearly *three billion dollars* in capital and interest (Lévesque 2001). As one writer put it: "Jean Drapeau [the Mayor behind the 'mega-events' strategy] wanted to create a monument to reflect Montreal's greatness. The Olympic Stadium and tower has proved instead to be an international, multibillion-dollar embarrassment" (Johnston 1999).

For a decade after the Olympics, these sentiments and the post-Olympics fiscal hangover precluded major investments in Montreal's tourism infrastructure (Levine 2002). The city did build a convention center in 1983 (the Palais des Congrès), aiming to capture a larger share of the growing global market in conventions in the wake of the city's heightened post-Olympics international profile. In addition, a number of festivals and sports events were begun during the 1980s: the Formula One Grand Prix auto race, the International Jazz Festival, the Francofolies music festival, and the Montreal Comedy Festival, "Juste pour rire." Nevertheless, the number of tourists visiting Montreal fell sharply through the mid-1980s, not returning to the Olympics-year level until 1986. Many of the hotels opened during the Olympics era closed during the early 1980s, and by 1985 the number of hotel rooms in downtown Montreal had declined to pre-1976 levels (Bodson, Samson, and Stafford 1988: 6). Numerous factors, of course, shaped the Montreal economy after the Olympics, but clearly there was no tourism-led economic boom in Montreal in the wake of the hosting of the 1976 Games.

Despite the post-Olympics letdown, however, Montreal did not abandon tourism. By the late 1980s, as Montreal faced chronic double-digit unemployment, a series of provincial and municipal government strategy papers recommended a renewed commitment to tourism as offering the city "some of the best prospects for development" (Gouvernement du Québec 1991: 58).[1] Thus, in this second phase of development, Montreal's tourism policy shifted away from mega-events to development of a diverse array of tourism attractions. Since the late 1980s, over $3 billion in public and private capital has been invested or planned in the staples of tourism-related redevelopment: sports, entertainment, culture, and hotels. Some of the major post-1987 investments included:

- Redevelopment of the city's heritage district, Vieux-Montréal, with over $250 million in public investments in museums and historic sites, to coincide with celebrations marking Montreal's 350th anniversary in 1992 (Linteau 1992: 504). The anchor project was the Vieux-Port, once a classically decayed North American urban waterfront, which was redeveloped as "récréo-touristique" district, with walking paths, boating, and some entertainment facilities (Société du Vieux-Port de Montréal 1999). The Vieux-Port quickly became one of Montreal's leading destinations, attracting over seven million visitors (residents and tourists alike) in 2000 (Tourisme-Montréal 2001a).
- The Casino de Montréal, built for $241 million in 1993–6 on the site of Expo 67.
- Expansion of the Palais des Congrès, slated to open in 2002 at a total public cost of $185 million.
- "Urban entertainment destinations," such as Planet Hollywood and Centre Métaforia (both now bankrupt) and an $85 million entertainment "mega-center" at the Forum (former home of the Montreal Canadiens hockey team).
- $175 million between 1997 and 2000 alone in private investment in hotel construction and renovation (Tourisme-Montréal 2001a).

- Sports facilities, including the privately financed $300 million Centre Molson, the new downtown home of the Canadiens hockey team; and Parc Jarry/Du Maurier, which was refurbished at a public cost of $24 million in 1995 to accommodate the Canadian Open Tennis tournament. Plans for a new, partially subsidized $250 million downtown stadium for the Expos baseball team were also unveiled in 1998, although by 2002 continuing financial troubles for the franchise had scuttled the project and made certain the imminent departure of major league baseball from Montreal.

In short, by the end of the 1990s, Montreål remained as heavily committed as ever to tourism as a keystone for local economic development. Between 1980 and 2000, the annual number of tourists – defined as overnight visitors to the city – grew by 19 percent, and annual spending by tourists increased by 62.5 percent, adjusted for inflation (Tourisme-Montréal 2001a). Hotel occupancy rates and property values soared during the 1990s (Benoit 1999), and the number of hotel rooms in downtown Montreal increased by 40 percent during the decade (Tourisme-Montréal 2001a).

Clearly, in the North American urban tourism market, Montreal is a "winner," with a "diversified tourism product" and sizable annual influx of visitors (ibid.). Although the fiscal balance sheet on Montreal tourism is highly dubious – dominated by the red ink of the Olympic Stadium and questionable finances of investments in convention centers and entertainment facilities – by 2000, nevertheless, tourism indisputably occupied a central place in Montreal's political economy. For example, taxes and fees on tourist spending now represent almost 7 percent of city revenues (Levine 2003), and a reasonable estimate is that tourism represents around 5 percent of metropolitan Montreal's "gross metropolitan product" (Levine 1999: 427). Nevertheless, for residents of Montreal, particularly workers in the tourism industry, a key question remains: what does being a "tourism winner" really mean?

The Tourism Labor Market in Montreal

How has the growth of the tourist industry shaped the Montreal labor market? Since the early 1970s, Montreal has been buffeted by the same economic forces facing most older, historically industrial North American big cities: deindustrialization, the suburbanization of metropolitan employment, and the loss of jobs to expanding metropolises to the west (such as Toronto, Calgary, and Vancouver). Moreover, Montreal's employment situation has been shaped by the city's unique linguistic character. The rise of Quebec's Francophone separatist movement in the early 1970s helped accelerate the departure of many English-Canadian controlled firms (and jobs) from the city – a process that had been underway since the 1930s as Toronto displaced Montreal as Canada's national corporate center (Levine 1997). In addition, Quebec's French-speaking labor force, because of linguistic and cultural barriers, has limited geographic mobility (unlike English-speakers who, in principle, are more able to pursue employment opportunities across North America). Consequently, there is a swelling of the Francophone labor pool in Montreal, as French-speakers are drawn to the metropole from the Quebec hinterland, and unemployed Francophones are likely to stay in the city rather than search for employment in Canadian cities outside of Quebec. This linguistic segmentation brings a certain sclerosis to the Montreal labor market and creates an upward bias in the city's unemployment rate.

The upshot of these structural and contextual trends is that Montreal has consistently suffered from chronically high unemployment since the mid-1970s. From full employment in the 1960s, the metropolitan area's unemployment rate steadily climbed throughout the 1970s, and, with just a few exceptions, in each year between 1982 and 1998 remained above 10 percent[2] (Martineau and Rioux 1994: 5; Martineau and Lamonde 1997: 2). Throughout the 1990s, Montreal's unemployment rate was consistently the highest among large North American metro areas (Martineau and Lamonde 1997).[3] Moreover, in each year throughout the 1990s the unemployment rate in the urban core – the City of Montreal – remained 2 to 3 percentage points higher than the metro area average (Ville de Montreal 2000). In an era in which the OECD vaunted the prolific job creation in US metropolitan areas, Montreal's labor market was marked by the persistently high unemployment associated with "Eurosclerosis" (OECD 1994).

Thus, in the context of a persistent unemployment crisis since the mid-1970s, tourism has assumed increasing importance in Montreal as a source of jobs. In 1993, for example, when unemployment in metro Montreal approached depression-era levels (14.3 percent), the soon-to-open Casino de Montréal received over 155,000 applications for 776 job openings. A random draw was conducted simply to reduce the applicant pool to manageable size (Marsolais 1998).

By 2000, tourism accounted for approximately 61,000 jobs in metropolitan Montreal, or about 5 percent of the region's employment base (Tourisme-Montréal 2001a).[4] According to an input–output analysis of the Montreal economy conducted by Tourisme-Montréal, almost two-thirds of the jobs attributable to tourism in Montreal are in accommodations, restaurants, amusements, and retail trade (Tourisme-Montréal 2001b). The remaining jobs are spread across sectors of the economy in which tourist

Table 9.1 Average annual employment income in key tourism occupations in metropolitan Montreal, 1990–1995 (in 1995 C$)

Occupations	1990 Income	1995 Income	% Change 1990–95
Hotel Desk Clerks	$16,689	$15,357	–8.0
Occupations in Travel and Accommodations	21,374	21,000	–1.7
Occupations in Food and Beverage Services	10,710	9,657	–9.8
Attendants in Amusements, Recreation, Sports	9,765	15,301	+56.7
Light Duty Cleaners	15,786	14,363	–9.0
Montreal Occupations (all sectors)	27,813	26,918	–3.2

Source: Statistique Canada (1998).

Table 9.2 Work, status, and gender composition of key tourism occupations in metropolitan Montreal, 1995

Occupations	% working full-time, 1995	% female 1995
Hotel Desk Clerks	42.4	62.2
Occupations in Travel and Accommodations	56.7	45.1
Occupations in Food and Beverage Services	27.4	71.0
Attendants in Amusements, Recreation, Sports	22.4	32.9
Light Duty Cleaners	37.4	56.7
Montreal Occupations (all sectors)	51.4	47.2

Source: Statistique Canada (1998).

spending has boosted aggregate demand and hence generated employment. For example, according to Tourisme-Montréal, tourism created around 1,700 jobs in transportation services in 1999 (or three percent of Montreal's "tourism-related" employment), presumably reflecting the taxi drivers and public transit employees who serve the metropolitan area's 5.8 million annual tourists (Tourisme-Montréal 2001c).

What is the quality of these tourism jobs? Tables 9.1 and 9.2 provide data on wages, work status, and gender composition in the core occupations of the Montreal tourism industry during the 1990s. On the whole, the situation in Montreal appears consistent with depictions of tourism as primarily low-wage, part-time, seasonal employment in which women hold a disproportionate number of jobs (particularly jobs in the lowest paid occupations of the tourism industry). Moreover, at least through the first half of the 1990s, real wages in most key Montreal tourism occupations

Table 9.3 Income in tourism occupations as a proportion of average employment income, Canada's three largest metropolitan areas, 1995

Occupations	Montreal	Toronto	Vancouver
Occupations in Food and Beverage Services	35.9%	35.9%	38.8%
Occupations in Travel and Accommodations	78.0	81.7	87.0
Hotel Desk Clerks	57.1	54.6	62.4
Attendants in Amusements, Recreation, & Sports	56.8	28.6	40.2
Light Duty Cleaners	53.4	46.5	50.6

Source: Statistique Canada (1998).

Table 9.4 Average wages in tourism occupations as proportion of average annual pay, selected US metropolitan areas, 1997

Occupation	New Orleans	Boston	Baltimore	Atlanta	New York[a]	San Francisco	Las Vegas
Hotel Clerks	55.3%	53.3%	50.5%	45.8%	51.9%	50.5%	69.5%
Amusement & Rec. Attendants	50.9	42.6	44.9	42.0	31.6	34.7	45.9
Housekeepers and Maids	47.9	49.9	51.0	41.3	47.3	44.4	60.1

Source: Bureau of Labor Statistics (1999).
[a] Note that these figures are for the entire metro area and thus differ from the figures in Chapter 8.

declined markedly. Although employment income in all occupations fell during these recession-wracked years, the decline was steeper in low-wage labor markets such as tourism, exacerbating wage polarization and reinforcing gender inequality in Montreal's overall wage structure.[5]

As tables 9.3 and 9.4 show, the wage structure of Montreal's tourism labor market is similar to tourism jobs in major urban centers in the United States and Canada, generally offering wages at a fraction of the metropolitan area's average employment income. There are some differences among the cities: Las Vegas's highly unionized hotel workers, for example, earn much closer to the metropolitan area's average pay than elsewhere, and Montreal's unionized casino workers help push the income of "amusement attendants" relatively higher than other North American metropolitan areas. But, by and large, the differences are small, and tourism occupations offer low-wage employment in urban centers across North America.

All jobs in the Montreal tourism labor market are not poorly paid. Croupiers at the Casino de Montréal, for example, earn $35,000 annually, and average wages for hotel and food service managers approach $30,000 – with managers at the city's largest hotels earning much more. Many jobs indirectly created by tourism – such as in transportation services – offer decent earnings. In fact, excluding food services workers – by far the lowest-paid Montreal tourism workers – average employment income in Montreal tourism jobs would approach 80 percent of the metro area's average for all occupations. Nevertheless, in Montreal as elsewhere, tourism is "an industry where 5 percent of the people are chiefs and 90–5 percent are Indians," in the words of a hotel industry consultant (Greenhouse 1998). In Montreal, as elsewhere, the majority of tourism jobs are occupations such as hotel front-desk clerks, housekeepers, waitresses, and kitchen prep workers, and these are among the city's lowest-paid workers.

The low wages and declining real incomes of Montreal tourism workers are particularly striking, because since the 1970s the city's labor market has been shaped by social institutions and public policies more favorable to workers than those found in other North American cities (Levine 1995). Historically, minimum wage laws provide an important boost for low-wage workers and consistently, since the 1970s, Quebec's minimum wage,[6] as a percentage of average hourly wages in Montreal, has been higher than comparable percentages in the United States and elsewhere in Canada.[7] Moreover, although the inflation-adjusted value of the Quebec minimum wage eroded between 1979 and 1999, the drop (11.5 percent) was around half the decline in the United States (21.1 percent) during this period (Mishel, Bernstein, and Schmitt 2001: 186–8). Presumably, this difference helps explain small variations between tourism labor markets: the real wages of hotel clerks in the United States, for example, fell more rapidly in the late 1980s and early 1990s (−15.6 percent between 1986 and 1996) than in Quebec (−1.5 percent between 1985 and 1995) (Statistique Canada 1998; Bureau of National Affairs 2001).[8] Nevertheless, although minimum wage policy has probably helped nudge wages in Montreal tourism occupations slightly closer to average pay than in most US cities (see tables 9.3 and 9.4), it has not altered the basic character of tourism as a low-wage industry in the city.

Labor relations in Montreal, particularly in the tourism industry, also differ from most North American cities. As table 9.5 shows, among major North American metropolitan areas – many of which are important tourist centers – Montreal is the most highly unionized. The strength of organized labor flowing from this relatively high union density in Montreal is further enhanced by "one of the most pro-union labor codes in North America" (*Montreal Gazette* 2000). Since 1977, Quebec province has had in place an "anti-strikebreaker" law, which prohibits firms from hiring "scabs"

Table 9.5   Unionization rates in selected North American metropolitan areas

Metropolitan Area	Unionized % of total workforce, 1999
Atlanta	7.3
Baltimore	11.8
Boston	16.3
Calgary	20.3
Chicago	18.3
Denver	8.9
Detroit	21.7
Houston	6.1
Indianapolis	11.2
Minneapolis	17.8
Montreal	**31.7**
New Orleans	8.8
New York	23.3
San Francisco	16.5
Seattle	18.9
Toronto	20.5
Vancouver	30.8

Sources: Bureau of National Affairs (2000); Board of Trade of Metropolitan Montreal (2000).

during strikes or lockouts (while allowing strikers to work elsewhere during a labor action). The Quebec labor code also protects collective bargaining agreements in the event of a merger or sale of a firm; and, in cases where companies subcontract work, the union wages and benefits of the firm must be extended to employees of the subcontractor (Dutrisac 2000; Godin 2001: 229).

In most cities in the United States, few workers in tourism occupations belong to unions. Nationally, in 1998, unions covered only 2.6 percent of waiters/waitresses, 4.2 percent of hotel clerks, and 13.0 percent of maids (Bureau of National Affairs 1999). Moreover, despite energetic organizing campaigns in recent years, membership in the country's major "tourism workers" union, the Hotel Employees and Restaurant Employees International Union (HERE), declined by almost 50 percent between 1975 and 1997 (ibid.). Although cities such as New York and Las Vegas have somewhat higher concentrations of unionized hospitality workers, fairly typical is New Orleans where "there are 174 hotels and motels in the tourist-laden region, but only one . . . has a unionized rank and file staff" (*Baltimore Sun* 1998). At Baltimore's Inner Harbor, site of one of the United States' most

Plate 9.1   Tourists in Old Montreal. *Source*: Corbis

heralded tourism-oriented urban redevelopment programs, hotels remain union-free and management fiercely resisted a 1990's campaign by labor and community organizations to pay hotel workers a "living wage."[9]

By contrast, there is a substantial union presence in the Montreal tourism industry. By 1999, the Confédération des syndicats nationaux (CSN) – one of Quebec's two largest unions – had 4,500 members at 23 Montreal hotels. An estimated 30 percent of Montreal's hotel employees are unionized. Moreover, the bargaining power of labor is enhanced beyond these numbers because union membership is concentrated in the city's major downtown hotels catering to the tourist trade; all of them – from the Ritz-Carlton and Queen Elizabeth to the Wyndham and the Intercontinental – are unionized (Normand 1999a). Workers at the Casino de Montréal are unionized, as well, as are employees at the Vieux-Port and Parc-des-Îles "récréo-touristique" facilities.

During the 1990s, labor mobilized on several fronts in the Montreal tourism industry. Downtown Montreal hotels saw profits rise significantly during the decade: revenue per available room, the most commonly used measure of hotel income,[10] increased by 64.4 percent between 1993 and 1998 (Blair 1999: 1). Between 1996 and 1998, the estimated market value of downtown Montreal hotels increased by almost 40 percent (Benoit 1999). In this context, the CSN launched a campaign to increase wages and improve working conditions at Montreal hotels (Aubry 1998; Girard 1999; Latraverse 1999). Despite the relative financial health of hotels, and concessions by hotel employees during the rocky early 1990s, the CSN encountered strong management resistance – in fact, at several hotels, management was demanding "rollbacks of non-monetary benefits to what they were at the beginning of the 1980s" (King 1999a).

Many Montreal hotels – such as the Sheraton, the Wyndham, the Radisson, L'Hôtel du Parc, and the Ritz-Carlton – had been sold to US interests in the 1990s, and union leadership attributed much of the intransigence to a new "culture of americanization" in hotel management (Normand 1999b). "It's night and day if we compare working conditions in the hotel industry in Quebec to the United States," said union leader Jean Lortie. "There, few hotels are unionized and the working conditions are wretched. In Quebec [in contrast], we almost look like communists" (ibid.). In short, the hotel sector in Montreal revealed yet another tension as global tourist enterprises crossed national boundaries: a clash between "modes of regulation" as US-based hotel operators sought to impose US-style labor relations on a Montreal labor market regime with very different institutions, history, and culture.

Labor mobilization in the hotel sector came to a head in summer 1999. As negotiations stalled, the CSN threatened strikes at 23 hotels, just as the tourist season was shifting into high gear; in fact, a 24-hour work stoppage did occur at several downtown hotels. A full-scale battle was averted, however, as the CSN and hotels concluded a new three-year collective agreement, providing modest wage increases, lighter workloads, and improved benefit packages. Union leaders proclaimed a major victory, noting that "hotel employees went from earning minimum wage plus 10 cents an hour in 1980 to becoming the highest-paid service-industry employees in North America" (King 1999b). Although that claim was hyperbole, the compensation and benefits package of Montreal hotel employees had improved since the 1980s and was somewhat superior to conditions in most other North American cities.

Despite these gains, by summer 2002 labor strife returned to the Montreal hotel sector. Notwithstanding continuing increases in revenue PAR and overall profitability (Van Praet 2002), Montreal's major hotels balked at CSN demands "for their fair share of a hotel industry in full growth mode" (ibid.). The union demands included 15 percent wage increases, additional vacation time, higher employer contributions to retirement, and reduced workloads for housekeeping staff. Despite CSN warnings of a "historical frontal collision" between the union and hotels, negotiations went nowhere (Corriveau 2002). Once again, at the height of tourist season, the CSN mobilized 4,000 housekeepers, bellhops, desk clerks, and cooks at 22 hotels (representing roughly half of the available rooms in downtown Montreal) for a 24-hour walkout (Rodrigue 2002). Continuing pressure and the threat of an all-out, unlimited strike finally produced settlements at all of the hotels, each of which included wages and benefits only slightly less than demanded by the union (Douet 2002). Clearly, the CSN had demonstrated its ability, despite the resistance of hotel management, to extract improvements in wages and working conditions in this core sector of the Montreal tourism labor market.

In addition to the hotel sector, there were several other episodes of labor militancy at businesses in the Montreal tourism industry in the 1990s. Among the most visible:

• Two bitter strikes at the Casino de Montréal, in 1995 and 1998: Each strike began with a lockout, ran about six weeks, and cost Loto-Québec about $40 million in revenues (Marsolais 1998). Both resulted in substantial pay gains, and improved fringe benefits and working conditions for employees. The disputes also underscored a potential tension in the political economy of tourism, pitting the state, as regulator of labor market protections for workers, against the state, as operator of a lucrative entertainment facility. Thus, some editorialists criticized the strikers, calling them "spoiled children who abused an artificial balance of forces to deprive the State of indispensable revenues" (Sansfaçon 1998), money necessary "to operate public services and narrow the budget deficit" (*Montreal Gazette* 1998).
• A two-week lockout and strike at La Ronde in 1999, a city-owned amusement park built for Expo '67 and operated by the city thereafter.[11] Some 520 employees – many of whom were students, working part-time – sought modest wage increases that would approach parity with other employees at the Parc-des-Îles public recreational facilities (Turcotte 1999). During the labor action, management brought in replacement workers from other parks, an action found by the courts to violate Quebec's anti-strikebreaker law. The strike ended with the workers, greatly aided by Quebec's labor law, receiving pay increases ranging from 9.3 percent to 15.4 percent over four years (Desrosiers 1999).
• Successful unionization campaigns at two McDonald's restaurants, making Montreal the only city in North America with such a record involving the notoriously anti-union multinational (Schlosser 2001: 76–7). Although McDonald's is not a tourist enterprise, *per se*, the restaurant sector, including fast food, is an integral part of the tourism industry; thus, the McDonald's campaign had important implications for the economic culture of tourism in Montreal. The labor victories at the Montreal-area "McDos," however, were short-lived. In 1997, three-quarters of the employees at a McDonald's in the suburb St Hubert voted to unionize; two weeks before certification, however, the 17-year-old restaurant closed, claiming that it was losing money. In 2000, 75

percent of workers at a downtown Montreal McDonald's joined the CSN and requested certification of their union; again, the restaurant was closed before certification, with the owners claiming a "sudden" 300 percent increase in rent that now made the franchise unprofitable (Corriveau 2001). "They want us to swallow that the decisions to close belong to the franchisees," said CSN president Marc Laviolette. "However, it's the multinational who orchestrates the whole affair" (Fortin 2001).

Conclusion

The level of labor mobilization in Montreal's tourism industry – combined with worker-friendly labor laws and a relatively generous minimum wage – indicates a different "mode of regulation" and economic culture than is generally found in North American cities. These are "small differences that matter":[12] as we have seen, unionized tourism workers have made some gains since the early 1990s, and the aggregate wage data suggest slightly greater social equity in the Montreal tourism labor market than in comparable North American cities.

But, since tourism labor market outcomes in Montreal have not been, to this point, radically different than elsewhere in North America, we must at least question the overall impact of these institutional variations. There are two schools of thought on tourism worker pay. One asserts that workers are compensated relative to their contribution to output. In the case of hotels, for example, an OECD report maintains that "productivity in this sector is relatively low. As a rule, the net value added per employee in a high-class urban hotel is three to four times less than in the case of a bank employee" (1995: 42). In short, so goes this argument, tourism pay is low because this is an intrinsically "low value-added" industry.

The other school argues that there is a "range of indeterminacy" in wages. Although there is a "range" set by the profitability of an economic sector, "different companies choose to set pay at different parts of the range, depending on their financial health, willingness to make do with high turnover and vacancies, and desire for a loyal, self-motivated work force" (Krueger 2001). And, of course, the "range of indeterminacy" is constrained by policies such as minimum wage laws and tax policy. Firms may not be free to pay whatever wages they please, but within a market range, economic culture and company strategy can produce different labor market outcomes.

The data do suggest a very modest "range of indeterminacy" in tourism sector wages, with Montreal's economic culture producing outcomes for tourism workers slightly closer to a "living wage" than in most cities. Unionization seems to be a critical variable: in cities such as Montreal,

Vancouver, and Las Vegas, with relatively higher rates of unionization and labor militancy in the tourism sector than other North American cities, tourism wages are somewhat (although not dramatically) closer to metro area average wages than elsewhere. Moreover, the successful mobilization of Montreal's hotel worker unions in extracting solid wage and benefit packages in 1999 and 2002 undoubtedly improved their labor market outcomes beyond what the data in this chapter, drawn from the most recent available (1996) Canadian census, have shown.

But management across North America – including, for the most part, Montreal employers – remains generally committed to the low-wage, high-turnover, non-union labor market model for the tourism sector. In the US, as the recent cases of Baltimore and New Orleans underscore, hotel operators remain fiercely anti-union and intractably opposed to living wage laws. Moreover, wage setting in tourism does not operate in an economic vacuum: Montreal has had a slack labor market since the early 1980s, with nearly continuous double-digit unemployment until very recently.[13] Older US cities that have vigorously pursued tourism development – such as Baltimore, Cleveland, St Louis, Philadelphia, and Milwaukee – face similarly distressed central city labor markets, with high rates of minority unemployment and poverty rates exceeding 20 percent. This is hardly a propitious environment in which tourism workers can bargain for "living wages." The Montreal case shows that even in a metropolis with a relatively solidaristic economic culture, if unemployment is high and employers take a "low-wage, high-turnover" approach to labor, it is difficult to raise wages in tourism significantly above the levels found in cities across North America.

On the other hand, as noted above, the successes of Montreal's hotel workers in 1999 and 2002 point out the promise of unionization in enhancing social equity in the tourism labor market. The conditions favoring mobilization of Montreal's hotel workers – a strong labor movement, a history of labor victories in the sector, a profitable hotel industry, and a city increasingly dependent on the tourism trade (thus enhancing the leverage of organized labor) – were in many ways unique to Montreal. Nevertheless, recent developments in the Montreal tourism labor market do offer at least some evidence of a "range of indeterminacy" in wage setting and the possibility that tourism need not be poverty-wage industry for urban workers.

NOTES

1   The RCM, which had been so critical of Drapeau's mega-events projects, took control of city hall in 1986. Ironically, by then, the RCM had long since

discarded its radical critique of tourism as an economic development strategy, and would preside over Montreal's second major phase of major public investments in tourism.

2   Except for 1988 and 1989, when it was 9.2 percent.

3   By 2000, as the North American economic boom reached its apogee, metropolitan Montreal's unemployment rate had fallen to just over 7 percent. In 2001, however, it began inching upwards again.

4   Montreal's tourism employment increased most rapidly in the 1970s, reflecting the 1976 Olympics. Tourism job growth was flat from the late 1970s through the early 1990s (Brodeur and Galarneau 1998: 42), with slight increases since then (Statistique Canada 1999).

5   Between 1980 and 1998, the proportion of metropolitan Montreal workers earning wages of less than $15,000 annually (in 1998 constant dollars) jumped from 30.5 percent to 36.3 percent. A full-time worker earning Quebec's minimum wage would make $14,352. (Statistique Canada 2001).

6   Provinces set minimum wages in Canada; thus, the Quebec provincial government sets Montreal's minimum wage.

7   In 1999, the minimum wage represented 38.9 percent of the average hourly wage in the United States as a whole, and 44.0 percent of the average hourly wage in Montreal. See Mishel, Bernstein, and Schmitt (2001), and Statistique Canada (1998). In both the US and Montreal, both of these figures represent a decline from 1979, when the minimum wage equaled 47.1 percent of the average hourly wage in the US, compared to 51.3 percent in Montreal.

8   As further evidence of the importance of the minimum wage in the hotel sector, in the United States between 1996 and 2001, real wages of hotel desk clerks rose by 9.6 percent. This period, of course, coincided with legislation in 1997 that increased the value of the minimum wage by 8.4 percent (from $4.75 to $5.15 an hour). The wage data are from Bureau of National Affairs (2001).

9   "Living wage" campaigns, designed to establish local minimum wages above the federal level, became common in US cities in the late 1990s. Although the campaigns achieved some victories – living wage ordinances establishing higher minimum wages for employees of firms receiving city contracts were passed in 63 municipalities – hotels and other tourist facilities have generally remained exempt from "living wage" laws (Sharpe 2001). On hotels' resistance to the Baltimore living wage campaign, see Butler et al. (1993). In New Orleans, a three-year campaign by labor and community organizations did result, in February 2002, in passage of a city-wide living wage ordinance raising the city's minimum wage to $6.15, including hotel workers.

10   Revenue PAR is measured by multiplying the rate per room by the hotel occupancy rate. If average room rates were $100 a night and the average annual hotel occupancy rate was 70 percent, revenue PAR would equal $70.00.

11   After accumulating $22 million in debt for the city, and facing the prospect of continually shrinking attendance, La Ronde was sold by the city in 2000 for $30 million to Six Flags, the world's largest theme park operator.

12   I have borrowed here from the title of David Card and Richard Freeman's (1994) seminal book on how differences in social institutions and public

policies have produced modestly different labor market outcomes in the United States and Canada.
13 By mid-2002, thanks largely to a high tech boom, metro Montreal's unemployment stood at just over 8 percent.

REFERENCES

Aubry, F. 1998: *La Conjoncture dans le secteur de l'hôtellerie au Québec*. Montréal: CSN.

Baltimore Sun 1998: 3 Unions trying to organize New Orleans hotel workers. November 23.

Benoit, J. 1999: Forte hausse de la valeur des hôtels du centre-ville. *La Presse*, March 3.

Blair, M. 1999: Downtown Montreal hotel market. *Canadian Lodging Outlook* (February).

Board of Trade of Metropolitan Montreal 2000: Unionization rate: Montreal overtakes Vancouver. *Trend Chart* (February).

Bodson, P., Samson, M., and Stafford, J. 1988: *L'Hôtellerie dans l'arrondissement centre de Montréal: Situation et perspectives d'avenir*. Montréal: INRS-Urbanisation.

Brodeur, M. and Galarneau, D. 1998: Three large urban areas in transition. *Perspectives on Labour and Income* 6: 4 (Winter): 37–45.

Bureau of Labor Statistics 1999: *Occupational Employment and Wage Estimates, 1997*. Washington, DC: Bureau of Labor of Statistics.

Bureau of National Affairs 1999: *Union Membership and Earnings Data Book*. Washington, DC: Bureau of National Affairs.

——2000: *Union Membership and Earnings Data Book*. Washington, DC: Bureau of National Affairs.

——2001: *Union Membership and Earnings Data Book*. Washington, DC: Bureau of National Affairs.

Butler, R. et al. 1993: A social compact that would attack poverty. *Baltimore Sun*, December 7.

Card, D. and Freeman, R. (eds.) 1994: *Small Differences That Matter: Labor Markets and Income Maintenance in the United States and Canada*. Chicago: University of Chicago Press.

Corriveau, J. 2001: McDonald's: une recette connue. *Le Devoir*, April 26.

——2002: Négociations dans l'hôtellerie – Les moyens de pression s'accentueront lundi. *Le Devoir*, July 21.

Desrosiers, E. 1999: La Ronde rouvre aujourd'hui. *Le Devoir*, August 12.

Douet, S. 2002: La menace de grève générale illimitée diminue. *La Presse*, August 1.

Dutrisac, R. 2000: Patrons et syndicats protestent . . . pour des motifs fort différents. *Le Devoir*, December 21.

Eaton, L. 1998: Tourism is helping put some back on the job, *New York Times*, August 30.

Fortin, K. 2001: Le bail courait jusqu'en 2006. *Le Devoir*, July 13.

Girard, M.-C. 1999: Des négos dans l'industrie hôtelière. *La Presse*, March 29.

Godin, P. 2001: *René Lévesque: L'espoir et le chagrin*. Montréal: Éditions du Boréal.

Gouvernement du Québec 1991: *Pour un redressement durable: plan stratégique du Grand Montréal*. Québec: Éditeur officiel.

Greenhouse, S. 1998: Labor eyes a prize: hotels of New Orleans. *New York Times*, August 18.

Johnston, D. 1999: O glory, O shame. *Montreal Gazette*, January 23.

King, M. 1999a: Hotel "hot time" promised. *Montreal Gazette*, July 14.

——1999b: Peace checks into hotel labour scene. *Montreal Gazette*, August 25.

Krueger, A. B. 2001: At colleges, as elsewhere, employer's prosperity lifts workers expectations. *New York Times*, April 26.

Latraverse, L. 1999: La richesse, ça se partage sur tous les étages. Montréal: CSN.

Lévesque, K. 2001: Une monstrueuse aventure financière. *Le Devoir*, July 25.

Levine, M. V. 1995: Globalization and wage polarization in US and Canadian Cities: Does Public Policy Make a Difference? In P. K. Kresl and G. Gappert (eds.), *North American Cities and the Global Economy: Challenges and Opportunities*. Thousand Oaks, CA: Sage Publications, 89–111.

——1997: *La reconquête de Montréal*. Montréal: VLB Éditeur.

——1999: Tourism, urban redevelopment, and the world-class city: the cases of Baltimore and Montreal. In C. Andrew, P. Armstrong, and A. Lapierre (eds.), *Les villes mondiales: Y-a-t-il une place pour le Canada?* Ottawa: Les presses de l'Université d'Ottawa, 421–50.

——2003: Tourism, urban infrastructure, and urban redevelopment in Montreal. In Dennis R. Judd (ed.), *The Infrastructure of Play: Building the Tourist City*. Armonk, NY: M. E. Sharpe, 245–70.

Marsolais, C. V. 1998: Deuxième conflit du travail au Casino en cinq ans. *La Presse*, June 4.

Martineau, Y. and Lamonde, P. 1997: Montréal et dix métro-poles nord-américaines. *La minute de l'emploi* 1 (4) (December): 1–4.

——and Rioux, P. 1994: *Le marché du travail dans la région métropolitaine de Montréal*. Montréal: INRS-Urbanisation.

Mishel, L., Bernstein, J., and Schmitt, J. 2001: *The State of Working America, 2000/2001*: Ithaca, NY: Cornell University Press.

Montreal Gazette 1998: Casino craps out. June 16.

——2000: Make Quebec competitive. April 15.

Morin, G. 1998: *La cathédrale inachevée*. Montreal: XYZ Éditeur.

Normand, F. 1999a: Un peu plus près de la grève. *Le Devoir*, July 29.

——1999b: Les employés d'hôtel accueillent mal la culture d'entreprise américaine. *Le Devoir*, July 20.

OCTGM (Office des Congrès et du Tourisme du Grand Montréal) 1998: *Report on Tourism in Montreal, 1997*. Montreal: OCTGM.

OECD (Organisation for Economic Co-operation and Development) 1994: *The OECD Jobs Study: Evidence and Explanations*. Paris: OECD.

——1995: *Tourism Policy and International Tourism in OECD Countries, 1992–1993*. Paris: OECD.

Rodrigue, S. 2002: Vendredi noir dans les hôtels de la région de Montréal. *La Presse*, July 21.

Sansfaçon, J.-R. 1998: Une grève injustifiable. *Le Devoir*, June 7.

Schlosser, E. 2001: *Fast Food Nation: The Dark Side of the All-American Meal*. Boston: Houghton-Mifflin.

Sharpe, R. 2001: What exactly is a "living wage"? *Business Week*, May 28.

Société du Vieux-Port de Montréal 1999: *Le Vieux-Port de Montréal*. Web site.

Statistique Canada 1998: *Population 15 Years and Over with Employment Income, by Sex, Work Activity, and Detailed Occupation, Showing Number and Average Employment Income in Constant (1995) Dollars*. Ottawa: StatCan.

——1999: *Labour Force Historical Review*. Ottawa: StatCan.

——2001: *Income Trends in Canada, 1980–1998*. Ottawa: StatCan.

Tourisme-Montréal 2001a: *Base de données sur le tourisme*. Montréal: Tourisme-Montréal.

——2001b: *Le tourisme à Montréal*. Montréal: Tourisme-Montréal.

——2001c: *Le tourisme d'affaires et de congrès à Montréal*. Montréal: Tourisme-Montreal.

Turcotte, C. 1999: Une bataille pour l'équité salariale. *Le Devoir*, July 26.

Van Praet, N. 2002: Sweet days for hotel trade. *Montreal Gazette*, July 20.

Ville de Montréal 2000: *Indicateurs économiques de Montréal*.

Part IV

Regulating the Tourism Industry

10   Mexico: Tensions in the Fordist Model of Tourism Development
Daniel Hiernaux-Nicolas

11   The New Berlin: Marketing the City of Dreams
Hartmut Häussermann and Claire Colomb

12   Museums as Flagships of Urban Development
Chris Hamnett and Noam Shoval

10

Mexico: Tensions in the Fordist Model of Tourism Development

Daniel Hiernaux-Nicolas

Introduction

In this chapter, I examine the growth and restructuring of Mexican tourism from 1945 to 1982 as an example of a Fordist model of development, and contrast it to the more recent post-Fordist approaches. Tourism has been pivotal to Mexico's development strategies and has been a substantial contributor to institutional, cultural, and economic changes. In the post-war period Mexico coped with the rapid growth of international tourism by developing resorts capable of serving large numbers of tourists who consumed standardized products and experiences. To guide the development of tourism as an accumulation regime, the Mexican government created specialized tourism agencies devoted to building centrally managed tourist enclaves. The institutions devoted to promoting tourism consumed significant public resources and their policies largely determined tourism development in Mexico.

In the past two decades, changes in international tourism have forced Mexico to redefine its approach to tourist development. At the beginning of the 1980s, falling tourist flows to resorts signaled a change in preferences, away from standardization and towards a variety of products and experiences. A move away from state-managed resorts and the privatization of the tourist economy have dispersed the sites of tourism and brought about a new emphasis on culture tourism, adventure tourism, ecological tours, and environmentally oriented activities. These post-Fordist tendencies have developed within Fordist-style tourism, however, because resorts and hotel clusters still characterize much of Mexico's tourist development, if not its approach to developing this sector.

Mexico: From Individual Experience to Mass Tourism

The early beginnings, 1920–45

As an organized activity, tourism hardly existed in Mexico before the 1920s. It took an adventurous and risk-taking state of mind to be willing to put up with the lack of infrastructure and the unpredictable social and political conditions in Mexico immediately preceding and during the 1910 Revolution. The road system was largely destroyed during the Revolution, and the railway network was also in poor condition. The improvement of communications and transportation became one of the main priorities of the Mexican government, a mission that became particularly clear during the Lázaro Cárdenas presidency from 1934 to 1940. The infrastructure developed in those years became essential for post-war tourism development.[1]

The Mexican government defined the legal status of tourist in the population law of 1921, when the tourist was recognized as a traveler with no intention to reside or to work in the country, but as a temporary visitor with specific rights. No restrictions existed in Mexico regarding the places tourists were allowed to visit (as in the Soviet Union during the same period). A Consulting Board for Tourism (in 1929, renamed the Mixed Commission Pro Tourism) was created to try to promote some cooperation between tourist entrepreneurs and the government. In 1931, in an attempt to facilitate the recent development of road tourism to Mexico, the Mexican Automobile Association was founded.

There were four major tourist destinations in the pre-war period:[2]

1 *Metropolitan Mexico City* was a destination for international tourists because of its extraordinary architecture, urban culture, its very significant National Museum (the National Museum for Anthropology), and because it provided connections to archeological sites and to Oaxaca and more distant locations (Hiernaux-Nicolas 2000b, 2001).
2 *Internal destinations* such as Oaxaca, Guanajuato, but also more remote places, such as Palenque, were attractive to adventurous "cultural" travelers who were willing to accept some level of risk and discomfort.
3 *Beach destinations* such as Acapulco, Cozumel, Veracruz, and various coastal zones, attracted bohemians in the 1920s and 1930s.

4   *Border destinations* in and around Tijuana developed in the 1920s. These were clearly related to Prohibition and to the movie industry in Hollywood. Because of the wealth of the Americans traveling to Tijuana, luxurious hotels, restaurants, casinos, and other amenities quickly developed there.

Because Mexico was cheap and accessible, especially to wealthy people in southern California, the tourism industry began to take off in the 1930s. In response, the Mexican government began to build a system of regulations and institutions to promote tourist development, beginning with Tourism Credit in 1935 (the first institution offering loans for hotel development), the National Council for Tourism, and the Mexican Tourist Association.

The government's interest in developing tourism was such that even World War II did not stop tourist flows; indeed, security was a crucial issue for US visitors, and Mexico was offering it. In 1939, 139,000 tourists visited Mexico, and with some ups and downs during the war, by 1945, 166,000 visitors traveled to Mexico. The Mexican government actively promoted tourism during the war. Foreign currencies were welcomed, and the government opened promotional offices in New York, San Antonio, Los Angeles and Tucson. But the infrastructure was lacking: only 636 hotels were available, with a total of 3,500 rooms. Major investments would be required to meet the growing demand. These substantial investments came immediately after the war: "the end of WW II is the birth of modern tourism" in Mexico (Jiménez 1993: 21).

Mass tourism and the primacy of Acapulco, 1945–75

Miguel Alemán, the president of Mexico from 1946 to 1952 (the first civilian president and only the third to serve a full six-year term), proposed a "Tourism Declaration" during his 1946 campaign. A sort of manifesto, this document emphasized that, at the beginning of the Cold War, Mexico was on the western side and that the country should make an effort to build connections with other Western countries by developing infrastructure and hotels, promoting tourist destinations, and preparing new generations of workers to work in tourism.[3] Officials in the Mexican government also thought that tourism provided a means of integrating the country by increasing contact among regions and building a national identity, *mexicanidad* ("Mexicanity").

Acapulco was a resort visited by the post-revolutionary Mexican bourgeoisie beginning in the 1920s, and during the war it also served as a central destination for American tourists. In the same way that Saint Tropez became famous for the French and American movie and show-business stars who spent time there – Johnny Weissmuller, for instance, spent many holidays there, and eventually died in the now declining Flamingo's. For a long time, Acapulco was *the* resort in Mexico, when Mexican and American celebrities took holidays side by side and eventually engaged in business or love affairs. Movies were essential to the international image of Acapulco. Promoted indirectly by Mexican and American cinema, Acapulco became a mythic resort that bundled together images of the tropics (sun, sand), beautiful people (sex, money), exoticism, and desire (Hiernaux-Nicolas 1994).

But Mexican tourism development was not focused exclusively on Acapulco. Mexico City remained one of the most popular destinations: By 1958, the capital city had 32.7 percent of the total number of hotel rooms in the country, and it received 60 percent of the credits offered by Mexico's national credit agency for tourism, FOGATUR (Jiménez 1993: 44–6). Founded in 1958 to offer loans for hotel building, FOGATUR evolved into a credit agency that offered loans for many aspects of tourism. At the same time, another institution, INFRATUR, was created to develop infrastructure. This institutional development reflected the fact that Mexico's government was making tourism central to its strategy for national economic development. The National Council for Tourism, dominated by Miguel Alemán, its CEO until his death, was the organization in charge of developing a national policy. It was also the chief vehicle for tourism policy, providing information and issuing reports to the government about the relevance and development of tourism.

On the demand side, two factors were very important in stimulating Mexico's efforts to promote tourism. First, as a neighbor of the United States, as geographers pointed out, there is a clear "basin" dimension in the expansion of international tourism: Mexico was located within the North American Basin of international tourism, easily accessible and yet quite different, with a subtropical climate in most of the country. Second, the Cuban Revolution of 1959 provoked a reorientation of tourism flows: Mexico was a safe destination with a clear ideological and economic integration into the Western Hemisphere, despite an official discourse that was often critical of the US and friendly towards Cuba.

It was clear that international tourism was looked on primarily as a strategy for economic development, even if official rhetoric made plenty of references to "tourism as a factor of peace" and "tourism as a factor of Mexicanity." Tourism was a business opportunity. Foreign capital poured into hotel investment, providing 22 percent of the capital by the end of the 1950s (MacDonald-Escobedo 1981). International tourism in Mexico grew rapidly, from 164,000 visitors in 1945 to more than 3.2 million in 1975, with an average annual growth rate of 10.4 percent over the 30-year period. Tourism grew far faster than did Mexico's average GNP (an average of about 9 percent from 1950 to 1975).

As in the developed nations, the "30 glorious years" ("les trente glorieuses") – the Fordist Age – began to decline in the late 1960s. Serious bottlenecks were affecting the Mexican economy: at the same time that Mexico was exporting raw materials and agricultural goods, its industrial and urban development needed expensive manufactured goods as machinery. The disequilibria in the trade balance grew dangerously. As a result, an inflow of foreign currency was needed to finance development. Tourism provided the best prospect for improving the flow; thus, the interest in promoting tourism intensified. The modernization of the Mexican economy also produced a rapid increase in tourism within the country. Time and money, images of modernity, and a desire to imitate the American way of life encouraged Mexico's growing middle class to take more holidays, a tendency reinforced by the Mexican Work Law, which required employers to provide for paid holidays.

Acapulco on the Pacific and Veracruz on the Gulf Coast were the preferred beach resorts. This encouraged changes in these places. Acapulco soon offered all kinds of "modern" amenities, from pizzas, hotdogs and hamburgers, to air-conditioned facilities, to American bars and martinis in the new high-rise hotels. Acapulco also transformed from a low-rise city of bungalows and two-story buildings owned and managed by local entrepreneurs to a coastal fringe of high-rise hotels with elevators, air conditioning, restaurants, bars and discos, with direct access to the beach. Two Acapulcos – a pre-Fordist city in the "Acapulco tradicional" style and a Fordist strip of "Acapulco dorado" (golden) began to co-exist (Hiernaux-Nicolas 2000a). For both international and national visitors, the new developments represented progress and success expressed through leisure and happiness. Acapulco was modernism transplanted into an underdeveloped country, a window opened to the world.

However, the modernist bubble was limited in scope. Mass tourism was focused narrowly on hotel accommodation and air transport. The Fordist development of tourism did not reach far into Mexican society, in contradiction to the rhetoric promising that it would nurture a national identity or promote national integration. Except for a very few programs sponsored by trade unions and the federal government to develop tourism for workers, tourism was clearly reserved for a better-paid population. Mexico's version of Fordist tourism was a pale copy of France's: Paid holidays were shorter, fewer workers were covered, and holiday options were much more limited. Rather than becoming a democratic force, Mexico's resort-centered tourism highlighted class differences.

Plate 10.1   Mexican beach scene. *Source*: Photdisc

The Fordist institutions

In 1962 the first National Plan for Tourism was submitted to the government. New resorts were proposed, but institutional changes were required before a truly integrated development strategy could take shape. In 1973 FOGATUR and FIDETUR were integrated into a single trust fund – FONATUR, el Fondo Nacional de Turismo, the National Trust Fund for Tourism. Together with the Bank of Mexico and the financial sector, FONATUR was responsible for developing the new resort of Cancún (Hiernaux-Nicolas 1999).

The Mexican government was interested in building five new resorts as a way of attracting more international tourists and obtaining badly needed foreign currencies. Mass tourism was seen as the way to secure the largest number of tourists and maximize profits for investors. Tourist development was patterned on Fordist industrial development: large-scale government institutions and private corporations, standardized tourist products, an unskilled workforce (in this case, with large proportion of women). A spatial division of labor was achieved on a national scale. Industrial production was concentrated in Mexico City, in industrial zones with large numbers of workers living far away in poor neighborhoods and suburbs; tourism was primarily located mainly in coastal areas, with a rigid spatial separation between workers who lived in neighborhoods outside the zone inhabited by tourists.

When young Mexican technocrats submitted their development plan for Cancún to the International American Development Bank (IADB), the proposal was quickly accepted, even though the studies supporting the proposal were quite sketchy. That was the kind of development that international financial institutions wanted, a kind of perfect utopian Fordist resort (see Hiernaux-Nicolas 1999). FONATUR developed all the infrastructure in Cancún: golf courses, a convention center, outdoor markets, hotels, a first-class airport, paved roads, all built to reinforce a sharp segregation between tourists and workers. The project was conceived by federal technocrats, paid for by federal funds, the IADB, and the World Bank, all of which leveraged money from private investors. The construction of Cancún began in 1970 and the resort opened in 1976, immediately followed by Ixtapa in 1978, and Loreto and San José in 1978 and 1980. Of these four resorts, only Cancún attracted a significant amount of private investment; for years, the three others were totally operated by the federal government agency's FONATUR.

FONATUR operated with nearly complete autonomy; it was the United Fruit of tourism in Mexico. It operated as a Fordist centralist agency, bypassing all local and provincial regulations, developing a federal project for federal purposes, to ensure benefits for the central economy and/or for investors. FONATUR also reinforced Fordist tendencies in tourist development elsewhere; it served as consultant to Cuba's and the Dominican Republic's tourist development. For many Latin American countries, it is still regarded as the best example of what a government should do to promote tourism on a national scale.

But the benefits from Fordist-style tourist development have been mixed for Mexico. From 1940 to 1985, Mexico secured a solid share of tourist flows and tourism receipts. Even the 1982 Mexican economic crisis did not deeply affect tourism development. On the contrary: after some ups and downs, a spurt of new growth occurred in response to the frequent currency devaluations after 1982. Tourism seemed to be a sector that was more or less immune from economic cycles because of its low salaries and operating costs.

Demand continued to grow, but the economic benefits and the benefits to the treasury seemed quite uncertain. For example, the balance of payments was sometimes negative in tourism, despite the growing number of visitors. This seemingly unlikely outcome could be traced, in part, to the

Fordist nature of Mexican tourism. Much Mexican tourism revenue was actually spent outside the country, for example, in payments to tour operators and airlines located elsewhere (especially the case with all-inclusive packages). In addition, Mexican citizens traveling outside their country tended to spend more during some periods than the average international visitor to Mexico.

From Mass Tourism to Flexible Organization, 1985–2002

After 1985, a new orientation began to influence Mexico's tourism policy. The 1985 earthquakes destroyed a large number of hotels and other infrastructure in Mexico City and frightened many tourists away. In response, the Mexican government initiated an emergency plan to attract tourists back. Differing from previous approaches, the new policies were adapted to the new realities of international tourism and the global economy that made Fordist-style tourist development less effective than before.

In the mid-1980s, Mexico was still in a stage of intense protectionism for its tourism industry. But cracks were beginning to appear in its wall of defense. Increasingly, tourist preferences were moving away from standardized tourist products and services. As with other economic sectors, consumers were developing a preference for unique, esthetically pleasing, highly variable products, and they were willing to pay more to get them. Resorts continued to attract large numbers of tourists, but these were proliferating all over the globe, leaving Mexico's Fordist version of tourism in a vulnerable position. It was becoming clear that Mexico would have to find ways to stay competitive and to improve returns on its investment.

Beginning in 1982, some large Mexican companies decided to invest some of their profits from the oil boom of the early 1980s in new hotels. Large hotel corporations also began to renovate or buy up existing hotels, often as joint ventures among several corporate partners. This movement came during a period of intense growth in Mexico's tourism, which was prompted, in part, by the Mexican government's devaluation of the peso in 1982. At least temporarily, Mexican resorts became very desirable because they represented an unusual bargain.

There was also a movement to diversify the tourism product. After the 1985 earthquakes, the Mexican government published a "Plan for Immediate Action to Reorder Tourism in Mexico." The plan proposed revolutionary changes in the government's tourism policy. It recommended that Mexican air traffic be opened to international competition and that the number of charter flights be increased. More far-reaching still, the report proposed that the government allow 100 percent foreign investment in tourist projects; up to that point, the law had imposed a 49 percent ceiling, with few exceptions. Foreign capital immediately began to flow to Mexico, though essentially through "swaps" mechanisms, (buying low-valuated debt as an investment). A large number of new hotel rooms were built close to existing resorts but also in or near some newer, smaller ones.

In opening up tourism to foreign capital and to unplanned investment, the Mexican State was taking a big step back from the Fordist tourism model and entering a new stage of globalization in tourism, anticipating the general opening of the rest of the economy (Hiernaux-Nicolas 1998). The end of the Fordist period became clearly visible when FONATUR decided in 1983 and 1984 to stop developing large projects. Subsequently Huatulco was developed by presidential decision, but it was the last of the state-managed resorts. At the same time more than 40 new resorts were proposed along the Pacific and Caribbean coasts by private investors, national and foreign. These projects, which ranged from a few hundred to more than 10,000 hotel rooms, were not all developed, but the number of private proposals revealed that the grip of the Mexican State on tourism policy had been loosened.

FONATUR began to slowly abandon its focus on new resort construction, though it continued to maintain close supervision of the operation and policies of the resorts. It increasingly turned its attention to the financing of new hotels. FONATUR also began to understand the growing importance of cultural tourism and its potential for bringing tourism to medium-size cities. The new "colonial cities tourism development" policy of dispersing tourism coincided with a larger government effort to relocate industry away from the big cities such as Mexico City, Guadalajara and Puebla to smaller cities. A growing international interest in Mayan history and art led to the development of a "Mayan Route," basically a tour between Central American countries and Mexico, so that tourists could visit Mayan archeological sites as well as traditional beach resorts such as Cancún and Cozumel. In addition, new environmental policies at the federal level provoked a renewed interest in ecotourism and adventure tourism.

Finally, it became obvious that urban tourism held great potential for growth. Visits to cities had always been an important aspect of Mexican tourism, but they had been relatively neglected in tourism policy. The opening of the Mexican economy and a sharp increase in business travel before and after the North Atlantic Free Trade Agreement (NAFTA) meant that even cities with few archeological or cultural attractions began to see increased flows of capital and visitors. FONATUR now helps to finance hotels in urban centers. In general terms, federal and local governments are more heavily involved in promoting the competitive advantages of Mexican culture than before, for example, the restoration of archeological sites in the historic center of Mexico City and the development of cultural tourism in Oaxaca, Zacatecas, Campeche and other traditional destinations, long ignored because of the Fordist orientation of the tourism model.

A repackaged tourism: Is it "post-Fordist"?

The new policy directions may seem like dramatic departures, but actually they constitute, at most, 10 percent of the tourist flows to Mexico (excluding travel to cities, much of which is only incidentally related to discretionary tourism). Mexico is still following a largely Fordist model, mainly because it offers short-term, obvious benefits. Selling low-priced rooms to tour operators and brokers in the developed countries is still the fastest and most reliable way to recover investment. Some 20 percent of the total room supply in hotels has shifted from room rent to time-sharing management during the past 15 years, a development that shows the interest of Mexicans and middle-class Americans in buying vacation property as a symbol of status and the integration of time-share management by such international enterprises as Resort Condominium International.

Another factor explaining the development of time-sharing is also the considerable increase in money laundering in the tourist sector in Mexico. Officials claim that drug money is not present in tourism, but any announcement of a drug dealer arrest and confiscation of properties includes some hotels and restaurants. In 1999, the government confiscated some hotels on the famous Paseo de la Reforma, the Mexican Champs Elysées.

Post-Fordist tendencies are present in the actual tourism model in Mexico, but they are still embedded within Fordist practices. Large hotels and resorts are willing to integrate cultural activities and new destinations with the usual sun, sand, and sea activities; on the other hand, individuals and social organizations offer new products competing with the traditional sand and sea practices. Meanwhile the new alternatives are scarce, and the Fordist shift to new practices is not very intense. Is this old wine in new bottles, or a real change? It may too soon to tell, but it is likely that the integration of Mexican tourism into the global system will lead to greater flexibility and variation. Multinational corporations are the main agents leading the transformation. This is particularly true for business tourism, but also for massive beach tourism: new reservation systems, computerization, international standards of quality, and flexible management are being progressively integrated into the Mexican tourist system. As elsewhere, the Internet has started to force change. Whatever tour operators or resort and hotel operators may wish to provide, consumers are often very well informed and aware of what they want. As Mexican tourism is becoming more genuinely international – more tourists, for instance, are coming from Europe – many of the new tourists want to see the "real" Mexico. Therefore, a shift from a supply-oriented to a demand-oriented tourism has appeared in recent years, a clear sign of an emerging post-Fordist orientation.

As a consequence, the traditional beach resorts, including even Cancún, are diversifying their activities. The beach is no longer the main attraction. Malls, cinemas, markets, and festivals are proliferating outside the resort, as are independent tourism entrepreneurs who offer guided visits to Mayan ruins and accommodations at other places along the coast. Investors would like to add casinos to the mix, but the Mexican government is afraid that might facilitate money laundering and mob activity. Mexican tourism is going through a transition. The foundation is still Fordist, with big resorts and large hotels at the center. But a complex mix of tourist activities and opportunities is being grafted onto this root stock as large corporations mix beach and archeological visits in "all inclusive-tours"[4] with ecotourism and cultural activities. An independent offer of alternative tourism products is also growing fast. In the future, the shape of tourism in Mexico will be determined less by government policy and more by what investors, tourists, and the people in Mexico want.

Conclusion

The events of September 11, 2001 have brought about an intense re-examination of tourist policy in Mexico. In the past the focus on resorts seemed to promise security to visitors who generally stayed within the safe confines of the tourist zone. Within Mexico, political turmoil and violence connected with the drug trade seem to have affected tourism very little, if at all. Even the Chiapas revolt was not seen as a major threat to tourism; indeed, the numbers of tourists increased in Chiapas after 1994.

However, after September 11 tourist flows declined in Mexico as else-where (WTO, 2001). If there is a vulnerability, it is introduced by the con-centration of North American tourists in a few places. These kinds of uncertainties have revived interest in diversifying tourism in Mexico. Historically, Mexico has promoted international tourism but largely ignored national and "backpacker" tourism that operates beyond the reach of tourism providers. Now the Mexican government is conducting studies of the diverse segments of internal or external tourism such as "social tourism" (low-income national tourism), conventions, meetings, business tourism, and urban tourism. There is a new awareness that visitors in general, and not only tourists in the official sense, must be part of the mix.

To achieve a reorientation of tourist policies, there are no plans to reinstall the Mexican government as the main regulator of funds and rules. In the place of regulations, the government now seeks to "facilitate" tourism and the industry that has grown up around it. A new regulation regime has appeared, in which local authorities are taking control of tourism promotion, relationships with investors, and the local infrastructure of tourism. The private sector is central to the new model. If this seems similar to developments in other nations, it is because international tourist flows and the practices of tourism entrepreneurs point the way from the Fordist model that has been favored by the Mexican government.

NOTES

1 According to Alfonso Jiménez, in 1925 Mexico had already 23,000 km of railways with severe management crisis. New roads were built by American contractors until 1928, when national suppliers began to participate; finally, air transportation started with a initial flight in 1921 (Jiménez 1993: 15).
2 The first organized group of tourists reached Mexico in 1929 (Jiménez 1993: 17).
3 Until the end of the Cárdenas presidency (1940), there was a strong leftist influence in Mexico. But Cárdenas failed to impose his "dolphin" on the presidential nomination, and a right turn started. Miguel Alemán represents a new bourgeois elite, further from the Revolution's ideology than Cárdenas and previous presidents.
4 For example, Club Méditerranée is now including more and more excursions to archeological sites than before; the new model is possibly breaking the "tourist bubble" tendency (Judd 1999).

REFERENCES

Hiernaux-Nicolas, D. 1994: En busca del Eden: turismo y territorio en las sociedades modernas. *Ciudades*, 23. Puebla: Red Nacional de Investigación Urbana, 24–31.
——1998: El espacio turístico ¿metáfora del espacio global? *Diseño y Sociedad*, no. 9. México City: Universidad Autónoma Metropolitana, 9–18.
——1999: The Cancún bliss. In D. R. Judd and S. S. Fainstein (eds.), *The Tourist City*. New Haven, CT: Yale University Press, 124–39.
——2000a: La fuerza de lo efímero: apuntes sobre la construcción de la vida cotidiana en el turismo. In A. Lindón Villoria (ed.), *La vida cotidiana y su espacio-temporalidad*. Madrid and Mexico City: Antropos-UNAM/CRIM y El Colegio Mexiquense.

——2000b: Tourisme et régulation urbaine: le cas de la mégapole de México. *Espaces et Sociétés*, 100, *Tourisme en villes*. Paris: L'Harmattan, 99–124.

——2001: Tourism and cultural Heritage in Mexico City. In G. Dubois-Taine and C. Henriot (eds.), *Cities of the Pacific Rim: Diversity and Sustainability*. Paris: PUCA (Plan Urbanisme Construction Architecture) and PECC (Pacific Economic Cooperation Council), 181–95.

Jiménez, A. 1993: *Turismo, estructura y desarrollo*, Mexico City: McGraw-Hill.

Judd, D. R. 1999: Constructing the tourist bubble. In D. R. Judd and S. S. Fainstein (eds.), *The Tourist City*. New Haven, CT: Yale University Press, 35–53.

MacDonald-Escobedo, E. 1981: *Turismo, una recapitulación*, Mexico City: ed. Bodoni.

Secretaría de Turismo 1962: *Plan Nacional de Turismo*. Mexico City: Secretaría de Turismo.

World Tourism Organization (WTO) 2001: *Tourism after 11 September 2001: Analysis, Remedial Actions and Prospects*, special report (November). Madrid: WTO.

11

The New Berlin: Marketing the City of Dreams

Hartmut Häussermann and Claire Colomb

Introduction

The fall of the Berlin Wall in 1989 marked the beginning of a period of dramatic economic, social, and physical transformation for Berlin. In addition to the specific issues raised by East Berlin's transition from a socialist to a market economy, and by reunification *per se*, the reunited city had to confront the same urban-economic problems faced by other Western industrialized cities since the 1970s under the pressures of global economic change. After reunification, Berlin quickly lost most of its industrial base due to the disruption of trade with Eastern Europe and the low capacity for innovation of the state-subsidized manufacturing sector. West Berlin also lost the special subsidies previously granted it by the West German government to retain firms (Häussermann and Kapphan 2002). Since the Wende – the transformation following the collapse of the GDR – Berlin has experienced the loss of the status of "exception" and the intensity of economic, physical, and social restructuring. Events after 1989 have triggered major changes in local politics and brought about new patterns of urban governance.

As was the case with other European cities attempting to stimulate their economies, the focus of local government in Berlin has shifted towards export-oriented policies designed to boost local economic growth in a context of de-industrialization, structural unemployment, and limited public finance. The coalition in power in the Berlin Council during the first half of the 1990s privileged an urban development strategy driven by the tertiary sector – services, research, culture, leisure, and urban tourism. The development of urban tourism has been part of a wider strategy to re-invent Berlin as a post-industrial service metropolis able to attract tourists, visitors, investors, and potential residents. Urban tourism has therefore become an increasingly important sector of the city's economy, a sector with a high future growth potential.

Ironically, for years the Wall was the city's best asset in attracting visitors. As the "advanced post of freedom" in a divided Germany, West Berlin did not really have to market itself. In order to transform itself into a first rank post-industrial European metropolis, however, Berlin had to break with the negative images associated with its past by constructing and presenting a new image of itself to three main target groups:

- Potential visitors and investors from outside Germany, in order to stimulate the urban economy (in particular the sectors of urban tourism, entertainment and culture);
- Germans throughout the Federal Republic, in order to improve the image of the city following the decision to move the federal capital from Bonn to Berlin. Berlin was distrusted for decades by old generations of West Germans who tended to perceive the city as the capital of two totalitarian regimes in German history.
- The Berliners themselves, in order to foster the acceptance of urban change and enhance "the visual and emotional integration of two populations differently socialized"[1] in a previously divided city (Süss and Rabe 1995: 20).

In the early 1990s several large-scale flagship developments were launched in the center of Berlin, on the former no man's land running along the Wall and in the historic city center. As the construction of the new government and parliamentary districts began, Berlin became the "largest building site in Europe." How the construction sites and the new urban developments were successfully established as a major attraction for both tourists and residents will be analyzed in this chapter. In our account of urban marketing campaigns in the new Berlin, emphasis will be put on both the *process* and the *actors* of urban marketing.

The process of urban marketing: regulating the city

In Berlin, the construction and marketing of "spectacular urban landscapes" (Hubbard 1996) have been a prerequisite for the stimulation of urban tourism and economic development. As discussed in the Introduction, this results from the recognition that few visitors come to a place because of its unmediated attractions. Rather, the attractions need to be packaged and advertised so that potential customers will perceive their attractiveness. This chapter will therefore analyze how, through carefully designed urban marketing policies relying on large-scale cultural and architectural events, the urban redevelopment of "the New Berlin" was staged and forged into a myth. This process will be illustrated through a spectacular example of how a tourist destination has been created *ex nihilo*: Potsdamer Platz, which became the central icon of the picture of "The New Berlin." The theme of this chapter is the regulation of the city for the benefit of visitors and the tourism industry, in particular through the staging of the urban landscape.

The actors of urban marketing: public–private partnerships and the regulation of the tourism industry

In Berlin investors and urban marketing professionals, supported by local policy-makers, the media, and cultural institutions, have managed to construct an image for "The New Berlin"[2] and spread it worldwide. We will first describe the formation of a public–private "tourism coalition," a coalition cooperating in marketing the city, organizing spectacular events, and reorganizing the urban space for the benefit of tourists. As outlined in the Introduction, four types of regulatory frameworks structure relations within the tourism milieu. This chapter particularly examines the theme of the regulation of the tourism industry – how, as local policy-makers have become aware of the economic and symbolic importance of urban tourism in Berlin, new types of planning, public relations, and promotional activities were strongly encouraged and developed in partnership with the private sector.

In the second part of this chapter we will focus on the cultural meaning of the staging and marketing of "the New Berlin" and on the material and cultural conflicts arising from that process. Urban marketing policies are part of the new "symbolic economy" devised by "place entrepreneurs," officials, and investors (Zukin 1995: 7). Local residents and other critics have contested these policies, highlighting their economic, ideological, and cultural role in the sometimes painful processes of urban restructuring and transition to a new post-Fordist urban economy. We also describe the potential tension between place-marketing policies directed at tourists and investors and urban policies geared at the local population. Our analysis of urban marketing policies in Berlin will consequently draw on a double approach – a *political-economic* and a *cultural* approach, which provides a unique insight into the complex relationships between material processes of urban restructuring and the symbolic economy (Harvey 1989; Zukin 1995; Fainstein and Gladstone 1997).

Staging "The New Berlin": Urban Marketing and Construction Site Tourism

A series of public–private partnerships, such as *Wirtschaftsförderung Berlin* (Business Location Marketing), *Berlin Tourismus Marketing* (Tourism Marketing) and *Partner für Berlin* ("Capital City Marketing"[3]) have been responsible for attracting outside investors to the city, promoting Berlin as a tourist destination and thereby stimulating local economic development. *Partner für Berlin* (PfB), an urban marketing agency set up in 1994, has a particularly original structure and set of activities. This public–private partnership has the legal status of a private company and a budget of around DM 20 million.[4] It comprises more than 130 shareholders from the private sector – major German corporations and local companies – which contribute to half of the agency's budget. The city government is not, strictly speaking, a shareholder of the company, but has commissioned the agency to design and implement broad urban marketing activities for the city as a whole and therefore provides half of the budget of PfB. Until 2001 the chief executive of PfB was a well-known civic leader who was Senator for Urban Development in the early 1990s and had kept strong contacts with both the Berlin Senate and major corporate interests in Berlin.

The primary task of the agency is to market Berlin as Germany's capital city and as a potential business location for foreign investors. PfB also seeks to promote Berlin within Germany as an exciting place to live in and visit. Also, at the regional and city level, the agency directs some of its promotional activities towards the local population to increase its interest, curiosity, and support for the major urban changes taking place in the city. Although the main task of PfB is not, strictly speaking, to promote the city for tourists, its activities have been core to the process of creation of an image for "The New Berlin." The agency has been extremely proactive in designing and launching city marketing campaigns and events in Berlin, Germany, and abroad: advertisements in the international and national press; multimedia presentations and exhibitions; sponsoring of major cultural events; open-air image campaigns in the city, etc. In this chapter we will focus on the image campaigns and cultural-architectural events organized to "stage" urban change and transform the image of Berlin abroad and within the city.

The program "*Schaustelle Berlin*"[5] ("Showplace Berlin") was launched for the first time in the summer of 1996 to transform "the largest building site in Europe" into a tourist attraction. Under the slogan "*Betreten erbeten*" ("trespassing [is] allowed"), the largest construction sites of the inner city were opened to the public through a series of more than 450 site visits and guided tours. The first edition of the *Schaustelle* focused on the new commercial developments along Friedrichstrasse and on Potsdamer Platz. A privately funded red building was erected to house an exhibition about the flagship structure under construction on Potsdamer Platz, organized by private investors. It became the ticket-selling point for all events related to the *Schaustelle*, as well as a world-famous landmark of late 1990s Berlin – the "Info Box." One of the major elements of the *Schaustelle* was the integration of a program of cultural events in and around the construction sites, in a remarkable new combination of arts and construction work featuring street music, theatre, dance performances, and fashion shows on building sites throughout the city center. Other cultural events were integrated under the banner of the *Schaustelle* in a 72-page program of festivities for the whole summer. A decision of the Berlin Parliament exceptionally authorized longer business opening hours during the *Schaustelle*.

The idea behind the *Schaustelle* was to allow the general public a glimpse "behind the scenes" of the new capital city while simultaneously transforming what was usually perceived as a disturbance – the building site – into an asset for attracting visitors. The new concept of "construction site tourism" (*Baustellentourismus*) quickly became a success. The number of tickets initially put on sale was doubled to cope with the demand, and the Info Box welcomed up to 10,000 visitors a day. In the local and national media, the *Schaustelle* was quickly praised as an extraordinary example of "making virtue of necessity," i.e. transforming the building sites and the negative perceptions usually associated with them into a dramatic and spectacular experience. The building sites were turned into "showplaces" and "showcases" worth a visit.

Following its initial success, the *Schaustelle* program has been organized every summer since its first edition in 1996. In 1997, more than a thousand tours and visits were offered. A promotional "Info-Bus" was sent to some of the most deprived districts of Berlin to promote the program. By January 1997, two million visitors had visited the Info Box. For the 1998 *Schaustelle*, the scope of the guided tours was broadened to reflect different aspects of the redevelopment of Berlin, ranging from the building of the new government quarter to major office developments, as well as residential and transport infrastructure projects. Again, a series of cultural and artistic events, the "Berlin Summer of Culture," accompanied the program. In May 1998, a massive outdoor advertising campaign was launched by *Partner für Berlin* on the walls of major buildings under construction and on buses and taxis, to celebrate the forthcoming election of the federal president in the Reichstag and the new capital city status of Berlin.[6]

Plate 11.1   "The largest building site in Europe." *Source*: Susan S. Fainstein

In 1999 and 2000, the *Schaustelle* program was integrated into a larger event organized by several agencies and institutions.[7] "Berlin Open City: The City as Exhibition," a DM5 million project, expanded the concept developed in the *Schaustelle*: the city itself, the city as a whole, was offered as an exhibition, open at all times and free of charge. The project was based upon the selection of ten routes across the city, punctuated by 187 city signs presenting the major urban development projects. A guide presenting the ten routes and over 600 buildings was sold at most newsagents and bookshops in the city (*Berliner Festspiele and Architektenkammer Berlin* 1999). Through the Open City exhibition, visitors and Berliners were taught how to "read" their "new" city:

> On routes and city-signs along the way, on tour maps, on a guidebook and a thematic book, The New Berlin is *made transparent*. An exhibition at a 1 : 1 scale, open all the time. "Berlin: Open City" stages the appearance onto stage of "The New Berlin" and *shows pathways* through the labyrinth of the big city.[8] (*Das neue Berlin* 1999)

A cultural program ran parallel to the "Open City" exhibition: *"Spiel-Räume: die Stadt als Bühne"* ("Spaces of Play: The City as a Stage"), featuring a series of cultural performances staged in unexpected locations across the city center (such as a concert in the new road tunnel under the Tiergarten). Finally, in addition to "Open City" and the 2000 *Schaustelle*, a series of urban development projects, including the Info Box, were selected for their relevance to the theme of the EXPO 2000 taking place in Hanover on "Man, nature, technique" and marketed as EXPO 2000 projects in Berlin. It was hoped that Berlin would get a share of the visitors' flows to the main EXPO 2000 site in Hanover.

Potsdamer Platz, the Creation of a Tourist Attraction *Ex Nihilo*

Within the framework of these wide-ranging urban marketing campaigns, a particular site has become the icon of the redevelopment of "the New Berlin": Potsdamer Platz. The marketing of this site is an exceptional example of "construction site tourism" and how a successful tourist destination can be developed from scratch through image and marketing policies. Potsdamer Platz, a mythical crossroads in the 1920s, was cut by the Wall in 1961 and became a no man's land located at a dead end of West Berlin between the Tiergarten and the Wall. In 1988, the then mayor of Berlin granted the site to the Daimler-Benz corporation. After the Wall came down, Daimler Benz and Sony, who together owned 80 percent of the land, started to invest DM 4 billion to turn the site into a seven-million-square-foot business and retail center (Strom 2001: 186–200). The Daimler-Chrysler area opened in October 1998. The contemporary development has little in common with the historical Potsdamer Platz, neither in terms of its urban fabric nor of its functions. The flagship development has stirred up heated controversies, praises and criticisms, as it stands on a centrally located and mythical historical space. It is now a busy shopping and business district and has attracted, even long before its completion, millions of visitors from Berlin, the rest of Germany, and abroad.

The attractiveness of Potsdamer Platz as a major tourist venue does not appear to stem from its urban functions or "use value." There are no restaurants or shops of exceptional quality on the site – mainly fast-food and retail chains which can be found elsewhere in Berlin or in Germany. There are scarcely any outstanding cultural facilities either, besides a musical theatre and large cinemas which are the only venues still open after office hours on the Marlene-Dietrich-Platz (the core of the development scheme), therefore attracting visitors at night. Finally, the site does not relate very well to the rest of the urban fabric. The development was described by the developers and some enthusiastic politicians as the "New Centre," the new "pulsating heart of the city," the "bridge between East and West." However, the site is cut off from the *City-West* by the Tiergarten park and a canal. On its eastern side, it currently has rather weak links with the *City-Ost* as the new developments planned for the Leipziger Platz are still under construction. It is thus very unlikely for a passerby to walk accidentally through the site. Visitors eager to see the new Potsdamer Platz deliberately have to make a special journey to the site, which is precisely what millions of visitors have been doing. What then lures people to this new urban development if not the specific qualities of the place or the amenities and goods on offer?

At this point it is necessary to make some remarks on the sociological and psychological explanations of tourism (Enzensberger 1958; Hennig 1999). From the sociological and psychological perspective, the meaning of tourism is the visit to a counter-world in which one is free from the routines and pressures of daily life. The common denominator between extremely different tourist destinations such as South Pacific islands and European metropolises is that they serve as spaces of experience which differ sharply from the daily routine and in which the normally valid regulations of individual behaviors are absent. A strong incentive for travelling is, therefore, imagination. The tourist perception relies on pictures and fantasies, the descriptions of writers or the pictures of painters who turn parts of the real landscapes into "destinations." The tourist "constructs" the place he is going to visit, creates an image of his destination beforehand and, once arrived at the destination, lives in an imagined world. A culture of "rediscovering," of "reconstructing" emerges, in which the tourist experience consists in seeing *in reality* what one had in mind before leaving. This is clearly demonstrated by tourist trips to locations which have served as the settings of famous movies.

Tourism is therefore based on the dissemination of *images* of landscapes, cultures or cities, which then turn into desirable destinations. In a post-industrial economy, symbols and images become commodities. If one can successfully implant images and visions of specific locations into the mind of a large number of people, then it becomes possible to organize travel to these locations and create a tourist industry. This is what has been witnessed in the case of Potsdamer Platz. Our hypothesis is that investors, with the support of the local press, local politicians, and local "cultural intermediaries," have produced and spread an attractive image of the future flagship and have thereby managed to nurture the collective representations of Berlin worldwide. Through a careful and expensive mix of cultural and architectural events staged on site as well as massive advertising and marketing campaigns, a building site of local importance was turned into a global event and one of the main symbolic icons of "The New Berlin." It is thus the *image* of the Potsdamer Platz development, rather than any of its functions, which has made the place attractive to tourists.

The image of Potsdamer Platz was produced, on the one hand, through an architecture associated with the names of internationally famous architects (I. M. Pei, Renzo Piano, Richard Rogers, Isozaki, and Helmut Jahn) and presented as innovative, forward-looking and attractive. An exhibition displaying the architects' models for the development was set up in the "Info Box." With the support of advanced computer simulation technologies, suggestive pictures of a future vibrant urbanity on the site were projected on screen. The development of the area was presented as the most important event in Berlin since the reunification. The Info Box quickly became a major attraction for urban planning and architecture professionals as well as a wider audience of foreign tourists, Germans, and local residents curious about the future face of "The New Berlin." Besides, throughout the construction period, receptions were organized on site with a carefully selected audience of intellectuals, "approved" experts, and prominent speakers from the local political, economic, artistic, and cultural spheres, invited to debate on the planning of the area.

Besides the architectural design of the development, the technical organization of the construction process itself was turned into a marketing event. The progress of the construction process could be observed live on the Internet through a 360° virtual panorama. In the press and in guided tours, the logistics of the large-scale building site were presented as an exemplary technical achievement. Special emphasis was given to the transport of huge quantities of building materials and to the innovative solutions for traffic management in and around the site – the construction of a huge underground car park, a new S-Bahn station, and a new road tunnel under the Tiergarten.

In addition to the promotion of the design and construction process of the new development, another crucial element in the production of the image of the new Potsdamer Platz was an expensive program of cultural events staged on site. The cultural promotion of the new development was facilitated by the fact that there was one large-scale developer for the site (Debis, working on behalf of the main investor, Daimler-Benz), as opposed to the many developers and investors who redeveloped neighboring areas in a more fragmentary way (e.g. on Friedrichstrasse). In 1994, Daimler-Benz set up an advisory committee in charge of public relations for the Potsdamer Platz development, whose members were executives of the corporation, the architect Renzo Piano, members of the federal government, leading figures of the Berlin cultural scene, the chief editor of a cultural newspaper and the director of the Berlin Philharmonic Orchestra. The task of the committee was, in its own words, to encourage the dialogue between the investors and the cultural scene and promote cultural events beyond the standard repertoire, events which would become "brand labels for the development."

On October 29, 1994, the laying of the foundation stone was organized as an official ceremony attended by the local political, business, and media elite. A major artistic event then turned the construction site into an icon of the skyline of the New Berlin: the display of large-scale "light installations" on the cranes of the Potsdamer Platz by the artist Gerhart Merz in August 1996. During that summer, a dance company as well as the Berlin Philharmonic Orchestra performed on stages set up inside buildings still under construction. A few weeks before the official opening of the new development, large-scale pictures printed on $1,000\,m^2$ posters were hung on the façades of the new buildings, displaying scenes of the "old" historic Potsdamer Platz. A series of advertisements presenting the future face of the "new urban quarter" were published in the local press. For the inauguration of the new development, in October 1998, 170 professional climbers took the posters down to make the entire quarter suddenly visible. The opening of the site involved a three-day program of events featuring a party for 5,000 invited guests and journalists and various performances for the general public. During the opening week alone, 1.5 million visitors visited Berlin's "New Urban Quarter."

The success of "construction site tourism," in particular the Potsdamer Platz, was praised by most media and local policy-makers. Turning the construction sites into a successful tourist asset, attracting and triggering the interest of thousands of visitors for architectural, planning, and logistic issues, is a phenomenon worthy of academic attention. The construction site does not seem to correspond to the desire for remoteness, exoticism and escape, those elements traditionally highlighted by theories of tourism. But tourist destinations are collective representations, imagined geographies and spaces of fantasy which appeal to potential visitors through images shaped and spread by writers, artists, travel agents, place marketing professionals, and the media. Maybe the success of urban marketing is precisely to have turned a mundane urban experience (the construction site) into an extraordinary event, a romanticized and glamorous landscape, a place of desire:

> Berlin is a construction site, so is life in Berlin: this syllogism reveals the pressing efforts of local marketing professionals to redefine the daily life [in Berlin] as a form of existence of a considerable cultural rank.[9] (*Darmstädter Echo* 1997)

> Building site tourism, the productive curiosity about the New, has since long imposed itself over the fear of dust and noise.[10] (Kleeman 1996)

The cultural and festive events staged around the building sites have contributed to turning the construction site from a place of disturbance and brutal change into a place of "play," as the very name of the program indicates.[11] This "festivalization" of the construction site has helped to soften the threatening image of an entire city center under (re)construction, a skyline spiked with cranes. Marketing campaigns have managed "to transform the silhouette of cranes on Potsdamer Platz into the skyline of change, to turn the noise of construction sites into a symphony of the changing times"[12] (*Darmstädter Echo* 1997).

The concept of "construction site tourism" is specific to Berlin but inscribes itself into a wider trend towards the "festivalization of urban politics"[13] in many European cities, i.e. towards an urban policy dominated by the staging of large-scale cultural/sports events and flagship developments (Häussermann and Siebel 1993). It was argued that, following Berlin's unsuccessful bid for the Olympic Games 2000, "Berlin: Open City" was another attempt to pursue an urban development politics characterized by a festive staging of urban change through flagship projects (*Scheinschlag* 1999). This "repackaging" of the city center through cultural and architectural spectacle can be interpreted as being part of a "speculative construction of place" (Harvey 1989: 8), in which the new "symbolic economy" plays a crucial role. Zukin highlights how contemporary cities owe their existence to a second and abstract economy, a "symbolic economy" devised by "place entrepreneurs, officials and investors whose ability to deal with the symbols of growth yields 'real' results in real estate development, new businesses, and jobs" (Zukin 1995: 7). It is within this framework that urban marketing policies are contested and opened to criticisms regarding their economic, ideological, and cultural role in softening painful processes of urban restructuring and transition to post-industrial urban economies.

Marketed Spaces, Living Spaces: Cultural and Material Conflicts over the Marketing of "The New Berlin"

Several academic analyses of the concept of urban marketing have highlighted that it has a double orientation (Kearns and Philo 1993; Ward 1998). It not only aims at attracting external flows of investment and visitors into the city to sustain the city's position on the global or regional stage. Urban marketing can also be directed at the local population as a potential tool to (re)create a sense of local identity, soften conflicts over new developments in the city, or stimulate the endogenous economic development potential. Communication towards the local population has indeed been a key preoccupation of urban marketing professionals and local politicians in Berlin, who assumed that the people from Berlin have a more negative vision of their city than outsiders (*Partner für Berlin* 1995). Therefore, interest and acceptance were stimulated through a series of events combining both a didactic and an entertaining approach – two elements strongly present in the *Schaustelle* and Open City programs, as demonstrated above. However, it is difficult to assess the impact and the meaning of those marketing events on the local population. The local press was generally very enthusiastic, regularly publishing reviews and event listings. Forty percent of the visitors on the various tours and exhibitions organized were from the city. However, whether those marketing activities have created an interest or responded to a pre-existing curiosity is a difficult question. Opening the building sites has allowed the local population to glimpse behind the fences of otherwise enclosed areas. It could be argued that this has contributed to improving the legibility of an area under complete change and making residents feel less estranged by the massive urban redevelopment projects taking place in their city.

However, there has been a degree of criticism regarding the cultural and political alienation potentially present in urban marketing events which stage local residents as "tourists in their own city." Can such events participate in the reconstruction of local identity and pride? On the contrary, do they carry a large degree of cultural bias and can they deepen the feeling of alienation of some segments of the population facing a brutal urban change? Rada (1999) questions whether the discourse on "the New Berlin" of urban marketing professionals, the media, and local politicians represents the feelings of the Berliners, and if so, of which parts of the population. We argue that there are clear arguments pointing at a series of cultural and material conflicts over the marketing of "The New Berlin":

1   Urban marketing campaigns have promoted an urban experience defined by consumption and high-income groups, in contrast with the urban experience of lower-income residents.
2   Conflicts also arise because the images and urban myths projected by marketing professionals potentially differ from the memories and cultural practices of local residents.
3   Finally, the focus on architectural spectacle has deflected attention away from crucial political, economic and distributional issues underpinning new urban developments such as Potsdamer Platz.

The urban experience defined by consumption and high-income groups

Potential conflicts arise because urban marketing campaigns do not only aim at "selling" new urban developments but also the corresponding lifestyle(s) and ways of consuming, thereby focusing on profitable uses and users such as the "new urbanite," the tourist, or the high-income young professional. In the case of Potsdamer Platz, Rada argues that

> it is not only the hardware, the image of the built city, the investors' architecture . . . which is offered here, but also the software, the codes of its use; a picture that the successful city-dwellers of tomorrow can already have today.[14] (Rada 1997: 9)

The urban marketing discourse thus tends to be dominated by high-income consumers' experiences and definitions of urban life (Mayer 1995; Rada 1997). This paves the way for potential conflicts between the "visions" and experience of the city of lower-income residents and those of tourists, potential in-migrant professionals, or corporations who are the targets of most marketing campaigns. Indeed the cultural events organized in and around the city center of Berlin, in particular on the Potsdamer Platz, have tended to focus primarily on sites of consumption. Although the Potsdamer Platz development has been promoted as the reinvention of the vibrant and lively heart of 1920s' Berlin, it is a pure site of consumption which caters only to business, entertainment and shopping. There are no public amenities or civic buildings on the site, no space for non-commercial uses. This post-modern version of an "urban center" is very remote from the tradition of the European city and its associated public spaces, in which the *Stadtbürger* (citizens) played a central political and cultural role.

Urban myths potentially differ from the memories and cultural practices of local residents

Several critics have emphasized that urban marketing has a very ambiguous relation to local cultures and history: the marketing process often encompasses a "repackaging" and "aesthetization" of the memories and cultures of the city (Kearns and Philo 1993). This is not a neutral process, as Zukin (1995: 1) argues: "Culture is a powerful means of controlling cities. As a source of images and memories, it symbolizes 'who belongs' in specific places." In Berlin, the cultural and historical references used in urban marketing campaigns have indeed been carefully selected; they work as a method of "social sorting." There seems to be only one "politically correct" past to refer to: the golden age of the mythical *Weltstadt*, i.e. the late nineteenth–early twentieth century (Rouyer 1997: 127). The GDR heritage is absent from the city marketing discourse, reflecting the sensitive question of the treatment of East German political and cultural memory in contemporary Germany. It was argued that the pre-eminence of the representation of the new Potsdamer Platz in media representations of the New Berlin and its "global-CBD imagery" corresponds to "a vision of the future that explicitly draws on capitalism's victory over the drab reality of East German communism" (Cochrane and Jonas 1999: 149). The question of the integration of East German history and architecture into the collective memory of the city has been epitomized by the controversy surrounding the fate of the *Palast der Republik*, a 1970s' "House of the People" which contained cultural facilities and the People's Parliament of the GDR (Ladd 1997). When, in the early 1990s, the Federal government decided to tear it down, there was a strong protest from East Berliners (and some West German intellectuals) who felt some sense of identification with the built environment of the former GDR. The controversy was fuelled by the proposal to reconstruct the Imperial Castle demolished by the Communist regime in 1951, which used to be located exactly on the same site. In 1994, a businessman from Hamburg sponsored the design of a spectacular painted mock-up simulating the Baroque façade of the old Castle to lobby for the reconstruction of the Castle. The future use of the site of the *Palast der Republik*/Imperial Castle has been under debate ever since. In 2002 the Federal (!) Parliament has decided to reconstruct the Castle – a decision that stimulates ambiguous feelings about a symbol of "the New Berlin."

The potential conflicts arising out of the discrepancy between the urban myths projected by marketing professionals and the vision and memories of local residents have also been illustrated in the old inner-city residential neighborhoods of Mitte (Scheunenviertel) and Prenzlauer Berg, famous in GDR times for hosting political dissidents, artists, and alternative lifestyles. Urban marketing campaigns not only focused on the spectacular, high-tech new urban developments of Potsdamer Platz. *Schaustelle Berlin* and Open City have integrated other parts of the city into their program, in particular these two neighborhoods which have been the object of intense pressures for urban renewal. Here the urban marketing discourse has sought to recreate a "staged authenticity" (Fainstein and Gladstone 1997; *Scheinschlag* 1998) through a reference to the traditional atmosphere of these neighborhoods, their artistic and cultural life, and their "typical" Berliner architecture. However, in the process of staging the "authentic" and the "local," the images recreated by marketing professionals can potentially conflict with the images held by local residents, in particular since they can, to a certain extent, contribute to a process of symbolic gentrification. Images and myths are a crucial component of the gentrification process and symbolic gentrification through image building and place marketing will often pave the way for physical gentrification (Smith 1992). Prenzlauer Berg has indeed witnessed a struggle over spatial images, as attempts at "framing" the local culture for urban marketing purposes were opposed by local residents who fought to retain a local festival (the *Walpurgisnacht* celebration) and control the development of cafés (the "Kneipen" war) (Häussermann, Holm, and Zunzer 2002). This type of struggle over spatial images ultimately aims at preventing the transformation of traditionally mixed neighborhoods into places of "controlled diversity," "eclectic conformity," "commodified ethnic culture and sanitised classlessness" (Holcomb 1993: 142). As Hubbard points out (1996: 1446), the process of myth-making not only involves "a commodification of landscape by developers and politicians" and the construction of media discourses, but also "the incorporation or contestation of these myths by people themselves" (ibid.; see also Goodwin 1993; Kearns and Philo 1993). Urban marketing policies have tended to convey a vision of Berlin closely associated with the strong pro-growth agenda of the local business and political elite, but other political and social movements have been challenging the vision of Berlin's future offered by the "global imagineers" (Cochrane and Jonas 1999: 160).

The focus on architectural spectacle has deflected attention from crucial political, economic and distributional issues

The dominance of issues of architectural design in the urban marketing discourse has tended to overshadow the debates on the political and economic conditions of production of the new urban spaces, i.e. "who builds what, where, for whom, with whose finance and at whose expense" (Crilley 1993: 251). Architectural debates have often hidden the fact that there was no in-depth discussion of the arguments for or against a new development. Potsdamer Platz is often cited as a case in point. Visitors were allowed to look behind the scenes of the construction site, but their gaze was focused on the project's technical and architectural achievements. The models and digital simulations of the "city of the future" presented in the Info Box served to channel the curiosity of the visitors on questions of technology, design, and logistics and deflected attention away from more crucial issues which could fuel protest (Ronneberger et al. 1999: 91; Rada 1997). The same interpretation could be made of the various cultural and artistic events staged on and around the building sites. These events can be read as "signs of cultural goodwill and public accountability" from investors and developers, so that space is "not experienced as a space of domination and power, but is intended instead to arouse a sense of comfort and play" (Crilley 1993: 241). Urban marketing activities in Berlin through cultural-architectural events have indeed been described by some critical voices as a "bread and circus" strategy to engineer social consent (*Süddeutsche Zeitung* 1995).

Urban marketing campaigns are an important element of the new "symbolic economy" and as such have contributed to the process of regulation and legitimization of urban physical and economic restructuring and of the types of policies conducted to transform Berlin into a post-industrial city. The ideological and cultural role of urban marketing policies in softening painful processes of urban restructuring and transition to a new post-industrial urban economy has been underlined by several authors. Harvey (1989) refers to urban marketing and the "mobilization of spectacle" as a tool for urban conflict management to mask an increasing socio-spatial segregation. Many critics have indeed argued that marketing campaigns have been a convenient "screen" allowing city leaders to divert public attention away from crucial questions of power distribution and social justice, such as the impact of flagship developments on local employment and housing, accessibility to local residents, the absorption of public resources into large-scale projects, and democratic accountability in urban decision-making. Criticisms have also been raised about the amount of public money invested in public–private partnerships responsible for economic promotion, urban marketing, and other promotional activities in Berlin (Rose 1998).

Conclusion

In Berlin, private investors, the city government, urban marketing professionals, the media and cultural institutions have formed a coalition geared towards the proactive expansion of urban tourism in the city. This coalition was responsible for the construction and promotion of an image for "The New Berlin" through carefully designed image policies relying on large-scale cultural and architectural events. The images constructed through place marketing have been directed both at potential visitors and at inhabitants of the city. It can be argued that urban marketing policies have played a crucial economic, ideological, and cultural role in processes of urban restructuring and transition to a post-Fordist urban economy. This has opened the way for material and cultural conflicts between the "city of dreams" staged for tourists and the "real" city experienced by its inhabitants; between the spaces of consumption for tourists and "new urbanites" and the living spaces of lower-income groups; between the re-packaged urban culture promoted by city marketing professionals and the various local cultures and memories that shape the city.

Whereas during the phase of unification, in the early 1990s, no coherent "urban regime" was formed in Berlin for the restructuring of the city as a whole (Strom 2001: 223), in certain areas of the urban economy specific coalitions have been created. The "tourism coalition" is one example, but there are similar public–private partnerships in the field of high-tech industries (Häussermann and Simons 2000) and new housing developments. In all these partnerships, the public administration is still playing a dominant role. But the local government of Berlin has been facing endemic financial difficulties since the beginning of the 1990s, culminating in a political crisis in the spring of 2001 leading to the resignation of the governing mayor. The increasing financial crisis of the city will force the public administration to rely more heavily on private initiatives. In this perspective the "tourism coalition" described above can be interpreted as a pioneer arrangement foreshadowing a new type of urban regime which is already emerging in Berlin. Such a regime will exchange the dominant role of the public administration in a traditional system of hierarchical government for a system of decentralized coordination between different public and private actors.

NOTES

1   Authors' translation from German.
2   "The New Berlin" was an expression used in the 1920s to promote Berlin. Its current use triggers reminiscences of the "Roaring Twenties," when Berlin was seen as the "capital of modernity."
3   *"Gesellschaft für Hauptstadtmarketing."*
4   This figure is for 2000.
5   In German, there is a phonetic pun between the word *Schaustelle* (showplace) and the word *Baustelle* (building site).
6   Most of the materials produced by *Partner für Berlin* for their advertising campaigns can be viewed on the agency's website at http://www.berlin.de/pfb.
7   *Partner für Berlin*; *Berliner Festspiele* on behalf of the Senate; Chamber of Architects; Federal Ministry for Building and Spatial Planning; Department of Building and Department of Urban Development of the City of Berlin.
8   Emphasis added. Authors' translation from German.
9   Authors' translation.
10   Authors' translation.
11   *"Spiel-Raüme: die Stadt als Bühne"*: "Spaces of play: the city as a stage."
12   Authors' translation from German.
13   Authors' translation.
14   Authors' translation.

REFERENCES

Berliner Festspiele and Architektenkammer Berlin 1999: *Berlin: Open City – The City on Exhibition*. Berlin: Nikolai.

Cochrane, A. and Jonas, A. 1999: Reimagining Berlin: world city, national capital or ordinary place? *European Urban and Regional Studies* 6(2): 145–64.

Crilley, D. 1993: Architecture as advertising: constructing the image of redevelopment. In G. Kearns and C. Philo (eds.), *Selling Places: The City as Cultural Capital, Past and Present*. Oxford: Pergamon Press.

Das Neue Berlin 1999: *Das neue Berlin erleben / Discover the New Berlin: Berlin offene Stadt, Programmheft 1*. Berlin: Das Neue Berlin.

Enzensberger, H. U. 1958: Vergebliche Brandung der Ferne: eine Theorie des Tourismus. *Merkur* 12: 701–20.

Fainstein, S. S. and Gladstone, D. 1997: Tourism and urban transformation: interpretations of urban tourism. In O. Källtrop et al. (eds.), *Cities in Transformation, Transformation in Cities: Social and Symbolic Change of Urban Space*. Aldershot: Avebury.

Goodwin, M. 1993: The city as commodity: the contested spaces of urban development. In G. Kearns and C. Philo (eds.), *Selling Places: The City as Cultural Capital, Past and Present*. Oxford: Pergamon Press.

Harvey, D. 1989: *The Condition of Postmodernity*. Oxford: Blackwell.

Häussermann, H., Holm, A., and Zunzer, D. 2002: *Stadterneuerung in der Berliner Republik: Beispiel Prenzlauer Berg*. Opladen: Leske & Budrich.

——and Kapphan, A. 2002: *Berlin: von der geteilten zur gespaltenen Stadt?* Opladen: Leske & Budrich.

——and Siebel, W. (eds.) 1993: Festivalisierung der Stadtpolitik – Stadtentwicklung durch grosse Projekte. *Leviathan* (special issue no. 13). Opladen: Westdeutscher Verlag.

——and Simons, K. 2000: Die Politik der großen Projekte – eine Politik der großen Risiken? Zu neuen Formen der Stadtentwicklungspolitik am Beispiel des Entwicklungsgebietes Berlin-Adlershof. *Archiv für Kommunalwissenschaften*, 39: 56–71.

Hennig, C. 1999: *Reiselust: Touristen, Tourismus und Urlaubskultur*. Frankfurt am Main: Suhrkamp.

Holcomb, B. 1993: Revisioning place: de- and re-constructing the image of the industrial city. In G. Kearns and C. Philo (eds.), *Selling Places: The City as Cultural Capital, Past and Present*. Oxford: Pergamon Press.

Hubbard, P. 1996: Urban design and city regeneration: social representations of entrepreneurial landscape. *Urban Studies* 33: 1441–61.

Kearns, G. and Philo, C. (eds.) 1993: *Selling Places: The City as Cultural Capital, Past and Present*. Oxford: Pergamon Press.

Kleeman, J. 1996: Bühne frei für Berlin. *Foyer*, no. 6.

Ladd, B. 1997: *The Ghosts of Berlin: Confronting German History in the Urban Landscape*. Chicago: University of Chicago Press.

Mayer, M. 1995: Urban governance in the post-Fordist city. In P. Healey et al. (eds.), *Managing Cities, The New Urban Context*. London: Wiley.

Partner für Berlin 1995: *Das Image Berlins*. Berlin: Partner für Berlin.

Rada, U. 1997: *Haupstadt der Verdrängung – Berliner Zukunft zwischen Kietz und Metropole*. Berlin: Verlag Schwarze Risse – Rote Strasse.

——1999: Die Rückkehr des Flaneurs. *Tageszeitung*, 5870, June 26, 21.

Ronneberger, K., Lanz, S., and Jahn, W. 1999: *Die Stadt als Beute*. Bonn: Dietz.

Rose, M. D. 1998: *Berlin, Hauptstadt von Filz und Korruption.* Munich: Droemer Knaur.

Rouyer, A. 1997: Berlin ou l'ambition métropolitaine: nostalgie ou renaissance de la Weltstadt? In P. Claval and A.-L. Sanguin (eds.), *Métropolisation et Politique.* Paris: L'Harmattan.

Smith, N. 1992: New city, new frontier: the Lower East Side as wild, wild West. In M. Sorkin (ed.), *Variations on a Theme Park: The New American City and the End of Public Space.* New York: Hill and Wang.

Strom, E. A. 2001: *Building the New Berlin: The Politics of Urban Development in Germany's Capital City.* Lanham, MD: Lexington Books.

Süss, W. and Rabe, H. 1995: *Stadtmarketing, eine Berliner Fallstudie.* Berlin: Freie Universität.

Ward, S. V. 1998: *Selling Places: The Marketing and Promotion of Towns and Cities, 1850–2000.* London: E. & F. N. Spon.

Zukin, S. 1995: *The Cultures of Cities.* Oxford: Blackwell.

Newspaper Articles

Darmstadter Echo 1997: Ein Wald aus Kränen als Skyline des Umbruchs. Ich bin ein Maurer. June 18.

Scheinschlag 1998: Authentizität als Kulisse. February.

—— 1999: Im Angebot: eine vollkommen neue Stadt. June.

Süddeutsche Zeitung 1995: Werbung für die alter Brot- und Spiele-Mentalität. July 8–9.

12

Museums as Flagships of Urban Development

Chris Hamnett and Noam Shoval

Once it [the museum] was a place that had instruction and the propagation of a particular view of the world as its underpinning. Now it [the museum] has come to be seen as an urban landmark – a replacement for the missing agora, a place devoted to spectacle. (Sudjic 1993: 143)

Introduction: The Growing Importance of the Cultural Economy of Cities

The late twentieth century has seen a dramatic transformation in the structure of western capitalist economies. The era of large-scale manufacturing production and employment in the nineteenth and early twentieth centuries has increasingly given way since the mid-1960s to a "post-Fordist" services-dominated economy. While industrial production is still important, employment in this sector has fallen sharply, and employment growth has been in financial, business, and personal services and what are termed the "cultural" industries. The scale and importance of this transformation have been most marked in old nineteenth-century cities which have been a locus of large-scale de-industrialization and economic restructuring. While some of these cities are still struggling with the legacy of economic and physical decline, others have been successful in transforming themselves into centers of post-Fordist production and consumption. In the process, the structure of their economies and their employment base has shifted away from manufacturing to a more strongly service and culturally based economy.

The significance of these developments has not gone unremarked. While considerable attention has been devoted to the growing financial importance of global cities (Sassen 1990), Zukin suggested in *The Cultures of Cities* that: "With the disappearance of local manufacturing industries and periodic crises in government and finance, culture is more and more the business of cities: the basis of their tourist attractions and their unique competitive edge" (1995: 1). Similarly, Scott argues in *The Cultural Economy of Cities* that "capitalism itself is moving into a phase in which the cultural forms and meanings of its outputs are becoming critical if not dominating elements of productive strategy." He states that: "the cultural economy is coming to the fore as one of the most dynamic frontiers of capitalism at the dawn of the twenty-first century" and he sees this as "especially evident in a number of giant cities representing the flagships of a new global capitalist cultural economy" (2000: 2–3). We are seeing a shift to an economy where stress is more on the production and consumption of experiences than on physical products. As such, the symbolic economy has become more important (see Rybcznski 2003).

Given these trends, it is not surprising that cultural industries and "cultural strategies" have become important elements in urban policies. As Harvey perceptively pointed out, there has been a reorientation in attitudes to urban governance in the past 20 years whereby the "managerial" approach so typical of the 1960s has given way to initiatory and "entrepreneurial" forms of action in the 1970s and 1980s (1989: 4). Harvey identified four main options for urban entrepreneurialism. The first involves the development of a competitive edge in the international division of labor; the second is the attempt to gain control over the key control and command functions in business and finance; and the third focuses on competitive edge regarding the redistribution of central state spending. It is the fourth one which particularly concerns us here. Harvey argued that the urban region can "seek to improve its competitive position with respect to the spatial division of consumption." More specifically, he argued that:

> Gentrification, cultural innovation, and physical upgrading of the urban environment (including the turn to post-modernist styles of architecture and urban design), consumer attractions (sports stadia, convention and shopping centres, marinas, exotic eating places) and entertainment (the organisation of urban spectacles on a temporary or permanent basis) have become much more prominent facets of strategies for urban regeneration. Above all, the city has to appear as an innovative, exciting, creative, and safe place to live or to visit, to play and consume in. (ibid.: 9)

Boyle and Hughes (1994: 467) point out that this shift has tended to be associated with the move of local government "away from the provision of items of collective consumption to the speculative use of local funds for local economic development," which can lead to a legitimation crisis. One way in which the local state may seek to restore legimacy is by high profile place marketing events which "help to consolidate support for entrepreneurialism by cultivating a new sense of place identity rooted in the idea of inter-locality competition for inward investment" (ibid.: 467). But, as Boyle and Hughes have argued in the context of Glasgow's 1990 designation as a European City of Culture, attempts to justify entrepreneurialism are not always without conflict.

In this chapter we are concerned with just one form of cultural consumption, that of the prestige museum or art gallery. Though there is now a considerable literature on the museum as a cultural phenomenon (Zolberg 1981), there is little specifically in the urban literature (but see Zukin 1995 for her analysis of the Massachusetts Museum of Contemporary Art). Our approach is based, in part, on the transformation which has taken place in the post-Fordist economy of cities and interprets the recent growth in the number of museums and visitors in terms of the growing importance accorded by city governments to new forms of cultural consumption as part of a new regime of regulation. We also argue, however, that changes in the social structure of advanced capitalist societies, particularly the growth of a new educated middle class with specific cultural demands, have also been important in enhancing the role of the museum. While museums may play a valuable function as a tool for modern urban development, they also serve other social and cultural functions, and their growing importance cannot simply be ascribed to the needs of urban governance. Rather, it can be seen as a coincidence of events between the "cultural logic of late capitalism" (Jameson 1989), the growing development of urban tourism, the search for cultural capital by the new middle class, a desire for spectacular architecture, and the growth of place promotion by cities.

The Emergence and Transformation of the Modern Museum

The establishment of the British Museum in 1753 and the transformation of the Louvre into a museum in the beginning of the nineteenth century marked a new era in urban cultural development in which museums of art, archaeology and natural science began to appear in most major cities in Europe and North America (Thomkins 1973; Feldstein 1991). Museum construction in this period was part of a strong national and municipal desire to establish the cultural credentials of cities and put them on the map in cultural terms. In this explosion of national and metropolitan cultural pride, no city was complete without its prestige art galleries and museums.

Until relatively recently, however, these museums tended to be elitist in outlook and saw their main tasks as the promotion of scholarship and conservation with exhibitions and displays mounted for a relatively small number of culturally knowledgeable visitors who would generally know what they were viewing and its wider significance (Richards 1996: 8). Such an audience did not need stylish displays or signposting. For other visitors who were not members of the cultural elite, museums were generally seen as boring, dull and old-fashioned, full of badly laid out and badly lit dowdy display cases (Burt 1977; Bourdieu and Darbel 1991). The past ten to twenty years, however, have seen a dramatic change in both the role, character, nature and design of museums and in museum visitors. In the late twentieth century, a growing number of museums have become centers of style and design, blockbuster exhibitions, corporate patronage, and cultural distinction. Museums are places to go: they are places to see and be seen. In addition, in the search for social distinction in a more populist age, marked by the expansion of a wealthy professional and managerial middle class, art and patronage of art museums have become powerful new sources of cultural distinction (Bourdieu 1984). Today museums are more customer-oriented since they frequently have to rely more on admission charges, corporate sponsorship and other commercial activities than on shrinking public funding. Finally, given the success of some spectacular new and refurbished museums in attracting large numbers of visitors, and generating jobs and visitor spending, museums now have a growing role as "tools" for urban regeneration.

The growing importance of culture in contemporary society together with the rising importance of tourism in the economic base of post-industrial cities has led in recent years to the construction of new "Flagship Museums" (in terms of both their size and spectacular architecture) in cities and the expansion of many existing museums. There are a number of well-known examples of such new museums like the Guggenheim Museum in Bilbao, the Getty Museum in Los Angeles, the Musée d'Orsay in Paris, and the newly opened Tate Modern in the former Bankside power station in London. Because of the radical, dramatic, and spectacular nature of the architecture of these buildings, they arguably function as tourist attractions in their own right in addition to, or even ahead of, the art they contain. Sudjic (1993: 145) comments that: "The collection has clearly taken second place to the idea of the museum as a place to be." We would also add "or to see."

Urban Cultural Tourism and Museums

The view that cities perform an important function as centers of urban tourism is now well established (Ashworth and Tunbridge 1990; Law 1993; Page 1995; van den Berg et al. 1995; Law 1996; Mazanec 1997; Judd and Fainstein 1999). But more generally, we would argue that the expansion of the professional/managerial educated middle class in Western capitalist economies, which has been documented by Myles (1988), Wright and Martin (1987), Butler and Savage (1995), Ley (1996) and others, has been crucial in underpinning the emergence of a expanded new interest in culture and the arts. In part, the interest can be seen as a reflection of the growth of liberal arts education and the greater attention devoted to the arts in the media, but in part it can also be interpreted as a search for a source of social distinction. Bourdieu (1984: 2) has argued that the socially recognized hierarchy of the arts "predisposes tastes to function as markers of class" and that "art and cultural consumption are predisposed, consciously and deliberately or not, to fulfil a social function of legitimating social differences" (ibid.: 6). The formation of private collections, the endowment of museums, and the distinction conferred by art appreciation and philanthropy have a long history. This can be seen in the endowment of individual pictures, whole collections, and new wings or buildings at the Metropolitan Museum of Art, the Tate and elsewhere (Thomkins 1973; Burt 1977).

These trends have consolidated a major new segment in urban tourism: that of cultural tourism. Visiting cities for the purpose of cultural consumption is not new, of course; the aristocratic European "Grand Tour" of the seventeenth and eighteenth centuries was mainly an urban phenomenon (Towner 1985, 1996). It was, however, elitist and small-scale, whereas today the expansion of the demand for new forms of cultural consumption has changed the character of tourism to cities, enabling localities to initiate strategies for urban development based on cultural consumption by tourists as well as the local population. In the process, visiting museums has become something of a mass consumption activity for many urban tourists. The Van Gogh Museum in Amsterdam and Rembrandt's "Night Watch" at the Rijksmuseum are now part of the mass tourist experience, along with Leonardo da Vinci's Mona Lisa at the Louvre for visitors to Paris.

The rapid growth in urban tourism in recent decades has led some cities to adopt tourism as a central tool in their strategies for achieving urban regeneration (Owen 1990; Page 1993; Judd 1995; Robertson 1995) as well as using arts and culture for the same purpose (Whitt 1987). Law (1992, 1993) has indicated that many European cities in the 1980s adopted an

Table 12.1 The ten most visited attractions (in millions of visitors) in London, Paris, and New York, 1997

	London		Paris		New York	
1	British Museum	6.1	Notre Dame	12	Ellis Island and Statue of Liberty	5
2	National Gallery	4.8	Montmartre	6	Metropolitan Museum of Art	5
3	Madame Tussaud's	2.8	Eiffel Tower	5.7	American Museum of Natural History	3.5
4	Westminster Abbey	2.5	Louvre	5.2	Empire State Building	3.5
5	Tower of London	2.6	Pompidou Center	4.4	World Trade Center Observation Deck	1.8
6	Tate Gallery	1.8	City of Science, La Villette	3.4	Museum of Modern Art (MOMA)	1.7
7	St Paul's Cathedral	2	Versailles	2.7	Guggenheim Museum	0.9
8	Natural History Museum	1.8	Musée D'Orsay	2.3	Brooklyn Museum of Art	0.6
9	Science Museum	1.5	L'Arc de Triomphe	1.2	National Museum of the American Indian	0.4
10	Chessington World of Adventure	1.8	Natural History Museum	1.1	Museum of the City of New York	0.4

Sources: Trew (1999: 59), Citrinot (1999a: 56), Citrinot (1999b: 72).

urban tourism strategy following the examples of such strategies in American cities like Baltimore and Boston in the 1970s, and within such an urban tourism strategy, urban cultural policy has become increasingly important. Museums have been seen as especially important in such strategies for several reasons. First, a "Flagship Museum" usually becomes a must-see attraction for visitors to the city and, by *extending* their average stay in the city, it results in more money being spent in the city. Second, a museum with constantly changing exhibits helps to attract *repeat* visitors. Third, in addition to the cultural importance of the museum collections, spectacular museums have become an attraction in themselves and often become icons for the city as a whole. Last but not least, museums also serve the local population and are not just geared towards visitors to the city. This helps to justify funding these costly institutions by the public. The importance of these large-scale museums in the overall tourist offerings of cities is reflected in table 12.1, which shows the ten most visited tourist sites in 1997 in London, Paris, and New York respectively. Of the top ten attractions in London and Paris, five are museums or galleries, as are eight of the ten in New York. This suggests museums are now a key part of urban cultural tourism, and Tate Modern in London, which opened in 2001, is now attracting over five million visitors a year.

The Changing Nature of the Museum

> The transformation of art museums in the 1980s from purveyors of a particular elite culture to fun palaces for an increasing number of middle class art consumers has to be seen within the dual perspective of government policies and business initiatives. (Wu 1998: 30)

As noted above, recent decades have witnessed a dramatic re-orientation of museums throughout the world. Museums traditionally focused on collection of artifacts, creation of scientific catalogues and the display of as much as possible of their collections and were mostly funded by the state or by wealthy individuals as a philanthropic activity. But as a result of shrinking support of the state and the need to find new sources of income for their activities, they face the inherent conflict of being rich in art and poor in operating budgets (Feldstein 1991: 2). This, together with the greater interest of the public in art and culture has led museums to a change of attitude in many respects. New ways of display have been introduced, more entrepreneurial strategies have been adopted, new sources of finance such as corporate funding have appeared, there has been a growing use of blockbuster exhibitions, and museums have become more and more consumer oriented. Januszczak (1988) has described Nicolas Serota's task at the Tate as being to make it "the biggest funpalace in Europe." Similarly, Wu (1998: 40) states regarding the tenure of Thomas Hoving as director of the Metropolitan Museum in New York, that Hoving:

> deliberately ventured into costly undertakings – new wings, blockbuster exhibitions and expensive acquisitions, forcing the museum into a desperate search for new sources of income. Hoving's regime at the Met successfully transformed the traditional operation of the art museum from a warehouse of art artefacts into that of an entrepreneurial undertaking.

The conversion of many museums into entrepreneurial undertakings has had several dimensions which we discuss below.

Museum shops and restaurants. Museum shops have turned from small places for selling books and artifacts related to the museum to a key retail attraction and a central component of the museum, selling a wide range of prod-

Plate 12.1 Inside the Musée D'Orsay, Paris. *Source*: Susan S. Fainstein

ucts, many of them not directly related to the museum itself. The leading museums have even developed chains of museum shops in different locations outside the museum (Aldin 2002). The same is true regarding museum coffee shops and restaurants, which have become an increasingly important element of the museum experience. As Sudjic (1993: 138) has cynically commented: "At the Louvre, one of the primary results of the I. M. Pei pyramid has been to create an elegant means of providing natural light for an underground shopping centre."

Hiring out the museum. An integral part of the trend towards the commodification of museums has been their use for private and corporate events and entertaining at the evening and weekends. Museums offer an unparalleled range of both spaces and exhibits and the possibility of hiring them for a party; a reception or meeting can raise the profile or exclusivity of the event. In addition, it offers a cultural cachet and private access to a cultural display, which would not be otherwise available.

Corporate sponsorship. Wu (1998) outlines how corporate capital is playing a growing role in the financing of art museums today. The corporate focus on art museums is, according to Wu, because their visitors rank higher in socio-economic terms than those visiting other types of museums, even though museum audiences in general are already disproportionately privileged in socio-economic terms compared to the population as a whole (ibid.: 36–7). Corporate sponsorship is also very prominent in prestige cultural events such as Covent Garden opera, and classical concerts at the Barbican and the Royal Festival Hall in London. The parallels with Bourdieu's analysis of distinction are strong.

Blockbuster exhibitions. The most significant effect of the shift in funding from public to corporate funding is the new emphasis being placed on "blockbuster exhibitions" (ibid.: 39). These exhibitions are a central theme of contemporary museum management and curatorship. They reduce vast and complicated museums to a defined and easily understood product, thereby making museums more accessible to the average visitor. Since they attract repeat visitors both locally and from abroad, they help the museum to increase the numbers of visitors. Such exhibitions generally charge a separate and relatively high entrance fee, and the exhibitions are usually backed with corporate sponsorship. In the process, the publicity surrounding such shows helps create a "must-see" cultural ethos among the museum-going public and helps to ensure that their success is aided by exclusive previews and viewings for the social elite.

Branding and franchising. There is a small but growing trend for museums to open branches in new locations. This arises as a result of several factors: Museums generally have much more art than they have the space to exhibit and they are keen to solve some of their problems due to lack of storage space and the high costs of preservation of artifacts in storage (Clarke 1991: 305). In Britain an official commission found that only about one-third of art collections are on display at any time (Lord et al. 1989). For small places outside the major global or national nodes of tourism and cultural production, a branch of an existing museum may seem to be more prestigious than a local museum. Using the name of a successful museum is valuable in terms of name recognition (*branding*). Another form of branding is the use of a world famous architect, so the museum is branded by its spectacular architectural design and not by the character of the display.

A new commercial strategy that has been adopted among museums recently is the idea of *franchising*. The most prominent exemplar of this strategy is the Guggenheim Museum of New York which, under the leadership of its then chairman Thomas Kren, had for several years been involved in franchising the Guggenheim name and collection to different cities in the world such as Berlin, Bilbao and, most recently, Las Vegas (*The Economist*, April 21, 2001). Kren's plans to create the "Museum of the Twenty-First Century" involved the Guggenheim selling itself as a brand, allowing local operators to pay for new premises in their locality, buying curatorial skills, and benefiting from a continuous circulation of the museum's stock (the central branch can display less than 5 percent of its total holdings at a time) (McNeill 2000: 480). Critics have termed this process McGuggenization, suggesting both the global franchising strategy and the extreme commodification of art (ibid.: 474).

Creation of Spectacle: Museums and Signature Architecture

Nineteenth- and early twentieth-century galleries and museums were built on monumental neo-classical lines. They embodied solidity and respectability. The last decades of the twentieth century have, however, seen the construction of what is arguably a wholly new phenomenon: museums as architectural spectacles. Because of the radical, dramatic and spectacular nature of the architecture of these buildings, they arguably function as tourist attractions in their own right in addition to the art they contain. It is possible to identify a series of such key futuristic buildings in major cities. The first was Frank Lloyd Wright's Guggenheim Museum in New York. This building broke the mold in terms of the architecture associated with museums and art galleries. Also some existing museums have chosen to redevelop in a dramatic way, creating the glass pyramids of the Louvre, the Great Court of the British Museum or the "bird in flight sculpture" of the Milwaukee art museum. A prototype of the use of spectacular architecture in regard to cultural buildings is the Sydney Opera House designed by Jørn Utzon in the late 1950s and the early 1960s, which has become one of Sydney's and Australia's symbols. It has become a must-see site of the tourist gaze (see Urry 1990). More importantly, these new urban landmarks like the Guggenheim in Bilbao can present an image of innovation and excitement which are transmitted far beyond the city. Indeed, the role of architecture and architects has become steadily more important. It is no longer sufficient merely to construct a large building to accommodate a collection. On the contrary, the buildings are now sometimes as important, if not more important, than the collection they are designed to house. They provide a bridge between the need of city governments for high visibility, prestige cultural projects and the needs of museums to generate greater public awareness and attendance. In figure 12.1, two sets of processes are depicted, one is regulation external to the museum and the second is regulation that is internal. The linkage between the two processes is the spectacular architecture which can be seen to serve the requirements of museums, their sponsors, visitors and city governments.

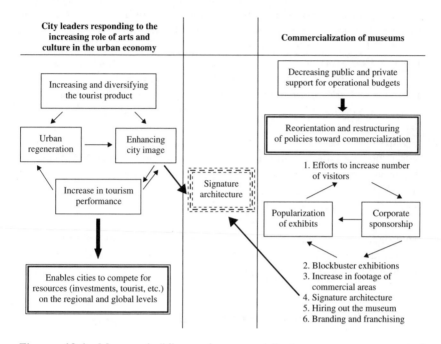

Figure 12.1 Museum building and commercialization process: a conceptual framework

Flagship Museums as Anchors of Regeneration

> Museums are pump primers, their presence can be compared to the opening of a subway station, or even an airport: an investment which has the effect of raising property values. They have the ability to raise the profile of a development, bringing life into an area. (Sudjic 1993: 141)

The new wave of museum buildings also highlights a new phase of location policy of museums in cities. The first phase emerged during the second half of the nineteenth century, when museum clusters in cities like London and Washington were established. These examples were later followed by many other cities such as Amsterdam, Frankfurt, Jerusalem, Cleveland, Stockholm, and Rotterdam.

The second, more recent, phase of museum location in large cities is characterized by the building of large museums outside the traditional clusters to enable regeneration and spatial expansion of the Tourist City. In London the new Tate in Southwark serves as an anchor for regeneration and cultural production on the South Bank of the Thames through a series of cultural institutions such as the Shakespeare Globe Theatre, the London Eye, the London Aquarium, the National Theatre, the Hayward Gallery, and the Museum of the Moving Image. The highly successful London Eye and the Tate Modern (3.5 and 5 million visitors, respectively in their first year of operation) create two anchors of activity that link the cultural attractions of the South Bank and foster expansion of the central tourist district of London through the new Millennium bridge and Westminster Bridge to this formerly peripheral part of the city (Teedon 2001). Most recently, the *New York Times* (Dunlap 2001) reported that: "Lower Manhattan has become a cultural destination in its own right capitalising on the growing popular interest in heritage and history. A dozen museums are now operating, and several important ones will be arriving in the next few years." In addition to the change in image, large cultural complexes are often said to have a direct impact on regeneration in nearby areas where secondary tourism services such as restaurants, hotels, shops and art galleries may emerge. The extent to which these secondary developments become a reality remains an open question.

Regime, Scale, and Museum Development

Given the decline of major cities as traditional centers of manufacturing production and the growing importance of the cultural industries and consumption in the economy of major cities (Pratt 1997; Scott 1997, 2000), it is not surprising that the business community and government have taken a stronger interest in the promotion of cities as centers of cultural production and consumption. In the new era of mobile international firms, investment, and visitors, the image of a city is becoming increasingly important, as is place promotion (Gold and Ward 1993; Kearns and Philo 1993; Ward 1998). As a result, different levels of government have become increasingly proactive in place promotional activities. Such activities now take a number of forms, ranging from competition for key international sporting and exhibition events such as the Olympics (Roche 2000; Whitelegg 2000; Burbank et al. 2001) to the cultural primacy manifested in the development of opera houses, symphony orchestras, and museums.

It is difficult, however, to identify a simple or consistent model of regulation which accounts for the variety of ways in which museums are founded, funded and promoted in different cities. In some cases, the key actors are wealthy individuals or philanthropic trusts, while in others the central or local state has been pivotal. Although there are some privately funded museums or galleries in Europe, the state has traditionally been more significant than in North America. The privately funded Getty Museum and Armand Hammer Gallery in Los Angeles and the Rock and

Roll Hall of Fame in Cleveland are unusual in a contemporary European context, where state patronage is far more important, directly or indirectly, through state-funded art organizations.

In Britain the Arts Council, a quasi-governmental organization for the development of arts policy and funding distribution, has traditionally played a key role. More recently, the National Lottery Commission has distributed large amounts of money to the arts, particularly to assisting the construction of new museums. These have included a £50 million grant toward the cost of the New Tate, as well as funding the rebuilding of Covent Garden Opera, the Scottish Museum of Modern Art in Edinburgh, and new galleries in Salford and Wolverhampton. In general, central government in Britain has not taken on responsibility for planning the location for new galleries and museums, but has instead responded to requests from below. In France, however, perhaps unsurprisingly, given its strong statist legacy and the strong political links between Paris and central government, central government has taken a stronger role. Sudjic (1993: 136) comments on the plethora of new museums in Paris: "To Mitterrand, it is the duty of the French state to build museums, for a variety of reasons, only one of which is the enlightenment of its citizens. An even stronger . . . factor is the recurring French mission of making Paris the unchallenged centre of European culture."

Intervention on the regional level is usually typical in federal states such as the United States, Germany, Australia, and Canada, where competition exists between different states or provinces for resources allocated by the central government or by the private sector. Each state usually has a leading city, which serves as its financial capital and sometimes as the administrative capital as well. Since this city is in most cases the "engine" for economic growth in the region, the state often tries to promote urban development schemes in the city, and today more and more of these are related to culture and tourism. In the case of museums, the hope is that their establishment will attract visitors from outside the region and thereby contribute to both the city and the regional economy.

Intervention at the local level is the most common practice among the three levels of regulation, and this reflects the shifting of the balance from the nation to the city and its region in terms of economic development and image (Harvey 1989; Bianchini and Parkinson 1993). Attracting international investment has become more important in the contemporary global economy, and cities have to create a civic image that will be attractive for investment. The creation of flagship museums is one potential tool for generating this image. They hopefully serve to convince prospective investors that the city has all that is good in civic life, including art, culture, and general quality of the social milieu (Robertson and Guerrier 1998: 218).

However, due to different systems of municipal organization, finance, and legislative rules, not all cities have similar possibilities for promoting museum development in their jurisdiction. Paris and New York possess both governing structures and potential demand that allows substantial initiatives. Thus, New York was considering donating land and money for a new $678 million Guggenheim Museum in Lower Manhattan (*The Independent*, November 29, 2000). The mayor of Paris has also been active in initiating major projects. In contrast, London has lacked an overall governing body since the Greater London Council was disbanded in 1987. A mayor for Greater London was recently elected, but his ability to promote major endeavors is restricted due to the limited budget of the newly established body. Moreover, notwithstanding the conventional wisdom of cultural regeneration, the degree to which such developments have proved successful appears very variable, particularly outside the major cities. In some cases, such as the Museum of Rock Music in Sheffield and the Royal Armories museum in Leeds, visitor numbers have proved disappointing. In general, despite the success of Bilbao, a critical mass of attractions seems essential for visitor numbers.

There remains, in addition, a question of who benefits from the creation of new urban "cultural" policies. Cities may now be "places to play" (Judd and Fainstein 1999), but Eisinger (2000: 317) argues that:

> building a city as an entertainment venue is a very different undertaking than building a city to accommodate residential interests. Although the former objective is often justified as a means to generate the resources to accomplish the latter aim, the two are not easily reconciled.

He suggests that:

> the city as a place to play is manifestly built for the middle classes, who can afford to attend professional sporting events, eat in the new outdoor cafes, attend trade and professional conventions, shop in the festival malls, and patronise the high and middlebrow arts. (ibid.: 317)

In Eisinger's view, courting the middle class as visitors may mean the creation of a very different sort of city from that designed to bring the middle classes back as residents or to serve the needs of the resident population. These issues were highlighted in the conflicts over the designation of Glasgow as European City of Culture in 1990 (Boyle and Hughes 1994). In our view, these issues have not yet been systematically addressed by city governments, which seemingly tend to see all cultural development as inherently beneficial.

Conclusion

Art gallery construction and conversion are major activities today. No self-respecting city is now complete without a major new gallery, preferably designed by a world famous architect which functions as a statement about its cultural pride, attraction, and status. In our view, the promotion of art and cultural visibility more generally is now a key component of urban policy in a wide range of major cities. To be without a symphony orchestra, opera house, and art gallery effectively condemns a city to the second rank. Culture is now a key element of urban competition, both in terms of civic pride and image and also in terms of its ability to attract both visitors and footloose national and multinational companies via the quality of urban life on offer to the large new class of educated professional and managerial workers. It is also an important prospective tool for urban regeneration, though how feasible or realistic it is to successfully translate this from major cities to smaller, older industrial cities with little in the way of cultural assets or existing visitors remains an open question. With a few exceptions, opening or relocating a new museum in a city far from existing centers and where there are few significant existing attractions is unlikely to prove successful, as visitor volume will not be there. But opening new museums in cities like Edinburgh or York (which already has York Minster, the medieval city, the National Railway Museum, and the Jarvik Viking Museum) can build on the existing critical cultural mass.

We have argued in this chapter that urban cultural tourism is now a significant element of urban tourism in general, and that the role of spectacular museum architecture, new museums and "blockbuster" exhibitions are now a key element in this. These trends can be argued to have met the needs of museums themselves, their sponsors and city governments. The cultural image of cities is important in increasing tourist numbers, in promoting the image of cities as place to live and work, in urban regeneration and as an element of interurban competition (Gomez 1998: 110). It is a key way for cities to insert themselves into the "space of flows" of global tourism, and the museum is now a key element in the symbolic image of place (Hannigan 1998) and in the regulatory regimes of many contemporary cities. In post-Fordist economies where cultural images and attributes are now a key element in inter-urban competition, prestige museums are increasingly a desirable commodity to be funded, sought, and competed for, rather than simply being seen as a drain on the budgets of hard-pressed city governments.

Prestige museums also offer a potential vehicle for reinforcing the legitimacy of city and regional governments in social, cultural, and economic terms. The development and success of such museums can be seen as an endorsement of the cultural policy of city governments, and they can also be promoted in economic terms as enhancing the cultural attraction of the cities concerned as a place to live and work. Even in the heyday of what has been termed "municipal socialism" in nineteenth- and early twentieth-century Britain, municipal success was measured not simply in terms of utility provision but also in terms of the provision of cultural facilities for the population. Briggs (1968: 64) states that: "In Birmingham, civic pride was the driving force of a whole civic philosophy" and the civic art gallery was built in 1876 on the profits of the municipal gasworks. The inscription in the entrance hall reads: "By the gains of industry we promote art." Today we might add "By the gains of art we also hope to promote industry." The legitimating role of museums is not guaranteed, however. For this, they have to be successful, and as we have shown, not all are.

REFERENCES

Aldin, R 2002: Pay and display: you've seen the exhibition, now buy the amphora. *The Times*, April 13.

Ashworth, G. J. and Tunbridge, J. E. 1990: *The Tourist-Historic City*. London: Belhaven.

Bianchini, F. and Parkinson, M. 1993: *Cultural Policy and Urban Regeneration: The West European Experience*. Manchester: Manchester University Press.

Bourdieu, P. 1984: *Distinction: A Social Critique of the Judgement of Taste*. London: Routledge.

——and Darbel, A. 1991: *The Love of Art: European Art Museums and their Public*. Cambridge: Polity Press.

Boyle, M. and Hughes, G. 1994: The politics of urban entrepreneurialism in Glasgow. *Geoforum* 25 (4): 453–70.

Briggs, A. 1968: *Victorian Cities*. Harmondsworth: Penguin.

Burbank, M. J., Andranovich, G. D., and Heying, C. H. 2001: *Olympic Dreams: The Impact of Mega-Events on Local Politics*. Boulder, CO: Lynne Reiner Publishers.

Burt, N. 1977: *Palaces for the People: A Social History of the American Art Museum*. New York: Little Brown and Co.

Butler, T. and Savage, M. 1995: *Social Change and the Middle Classes*. London: UCL Press.

Citrinot, L. 1999a: Paris. *Travel and Tourism Intelligence City Reports* 1 (1): 53–75.

——1999b: New York. *Travel and Tourism Intelligence City Reports* 1 (3): 53–73.

Clarke, R. 1991: Government policy and art museums in the United Kingdom. In M. Feldstein (ed.) *The Economics of Art Museums*. Chicago: University of Chicago Press.

Dunlap, D. 2001: New melting pot of museums downtown. *New York Times* (Metro), August 5.

Eisinger, P. 2000: The politics of bread and circuses: building the city for the visitor class. *Urban Affairs Review* 35 (3): 316–33.

Feldstein, M. (ed.) 1991: *The Economics of Art Museums*. Chicago: University of Chicago Press.

Gold, J. and Ward, S. V. (eds.) 1993: *Place Promotion: The Use of Publicity and Public Relations to Sell Cities*. Chichester: John Wiley & Sons.

Gomez, M. V. 1998: Reflective images: the case of urban regeneration in Glasgow and Bilbao. *International Journal of Urban and Regional Research* 22 (1): 106–21.

Hannigan, J. 1998: *Fantasy City: Pleasure and Profit in the Postmodern Metropolis*. London: Routledge.

Harvey, D. 1989: From managerialism to entrepreneurialism: the transformation in urban governance. *Geographiska Annaler* 71 (B.1): 3–17.

Janusczak, W. 1988: The shock of Serota. *Guardian*, November 26.

Jameson, F. 1989: Postmodernism or the cultural logic of late capitalism, *New Left Review* 146: 53–92.

Judd, D. R. 1995: Promoting tourism in US cities. *Tourism Management* 16 (3): 175–87.

——and Fainstein, S. S. (eds.) 1999: *The Tourist City*. New Haven, CT: Yale University Press.

Kearns, G. and Philo, C. 1993: *Selling Places: The City as Cultural Capital, Past and Present*. Oxford: Pergamon Press.

Law, C. M. 1992: Urban tourism and its contribution to economic regeneration. *Urban Studies* 29 (3–4): 599–618.

——1993: *Urban Tourism: Attracting Visitors to Large Cities*. London: Mansell.

——1996: *Tourism in Major Cities*. London: Routledge.

Ley, D. 1996: *The New Middle Class and the Remaking of the Central City*. Oxford: Oxford University Press.

Lord, B., Lord, G. D., and Nicks, J. 1989: *The Cost of Collecting: Collection Management in UK Museums*. London: HMSO.

Mazanec, J. A. (ed.) 1997: *International City Tourism: Analysis and Strategy*. London: Pinter.

McNeill, D. 2000: McGuggenisation? National identity and globalisation in the Basque country. *Political Geography* 19 (4): 473–94.

Myles, J 1988: The expanding middle: Canadian evidence on the deskilling debate, *Canadian Review of Sociology and Anthropology*, 25, 335–64.

Owen, C. 1990: Tourism and urban regeneration. *Cities* 7 (3): 194–201.

Page, S. J. 1993: Urban tourism in New Zealand: the National Museum of New Zealand project. *Tourism Management* 14 (3): 211–17.

——1995: *Urban Tourism*. London: Routledge.

Pratt, A. 1997: The cultural production system: a case study of employment change in Britain, 1984–91. *Environment and Planning A* 29: 1953–74.

Richards, G. 1996: Introduction: culture and tourism in Europe. In G. Richards (ed.), *Cultural Tourism in Europe*. Wallingford, UK: CAB International.

Robertson, K. A. 1995: Downtown redevelopment strategies in the United States: an end-of-the-century assessment. *Journal of the American Planning Association* 61 (4): 429–37.

Robertson, M. and Guerrier, Y. 1998: Events as entrepreneurial displays: Seville, Barcelona and Madrid. In D. Tyler, Y. Guerrier, and M. Robertson (eds.), *Managing Tourism in Cities: Policy, Process and Practice*. Chichester: John Wiley & Sons.

Roche, M. 2000: *Mega-Events and Modernity: Olympics and Expos in the Growth of Global Culture*. London: Routledge.

Sassen, S. 1990: *The Global City: New York, London, Tokyo*. Princeton, NJ: Princeton University Press.

Scott, A. J. 1997: The cultural economy of cities. *International Journal of Urban and Regional Research* 21 (2): 323–40.

——2000: *The Cultural Economy of Cities: Essays on the Geography of Image-Producing Industries*. London: Sage.

Sudjic, D. 1993: *The 100 Mile City*. London: Flamingo.

Teedon, P. 2001: Designing a place called Bankside: on defining an unknown space in London. *European Planning Studies* 9 (4): 459–82.

Thomkins, C. 1973: *Merchants and Masterpieces: The Story of the Metropolitan Museum of Art*. New York: E. P. Dutton.

Towner, J. 1985: The Grand Tour: a key phase in the history of tourism. *Annals of Tourism Research* 12 (3): 297–333.

——1996: *An Historical Geography of Recreation and Tourism in the Western World 1540–1940*. Chichester: John Wiley & Sons.

Trew, J. 1999: London. *Travel and Tourism Intelligence City Reports* 1 (2): 37–63.

Urry, J. 1990: *The Tourist Gaze: Leisure and Travel in Contemporary Societies*. London: Sage Publications.

van den Berg, L., van der Borg, J., and van der Meer, J. 1995: *Urban Tourism: Performance and Strategies in Eight European Cities*. Aldershot: Avebury.

Ward, S. V. 1998: *Selling Places: The Marketing and Promotion of Towns and Cities, 1850–2000*. London: E. & F. N. Spon.

Whitelegg, D. 2000: Going for gold: Atlanta's bid for fame. *International Journal of Urban and Regional Research* 24 (4): 801–17.

Whitt, A. J. 1987: Mozart in the Metropolis: the arts coalition and the urban growth machine. *Urban Affairs Quarterly* 23 (1): 15–36.

Wright, E. and Martin, B. 1987: The transformation of the American class structure, 1960–1980, *American Journal of Sociology* 93: 1–29.

Wu, C. 1998: Embracing the enterprise culture: art institutions since the 1980s. *New Left Review* 230: 28–57.

Zolberg, V. 1981: Conflicting visions in American art museums. *Theory and Society* 10: 103–25.

Zukin, S. 1995: *The Cultures of Cities*. Oxford: Blackwell.

Part V

Conclusion

13 Making Theoretical Sense of Tourism
   Susan S. Fainstein, Lily M. Hoffman, and Dennis R. Judd

13

Making Theoretical Sense of Tourism

Susan S. Fainstein, Lily M. Hoffman, and Dennis R. Judd

Why Regulation Theory?

New York City wants to host the 2012 Olympic Games. The city first had to apply to a national organization which processed the bids from US cities and selected a finalist. Having been chosen, New York must now compete with cities in other countries before an international organization (the International Olympic Committee), which is governed globally. Both public and private sectors are active partners in NYC's application and lobbying takes place in local, state, federal, and international arenas. The NYC Olympic committee raised and spent over $11.5 million on its bid, and the former president of the "NYC2012" campaign is now deputy mayor for economic development (Bagli 2002). The stakes are high: NYC's Olympic plan calls for over $4 billion in construction and includes a new stadium, an extension of the subway system, waterfront development, and an Olympic Village. Along with infrastructure planning, NYC prepared a detailed security plan, widely considered to be among the strong points of the proposal (Sandomir and Bagli 2002).

At the same time, neighborhood and civic groups have mobilized against the Olympic bid or against specific components of it – the proposed stadium is a popular target. They are concerned about: the destruction of a working-class neighborhood on Manhattan's West Side, traffic congestion and density, the diversion of scarce state and city funds from

Plate 13.1   Resistance to plans for a stadium to house Olympic competition on Manhattan's West Side. *Source*: Andrew Schwartz

other uses, and the ratio of taxpayer costs to benefits (Bagli 2002; Chernikoff 2002). Supporters have mounted a media and public relations drive, promoting the competitive advantages of the city, the symbolic value of hosting a mega-event, and the potential gains in terms of infrastructure, visitors, and export dollars, for local and national economies.

This scenario places tourism within a complex matrix of economic, political, cultural, and spatial interactions and illustrates the interplay of sectors and scales – local, regional, national, and international. In adopting a broadly conceived regulation framework, our objective has been to examine these linkages and processes without sacrificing the possibilities of agency or overlooking the complex role of culture. Regulation theory, by stressing linkages rather than simple hierarchies, avoids collapsing the multi-dimensional flux of actors, sectors, geographic places, institutions, and levels of governance. It therefore enables "thick" analysis.

Non-deterministic structural analysis

First and foremost, regulation theory permits a non-deterministic form of structural analysis. The usual critique of structuralism is that it excludes agency and provides us with an economically determined account of institutions and outcomes. But regulation theory *builds in agency* while accepting that a given regime of accumulation structures systems. Take, for example, the analyses of the Olympic Games in Barcelona or the World Soccer Cup in France. These studies show that mega-events can be used in both a liberating and a repressive manner. In Barcelona, García and Claver found that the Olympic Games were used to benefit local residents as well as visitors, but that doing so was far from simple. They credit the local governing coalition for this achievement, a finding that underlines their criticism of the tendency to "overemphasize economic and industrial restructuring *per se*." In France, Body-Gendrot describes how a reformist mayor in St. Denis used the World Soccer Cup to address the social problems of the inner city. He was able to build a new stadium, control two-thirds of the new jobs related to the event, and involve high-risk kids from public housing projects in the events. Among the outcomes she also lists new linkages and lines of communication within the community. In neither case, however, were these outcomes typical of experiences with these kinds of events. The "Barcelona model" of restructuring was historically contingent, and as we move towards the present, we see Barcelona's governing coalition and political economy more closely resembling those of other European and US cities. St. Denis was a single example within a larger set, and the long-term results can be debated. All the same, the existence of these cases indicates the potential of using mega-events to promote progressive outcomes within a constraining political-economic structure.

Culture and political economy

A second analytic strength is that a regulation framework allows us to explore the relations between political economy and culture in a non-reductive fashion. Along these lines, the chapters in this book present a range of situations relevant to emerging post-Fordist urban economies, in which culture plays an independent as well as a mediating role. These include examples of cultural revalorization, the use of local culture as a political and spatial resource, and the creation of culture *de novo*.

Comparing places and sectors

Regulation theory also gives us a powerful methodological tool for comparative analysis of phenomena such as urban tourism. Breaking down regulation into several dimensions, as outlined in the Introduction, allows us to compare sectors and places as well as to trace back similarities and differences to a global system. The typology identifies four types of regulation or regulatory frameworks that structure relations within the tourism milieu: (1) regulation of visitors to protect the city; (2) regulation of the city for the benefit of visitors and the tourism industry; (3) regulation of labor markets for the benefit of capital, labor, and place; and (4) regulation of the industry for the benefit of place, consumers, and labor. Judd provides a general description of the first category — the forms of tourism regulation. The case studies then depict the emergence of urban tourism regimes, the processes by which they are supported and legitimated, and the shift from mass tourism to hypertourism and post-tourism. The issues raised by the regulation of visitors as well as of residents are particularly prominent in Judd's examination of the form of the tourist city and Body-Gendrot's discussion of the activities of the French state. The typology also allows us to compare the regulation of tourism labor markets in Los Angeles and New York with Montreal. Finally, the question of how the industry is regulated runs through the various discussions of the role of the state and of the changing tastes of tourists. We thus return to the scenario of NYC's Olympic bid, where we see the interplay of scales and sectors as localities lobby nationally and globally to capture events, in a competition which itself serves as a regulating force at the local level.

Changing Social Structure and its Impact on the Uses of the City

The authors in this book document the growing importance of visitors and tourism-related development to the political economy and culture of major cities. These empirical trends, which raise the issue of "whose city?", are often portrayed simplistically in studies of tourism, which typically posit a dichotomy between local residents and visitors. Recent scholarly work on transnational urbanism and city users overcomes this binarism to regard migrants and transients as authentic components of urban culture (Martinotti 1999; Smith 2001; Costa and Martinotti, this volume). For these scholars, local residents are not uniquely privileged in terms of defining the city; rather, the emphasis is on connections across the boundaries of localities and nations. This redefinition of the city – from a site of production or collective consumption to a node within global flows of people and capital (Castells 1977, 2000) – is not just based upon economic globalization, but takes into account transforming occupational structures, cultural assumptions, and social relationships.

Central to the political economy and symbolic representation of the transient experience are groups at various locations within the social structure: a greatly enlarged, educated group of consumers, drawn primarily from wealthy countries but also from the middle and upper strata of developing nations, who travel for business and pleasure; migrants and immigrants who fill the low-wage jobs in the expanding urban service sector and make frequent trips back to their home countries; students and "drifter tourists" who manage, on low budgets, to colonize certain urban neighborhoods (Gladstone 2001). They all belong to the cities they visit as well as to the locations of their primary residence or origin. We can trace the growth of a cosmopolitan consuming class and the structure of consumption within which it operates to recent changes in the global regime of accumulation. The expansion of industries and occupations primarily requiring symbolic manipulation (finance, producers' services, the professions, management and marketing echelons of manufacturing, computer content producers, etc.) and therefore higher levels of education, has led to more sophisticated tastes – particularly for travel and cuisine – and to the demand for cultural amenities. In addition, changes in the mode of production have required managers and technicians to move around the world rather than just down the hall to exercise their supervisory responsibilities. And, as businesses serve ever more dispersed clienteles, sales and marketing forces grow larger and travel more.

Well-to-do, highly educated consumers are not the only basis for an enlarged urban tourism. Working- and lower-middle-class populations have also gained greater access to travel as the costs have dropped and the market segmentation and deregulation of the post-Fordist period have expanded this sector of the market. In Europe, where air travel within the continent used to be extremely expensive, one may now purchase a cheap return ticket so that one can go from London to Paris or Amsterdam and back for a night on the town or a sporting event. Indeed, Amsterdammers complain that such visitors often avoid the expense of a hotel and choose to spend the entire night noisily partying. But in the merging of high-brow and low-brow cultures that characterizes the present age, some of these travelers, as Terhorst et al. note herein, may visit a museum the next day.

Overall, this regime of accumulation is characterized by the interpenetration of work and leisure. The result is the synergy of users and uses seen in Amsterdam, Barcelona, and New York City, as well as Australia's Gold Coast. Although post-modernists have recast the city as a site of "consumption" rather than production, this label is inaccurate in that the contemporary city *combines* work and play. In contrast to the industrial city where these boundaries were relatively rigid, they are relaxed due to the importance of relationships among the highly educated professionals at the heart of the expanded financial and producers services sector. This life style is epitomized by such institutions as the "business lunch" and corporate-funded cultural events that provide opportunities for networking. Hiernaux-Nicolas, writing about Mexico, and García and Claver, on Barcelona, note that during the Fordist era, tourism was a functionally discrete activity – you worked, then you played ("ritual inversion," in Costa and Martinotti's terminology). Mass (Fordist) tourism was, for the most part, non-urban – sun and sea – with perhaps a side trip to a nearby city.

Under post-Fordism, tourism is more integrated – even embedded – in everyday life for a growing segment of the population in affluent societies. This has resulted in growth in the number of city users, since residents ("as-if tourists") are also drawn to the sites that attract visitors (Judd, this volume). In this sense, diverse city users are reshaping the city even as they are responding to structures and stimuli produced by global and local regimes of accumulation. These trends, which have made for a new fit between cities and the global political economy, have social, political and spatial consequences. How have cities responded to these new opportunities and new threats?

As with previously emerging economic sectors, tourism requires various forms of assistance and support; is associated with large-scale change in forms of regulation and governance; and gives rise to opposition and resistance. Drawing on the case studies in this volume, we turn to two of the most important tasks of tourism regimes: promoting cities as places to visit, and providing stability and security in the face of change.

Promoting Cities – Cultural Capital and Place

Culture is the source of urban attraction and the key to a distinct and marketable identity. As tourism has become a growth industry, city marketing has taken off, and the need to signpost and brand attractions has increasingly led tourism regimes to emphasize performance and the ephemeral. The mere existence of local attractions, whether it be significant architecture, waterfront parks, or priceless art collections, does not guarantee a sufficient flow of visitors. So events are constantly being created and staged as cities compete with elaborate weekly schedules for a growing number of malls, parks, plazas and waterfronts. Representation and spectacle have become necessary aspects of city marketing.

But representations and symbols of culture can be multiple and conflicting as well as open to manipulation. The debates are then fought out not just at the level of theory, but also at the level of communities of place. Tourism's double-edged quality can also engender conflict. The emphasis on uniqueness, which may reinvigorate local traditions, also threatens to vulgarize those traditions by making them into commodities for sale. The tension between these tendencies is always present.

In the chapter on Harlem, Hoffman notes that the development of an economy based on representations of African-American identity and history makes for new opportunities for Harlem and its residents. She concludes that "cultural capital is the engine of growth in Harlem, with multiplier effects for residential and commercial development as well as retail and services." But exploiting cultural capital for the purpose of economic regeneration is a delicate matter. For some, the issue is economic ownership and control; for others it is preserving what they regard as authentic and evading the tourist gaze.

Nowhere, perhaps, is this issue of identity formation more strongly in question than in Berlin, as Häussermann and Colomb's chapter makes clear. The authors examine Berlin's efforts to move beyond its history as the capital of the Third Reich and its division into two sectors, to create something out of nothing – construction site tourism at Potsdamer Platz – and to build "spectacular urban landscapes" based upon large-scale cultural and architectural transformations. They conclude: "This has opened the way for material and cultural conflicts between the 'city of dreams' staged for tourists and the 'real' city experienced by its inhabitants."

Barcelona's modernization illustrates the synergy between two seemingly contradictory strands – the preservation and marketing of its history, architecture, and culture, and the construction of new tourist areas and of a modernized transportation infrastructure. According to García and Claver, these elements have increased the city's capacity for international competition for business as well as tourism, while reinforcing its unique local identity and civic pride. Barcelona's modernist culture is now known (and marketed) world-wide. The locally owned hotels and restaurants continue to make it a special place, but the relaxation of regulations that have protected local businesses and kept international firms at bay may bring unforeseen changes.

In Amsterdam, a permissive liberal culture has given rise to a dual image – the city of culture and the city of sex, drugs, and fun. Although this dualism was not devised for the purpose of attracting tourists, it has nevertheless had that effect. The dual image has survived differing urban regimes, although Terhorst et al. suggest that the present exponential growth of tourism may undermine the balance by diminishing public tolerance.

In answer to the question we posed in the Introduction – whether cities are becoming more alike or more differentiated – we find both processes occurring. Urban tourism promotes cultural differentiation as well as homogeneity or standardization. This is partly due to the nature of contemporary (post-Fordist) tourism, which requires a combination of the standardized and the unique, as well as to the interplay of scales and sectors discussed above. The case studies show that local actors do not act autonomously: local accumulation regimes incorporate state policy; local players may be attached to global interests; and global forces structure and constrain local activities. At the same time, place competition motivates local actors to draw upon local resources – history and culture but also social demography and politics – to fashion place-specific and even progressive responses. Furthermore, the mix of large- and small-scale providers within the industry, as well as the differing motives and wealth of visitors, acts to preserve local difference.

Despite the stereotype of the guided tour as the vehicle for mass tourism, most people travel by car or purchase cheap tickets. The flexibility and choice provided by these common modes of transportation mean that the majority of city visitors proceed without benefit of programmed activities or partake of guided tours for only part of their stays. The popular hop-on, hop-off tour buses and the numerous and popular, small walking tours exemplify the new flexibility grafted onto an older, more rigid form of mass travel. In sum, not only does the local component vary. The resulting *mix* of local and global varies from place to place and time to time, with the authors suggesting that there may be *more* rather than less differentiation.

The tension between differentiation and homogeneity makes for contradiction and conflict in urban tourism regimes. For example, difference attracts but is hard to maintain in a world linked by global flows of information, media, marketing, and finance. Although ethnic products and production will reach global markets just as surely as Disney will locate locally, the logic of flexible production, with its push towards product differentiation, raises issues of commodification and control as in Harlem or in Hamnett and Shoval's discussion of museums. The synergy among uses and users, one of the strengths of tourism as an urban development strategy, is itself contradictory for reasons related to differentiation/homogeneity. It works up to a point. But too much in the way of mixed-use development can destroy the often delicate balance of interests and thus consensus among the different city users. We see evidence of tip-over effects in Harlem, Barcelona, Amsterdam, and Venice.

Cities, defined historically by their diversity and difference, are challenged by tourism not to become tourist bubbles. In his chapter, Judd concludes that such tourist constructions have been developed in many places but do not necessarily take over the city, and he argues that among the attractions of urban tourism are the many opportunities for evading standardization and control.

The Politics of Regulation

Despite the fact that tourism is embedded within other economic sectors and in the everyday life of cities, it is recognized as a separate activity and industry by international development agencies and by governments at all levels. As a consequence, it is the object of regimes of accumulation, defined as the political-economic structures underlying production. Tourism regimes have recently become more elaborated and have also begun to converge in important ways. Governments administer a variety of policies to promote and protect tourism, and these policies reflect cultural and institutional norms and political realities. In countries like Mexico, France, Germany, and Spain, where the public sector has traditionally assumed the primary role of marketing, planning, and infrastructure development, there is a marked movement towards greater market involvement and privatization. In countries like the United States, where the market has been the main driving force, state involvement has been increasing, especially at the local level. As tourism has become a more important sector of urban as well as national economies, both sectors have been brought into play; top-down approaches have given way to the development of an increasingly complex economic sector, and as noted above, local authorities have assumed greater responsibility for tourism policy.

Mexico – the first developing country to develop mass tourism – is in transition from a state-directed, Fordist tourism regime to a more fully developed sector with a mix of public and private actors. The development of mass tourism was led by the central government and funded by international agencies such as the World Bank. After the North Atlantic Free Trade Agreement (NAFTA), there have been signs of a shift in demand and activity – a more open economy is bringing more foreign investment and business travel. While this has enhanced the influence of the international tourism industry, it has also opened spaces for individual entrepreneurs. Mexico is still searching for a new regulatory regime, which is likely to be characterized by a shift from state to local regulation and more private sector participation.

The globalized accumulation regime of tourism may tend towards uniformity, but irregularities are introduced because the institutions that compose it must respond to a complex geography of differing national and supra-national (European Union, NAFTA) policies and regional and local regimes (Goodwin and Painter 1997). Governments and business groups spend considerable resources on place promotions that emphasize particular features of locality (Britton 1991: 458). These efforts are produced by local regimes of accumulation that specify "the broad relationships between production, consumption, savings and investment, and the geographic extent and degree of autonomy of the capital circuits" of urban tourism (Lauria 1997: 6). The Australian case illustrates how globalized forces become mediated by local influences. As described by Mullins, the tourism urbanization that has sprung up along Australia's northeastern coast was facilitated by institutions that had long nurtured a land and resource-based economy. Urban tourism that depended upon the natural environment was a logical extension of previous modes of regulation. The existence of international flows of tourism provided the opportunity, but the way that Australian cities responded was related to local traditions.

Attempts at authoritarian control of the urban milieu have been challenged. In Berlin, repressive, top-down planning gave rise to struggles over spatial images. In Venice, the impetus for a more collaborative "bottom-up" approach to tourism came from concerns about sustainability. Residents in Amsterdam, Barcelona, and Harlem have become, to varying degrees, participants in regimes of accumulation. Conflicts over the costs and benefits of tourism require the capacity to manage and mediate conflict. This enhances the role of the state. At the same time the opening up of entrepreneurial opportunities requires that market forces be allowed to operate.

Who Benefits?

A recent book on Las Vegas describes the "grit beneath the glitter" of that city's entertainment economy – the negative impacts on the lives of ordinary workers, the environmental degradation resulting from rapid growth, and the social and cultural distortions caused by tourism (Rothman and Davis 2002). Writing about Venice, Costa and Martinotti speak of the "threat of deterritorialization" due to the prevalence of city users over residents. Every city with a significant presence of visitors has its own set of concerns, given the limited nature of urban resources such as space and funding. Thus, an analysis of tourist cities must deal with the question – who benefits?

There are some clear trade-offs between the interests of residents and visitors. Costa and Martinotti note that a city like Venice, which is in danger of being inundated by visitors, must take aggressive measures to preserve the physical city and the rights of people who live there. Similarly, Mullins observes that Australia's Gold Coast is faced with the problem of preserving the natural attractions that distinguish Australia's tourism product. Conflicts between local residents and visitors have emerged in Amsterdam and Harlem. In fact, striking a balance between the demands of different city users is the animating force behind many of the conflicts that tourism regimes are called upon to manage.

Still, the chapters in this book illustrate that residents frequently do benefit from investment in tourism facilities, particularly when investment has moved beyond the tourist bubble to touch more far-flung parts of the city. In Barcelona, García and Claver show that residents throughout the city profited from facilities provided for the Olympic Games. And locals frequent the stadiums, hotels, festive malls, and convention centers constituting the purpose-built tourist milieu. In general, the synergy between different types of users and the multi-functional uses of spaces in the city means that a higher level of amenity becomes available to both visitor and resident than would be true for either group alone. In the case of museums, Hamnett and Shoval point out that their development as tourist attractions, merchandising and dining locations, events venues, and sites of blockbuster exhibits has greatly widened their appeal even while distressing those who wish to maintain them as repositories for high culture. Tourism-related activities may have other positive economic effects: an emerging literature connects the presence of a "creative class" to place-specific economic development (Florida 2002); informal as well as formal cultural attractions, tourism sites among them, act as magnets for this social grouping, identified as the engine of growth.

Tourism also benefits local land markets, elevating property values by increasing demand for centrally located sites and by creating positive externalities for spaces adjacent to tourist sites, wherever they are located. In cities or parts of cities suffering from the withdrawal of investment and population decline, tourism has frequently brought about revitalization. In addition to supporting museums, convention centers, malls, large hotels, and themed retail outlets, tourism gives rise to a broad assortment of entrepreneurial start-ups and small-scale businesses, ranging from bed-and-breakfasts and restaurants to street vendors and souvenir shops, and can also expand the opportunity structure for ethnic products and activities. Though such uses may be less desirable, Amsterdam's multitude of sex and soft drug shops illustrates the point concerning the breadth of opportunity.

The impact on land prices, however, can have negative distributional consequences. Related as tourism is to overall economic and residential development, in cities where land markets are tight, tourism can cause both primary and secondary displacement. This has been the case in London, Paris, and New York. Furthermore, there is a suggestion in the case studies of Barcelona and Berlin that as tourism becomes a leading sector of the urban economy and as cities become more dependent on it, the synergy of uses and users may begin to decline. Nevertheless, the example of Amsterdam, as the chapter by Terhorst et al. shows, indicates that regulatory restraint, when appropriately applied, can prevent tourism from crowding out other uses, even in a city that is extremely popular and densely developed.

One of the most significant issues regarding the distribution of benefits resulting from tourism development concerns its impact on employment. The chapters by Gladstone and Fainstein and by Levine indicate that even where there is labor organization, tourism is a low-wage sector with a truncated career ladder. On the other hand, it is labor-intensive, offering jobs for the low skilled. It is particularly able to provide entry-level positions for immigrants, who cluster in central cities. Although the industry is frequently criticized for producing only episodic, seasonal employment, this criticism applies more strongly in resort areas than in central cities which are also business centers. Given the limited options available for providing employment to those with limited skills, tourism, particularly if other cities follow the Los Angeles model of organizing around a living wage, can potentially provide relatively steady, decent employment with assured benefits. Moreover, a professionalized spectrum of jobs related to web page creation, place and facility marketing, and convention and business travel arrangements is expanding, making quick judgments about tourism employment structures hazardous.

Prospects and Limits of Tourism

As of this moment, we cannot confidently predict the future of tourism. It is an industry especially sensitive to social disorder, because it relies on the unimpeded movement of large numbers of people who cluster in vulnerable places (airports, public spaces) and stand out in many circumstances, making them obvious targets. Targets with high symbolic value are concentrated in cities, as affirmed by the attacks on the World Trade Center, the IRA bombings in Birmingham and London's Canary Wharf, and the sarin gas attack in the Tokyo metro. And because they are centers of international media, "a terrorist attack in a strategic urban core is a shot heard instantly around the world" (Savitch and Ardeshev 2001).

Because of this vulnerability, cities have redoubled their efforts at security in the wake of September 11, 2001. Peter Marcuse has predicted that fears of terrorism will lead to a proliferation of walls, barricades, and intensified security and surveillance (Marcuse 2002). For a time, security at museums, sports stadiums, and similar venues mimed the security procedures imposed at courthouses and airports, reminding us of the elaborate preparations described by Body-Gendrot for mega-events such as the World Soccer Cup in Paris in 1998. Authorities felt that an attack on any of these urban facilities would affect all cities with significant tourism flows, and in the weeks following September 11 there was, in fact, a widespread fear that such venues might be targeted by terrorists. At the same time, the very measures designed to protect tourists and tourism can serve as reminders of vulnerability and of the limitations of security.

The attacks of 9/11 dealt a sharp blow to the travel industry around the world. In the US, all airlines were grounded for two days following the attacks, and travel on US-based air carriers declined sharply, down 35.6 percent from November 2000 to November 2001 (Devol et al. 2002: 3). The International Labor Organization estimated a loss of 9 million jobs in tourism-related sectors, most of them outside the United States and Europe (Mastny 2002, p. 26).

It is difficult to isolate the effects of terrorism from the general economic slide that began in 2001. In New York City, jobs in hotels and lodging fell 8.6 percent from September 2001 to September 2002, and there were much milder declines in museums, zoos, and gardens (−2.7 percent). But eating and drinking establishments lost less than 1 percent of jobs (−.8 percent), and amusement and recreation actually gained (+8.5 percent). During the same period manufacturing employment fell by 11.3 percent in the city, wholesale trade declined by 5.1 percent, and finance, insurance and real estate (FIRE) by 6.5 percent (New York Department of Labor 2002). On the opposite coast, the picture was equally mixed. In Los Angeles County, manufacturing employment fell by 7.6 percent from September 2001 to September 2002, which far outpaced the declines in hotels and lodging (−3.5 percent), and which contrasted with gains in employment in eating and drinking places (+3.2 percent) and amusement and recreation (+4.3 percent) (CEDD 2002). Together these data imply that in the United States, the country most directly affected by the 9/11 attack, the slide in tourism was attributable at least as much to general economic recession as to fear of further terrorist strikes. In fact, tourism was not more negatively affected by the insecurity caused by the combination of the two factors than other economic sectors. Moreover, worldwide in 2001 the number of international tourist arrivals fell by just 0.5 percent, and in 2002 they grew by 3 percent despite the generally worsening world economy (WTO 2003).

Repeated terrorist attacks, however, would exert a far-ranging, long-lasting effect on travel and especially affect cities identified primarily as tourist destinations. The bombing of a nightclub in Bali in 2002, killing nearly 200 people, pointed to a strategy of targeting just such places. Other tourism-dependent locations, even if not directly hit, are hostage to social disorder. Thus, Egypt, which relies on tourism for one-eighth of its economy, had barely begun to rebound from the effect of the September 11 attack at the onset of the war in Iraq. Once US bombardment of Iraq began, hotel occupancy plummeted to 20 percent in Luxor and Aswan and to 40 percent in Cairo (*New York Times*, March 21, 2003).

The Future of Tourism?

The future of tourism is strongly intertwined with all other economic sectors, and it has become a defining component of urban culture. Moreover, the infrastructure of tourism and the activities that tourists consume are simultaneously used by local residents to such a degree that there are few exclusively "tourist" venues or activities in most cities. The threats posed by terrorism – and disease, as revealed by the recent SARS epidemic – exact a price in heightened surveillance of visitors and visited alike. And there are further costs in environmental deterioration and loss of authenticity as well. Nevertheless, tourism is so deeply embedded in the urban fabric that we do not envision more than temporary hiatuses.

For particular cities, perhaps the greatest danger is related to the intense competition for tourists. The responsibility for ensuring that cities continue to attract visitors, as the case studies in this volume confirm, is assumed by regimes of accumulation which have become embedded in cities with the rise of urban tourism. A city may lose its allure because of changing tastes or preferences, because another city offers a similar experience, or because it has failed to modernize its facilities. Thus tourism gives rise to demands for a large and continuing investment in marketing and infrastructure. Once on this treadmill, a city cannot easily get off. This brings us back full circle to New York City's Olympic bid.

REFERENCES

Bagli, C. V. 2002: Dreaming of stadiums and souvenirs. *New York Times*, August 28, B, 4.

Britton, S. 1991: Tourism, capital, and place: towards a critical geography of tourism. *Environment and Planning D: Society and Space* 9: 451–78.

California Employment Development Department (CEDD). 2002: www.calmis.ca. gov/htmlfile/subject/indtable.htm#table

Castells, M. 1977: *The Urban Question*. Cambridge, MA: MIT Press.

——. 2000: *The Rise of the Network Society*, 2nd ed. Oxford: Blackwell.

Chandler, S. 2001: A blow for reeling industry. *Chicago Tribune*, November 13, 3, 1.

Chernikoff, H. 2002: West Side waits for Olympic Committee's 2012 decision. *West Side Spirit*, August 1, 1.

Devol, R. C., Bedroussian, A., Fogelbach, F., Goetz, N. H., Gonzalez, R. R., and Wong, P. 2002: *Research Report: The Impact of September 11 on US Metropolitan Economies*. Santa Monica, CA: Milken Institute.

Florida, R. 2002: *The Rise of the Creative Class*. New York: Basic Books.

Gladstone, D. L. 2001: From pilgrimage to package tourism: a comparative study of travel and tourism in the third world. PhD dissertation, Rutgers University. New Brunswick, NJ.

Goodwin, M. and Painter, J. 1997: Concrete research, urban regimes, and regulation theory. In M. Lauria (ed.), *Reconstructing Urban Regime Theory: Regulating Urban Politics in a Global Economy*. Thousand Oaks, CA: Sage Publications, 13–29.

Lauria, M. 1997: Introduction: reconstructing urban regime theory. In M. Lauria (ed.), *Reconstructing Urban Regime Theory: Regulating Urban Politics in a Global Economy*. Thousand Oaks, CA: Sage Publications, 1–10.

Marcuse, P. 2002: Afterword. In P. Marcuse and R. van Kempen (eds.), *Of States and Cities: The Partitioning of Urban Space*. Oxford: Oxford University Press.

Martinotti, G. 1999: A city for whom? Transients and public life in the second-generation metropolis. In R. A. Beauregard and S. Body-Gendrot (eds.), *The Urban Moment*. Thousand Oaks, CA: Sage, 155–84.

Mastny, L. 2002: Traveling light: New paths for international tourism. World Watch Paper 159 (December). Washington, DC: Worldwatch Institute.

New York Department of Labor 2002: *Economic Data* (http://64.106.160.140:8080/lmi/index.html).

Rothman, H. K. and Davis, M. 2002: *The Grit beneath the Glitter: Tales from the Real Las Vegas*. Berkeley, CA: University of California Press.

Sandomir, R. and Bagli, C. V. 2002: New York City makes a cut in Olympic bid. *New York Times*, August 28, B, 1.

Savitch, H. V. and Ardashev, G. 2001: Does terror have an urban future? *Urban Studies* 38 (13): 2515–33.

Smith, M. P. 2001: *Transnational Urbanism*. Oxford: Blackwell.

World Tourism Organization (WTO) 2003: War in Iraq may postpone tourism growth but will not cause collapse. Http://www.world-tourism.org/newsroom/Releases/2003/marzo/iraq.htm, March 21.

Index

Abyssinian Development Corporation
(ADC), Harlem 95–6, 104,
109n3
Acapulco, tourism development
189–90, 191
Agenda 21 59
airline industry, Australia 134, 136
Alemán, Miguel 189, 190, 198n3
Amin, Ash 92
Amsterdam
drugs policy 86–7
gentrification 81, 85
history 76–7
housing policy 81
image of 85–8, 245
museums 223
restructuring (1870–1974) 78–9
restructuring (1974–present) 79–81
social movements 81–3
tourism crisis 83–5
tourism market 87–8
tourism planning 31
tourist attractions 75–6
Apollo Performing Arts Center,
Harlem 100–2, 104
architecture
Barcelona 113

museums 228
art galleries 233
see also museums
Arts Council, Britain 231
"as if" tourists 31–2, 36n2, 211, 244
Ash, J. 54
Atlanta, Olympic Games (1996) 49
Augé, M. 54
Australia
land economy 131–2
tourism urbanization 126–40, 248
authenticity 57–8

Baltimore
living wage campaign 175–6,
181n9
tourist enclave 24, 30
Barcelona
benefits to residents 249
Fordism 124n3
hotels 121–3
labor market deregulation 121–3
local leadership 115–19
modernization 5, 114–21, 245
Old Town regeneration 117–19
Olympic Games (1992) 113,
116–17, 241

tourism policy 119–21
Universal Forum of Cultures (2004)
    120
Barthel-Bouchier, D. 55
Baudrillard, J. 28
Bauman, Z. 55
Benjamin, Walter 35
Berlin
    construction site tourism 201,
        203–10
    memories and myths 212–14
    "New Berlin" 202, 203–6, 211,
        215, 216n2
    "Open City" exhibition 205–6,
        211, 213
    Potsdamer Platz 202, 204, 206–10,
        212, 245
    public–private partnerships 202,
        203
    reunification 200–1
    Schaustelle Berlin 203–6, 213
    urban marketing 201–6, 210–15,
        245
Bingham, R. D. and Zhang, Z. 95
Birmingham, tourism planning 31
blockbuster exhibitions, museums 227
Boorstin, Daniel 24, 54
Boston 24
Bourdieu, P. 28–9, 223
Boyle, M. 221
Briggs, A. 234
Brisbane, Australia, tourism 129–31
Britain, museum funding 231, 232
British Museum 221–2, 228
Brown, Ron 102
Bruges 5
Brundtland Commission 59

Cairns, Australia, tourism
        urbanization 126, 128–31
Canada *see* Montreal
Canberra, Australia, tourism 129–31
Cancún, development plan 192–3
Cárdenas, Lázaro 188, 198n3
carnival-feast 56–7
Casino de Montréal, strikes 178
Castells, M. 138

Chicago World's Fair (1893) 26, 27
cities
    regulation of 8–9, 242
    social structure 242–4
    types of 5, 16n1
    see also inner cities; *under* urban
Cities of Culture, Europe 6
city users and hypertourists theory
        60–3
Cohen, E. 57, 60
collaboration theory 67–8
commodification, museums 225–8
community tourism 99
Confédération des syndicats nationaux
        (CSN), Montreal 176–9
construction site tourism, Berlin 201,
        203–10
consumer culture, globalized 32–3,
        243
Cook, Thomas, mass tourism 26
corporate sponsorship, museums
        226–7
Costa, N. 57, 61
costs, of travel 243
creative class 249
critical theory, tourism 54–6
cultural capital 106, 244–6
cultural differentiation 12, 245–6
cultural economy, post-Fordist
        219–21, 241
cultural flows, global 12
cultural standardization 245–6
cultural tourism
    Harlem 98–9, 104, 107, 245
    marketing of 244–6
    Mexico 195–6
    and museums 223–5
culture and inequality 13
culture of consumption, globalized
        32–3, 243–4

de Certeau, M. 34
deregulation
    Australia 134
    labor market 121–3
Detroit, tourist enclave 30
differentiation 10–13, 246

disaggregation 10–11
diversity 13, 16
  marketing of 91
"drifter tourists" 12, 243
drugs policy, Amsterdam 86–7
Durazo, Maria Elena 158

East Germany
  memories and myths 212–14
  see also Berlin
Edensor, Tim 23, 29, 34
Egypt, Iraq war impact 251
Eisinger, P. 232
employment *see* labor market
enclaves, urban *see* tourist enclaves
entertainment complexes 27, 31–2
entertainment industry, New York City
  100–2
entrepreneurialism 220–1
Europe
  Cities of Culture 6
  Grand Tour cities 25
Expo 67, Montreal 168

flâneur 34–5
Florida, Richard 33
FOGATUR, Mexico 190
FONATUR, Mexico 192–3, 195
football *see* World Soccer Cup
Fordism
  Mexico 191, 192–4
  paradigm 11, 92
  and tourism 57, 66–7, 244
  United States inner cities 104–5
  see also post-Fordism
France
  Millennium celebrations 41, 46–8
  museum funding 231
  security policy 39–41
  World Soccer Cup (1998) 41–6,
    48–50, 241
franchising, museums 227–8
Franco regime, Spain 114–15
future prospects, of tourism 250–2

gentrification
  Amsterdam 81, 85

Harlem 103
Germany *see* Berlin
Geron, K. 158
Getty Museum, Los Angeles 222
ghetto economies 94–5
Glasgow, European City of Culture
    (1990) 232
global forces
  entertainment industry 100–2
  local influences 247–8
  tourism 11–12
globalization 4–5, 11–12
  culture of consumption 32–3,
    243
Gold Coast, Australia
  criminal activity 138
  development of 126–7, 132–8
  Japanese tourists 134, 135
  regulatory system 136–8
  schoolies week 137–8
  tourism urbanization 126, 128–31
  transport 136–7
governance, local 113–14
Graburn, N. H. H. 55
Graham, Stephen 27, 34, 35
Grand Tour cities 25–6
Greenberg, Miriam 32
Guggenheim Museum, Bilbao 222,
    228
Guggenheim Museum, New York
    227–8, 232

habitus 28–9
Hannigan, John 24
Harlem, New York
  cultural capital 93, 106
  cultural tourism 98–9, 104, 107,
    245
  economic development 94–102,
    106
  entertainment industry 100–2
  Internet marketing 99–100
  marketing diversity 96–8
  September 11 impact 107–8
  tourism development 91, 102–9
Harvey, David 23, 119, 215, 220
Higazy, Abdallah 16n2

Hotel Employees and Restaurant
    Employees International Union
    (HERE) 157, 162, 175
hotels
    Barcelona 121–3
    Montreal 176–9
    New York and Los Angeles 150–1
housing policy, Amsterdam 81
Hoving, Thomas 225
Hubbard, P. 214
Hughes, G. 221
hypertourism
    theory 60–3
    Venice 63–7

image-making *see* tourism, images
industrial cities, tourist infrastructure
    5–6, 16n1
Info Box 204, 206, 214
INFRATUR, Mexico 190
Initiative for a Competitive Inner City
    (ICIC), Harlem 95
inner cities
    Fordism 104–5
    political economy 94–6
International American Development
    Bank (IADB) 193
international cooperation, World Cup
    security 42
Internet 10
    tourism marketing 99–100
ironic stance 34

Januszczak, W. 225
Japanese tourists, Gold Coast,
    Australia 134, 135
Johnson, Derek 97
Judd, D. 131–2, 242

Krapf, Kurt 60
Kren, Thomas 227

La Ronde, Montreal 178, 181n11
labor market
    Barcelona 121–3
    local policies 167–8
    militancy 176–80

Montreal 167–8, 170–80
New York and Los Angeles 151–64
regulation 9–10, 121–3, 160–4,
    242
tourism industry 145–7, 250
wages 156, 173–4, 179–80,
    181nn5–9
land prices, tourism impact 249
Las Vegas 5, 16n1
    tourism impacts 248
    tourist enclave 24, 30
Lefebvre, H. 23–4
lifestyle culture 32–3
Lisbon, tourism planning 31
Lloyd, Richard 33, 36n2
local policies, labor market 167–8
local regulation and governance,
    Barcelona 113–14
local variations
    cities 12–13
    global forces 247–8
London
    museum funding 232
    Tate Modern 222, 225, 229–30
    tourism industry 128
    visitor attractions 224–5
Lortie, Jean 177
Los Angeles
    labor regulation 160–4
    museums 230
    September 11 impact 251
    tourism employment 151–60
    tourism establishments 150–1
    tourism industry 147, 148–51
    tourist enclave 24
Los Angeles Alliance for a New
    Economy (LAANE) 159
Louvre, Paris 221–2, 223, 226, 228
low-income travelers 12

MacCannell, D. 8–9, 54, 57–8
mass tourism 244–7
Marcuse, Peter 250
market demand, inner cities 95
marketing
    cultural tourism 244–6
    Venice 65–6

Marseilles, World Soccer Cup (1998)
    45
Marvin, Simon 27, 34, 35
Mayan Route 195
McDonald's, Montreal 178–9
mega-events
    France 41–50
    impact 48–50, 241
    Montreal 168–9
    security issues 39–50, 250–1
    tourism marketing 62–3
memories and myths, Berlin 212–14
Metropolitan Museum, New York 225
Mexico
    Acapulco 189–90, 191
    cultural tourism 195–6
    Fordism 191, 192–4, 247
    foreign investment 195
    post-Fordism 194–7
    resort development 192–3, 195
    tourism development 187–98, 247
Mexico City, tourism development 31,
    190
migrants 12
Millennium celebrations, France 41,
    46–8
Milwaukee art museum 228
Montreal
    labor militancy 176–9
    linguistic segmentation 170–1
    mega-events 168–9
    tourism development 31, 168–70
    tourism labor market 167–8,
        170–80
    wages 173–4, 179–80, 181nn5–7
Musée d'Orsay, Paris 222
Museum of African Art, New York 97
museum shops 225–6
museums
    as anchors of regeneration 229–30
    architecture 228–9
    blockbuster exhibitions 227
    branding and franchising 227–8
    changing nature of 225–8
    commodification 225–8
    corporate sponsorship 226–7
    cultural tourism 223–5

development of 221–2
    "Flagship Museums" 222, 224
    regulation 230–2
    role of 233–4
    shops 225–6
myth-making, Berlin 212–14

National Labor Relations Board
        (NLRB) 162
New Orleans, living wage campaign
        175, 181n9
New York
    labor regulation 160–4
    Millennium celebrations 48
    Olympic Games bid (2012) 239–40
    September 11 impact 251
    tourism employment 151–60
    tourism establishments 150–1
    tourism industry 147, 148–51
    tourists 11, 33
    urban regeneration 230
    visitor attractions 224–5
    World Financial Center 29–30
    see also Harlem
niche marketing, Harlem 96–7
North Atlantic Free Trade Agreement
        (NAFTA) 247

Olympic Games
    1976 (Montreal) 168–9
    1992 (Barcelona) 113, 116–17, 241
    1996 (Atlanta) 49
    2012 (New York bid) 239–40

package tourism 26–7
Paris
    Millennium celebrations 46–7
    security issues 51n7
    visitor attractions 224–5
    World Soccer Cup (1998) 49
Parsons, Richard D. 100
Partner für Berlin (PfB) 203
Pataki, George 99
pillarization, Amsterdam 82
political economy
    inner cities 94–6
    of regulation 247–8

Porter, Michael 95
post-Fordism 11, 92, 246
  Barcelona 120
  culture 219–21, 241
  Gold Coast, Australia 132–3
  Mexico 194–7
  and tourism 244
  United States inner cities 105–6
  see also Fordism
post-structuralism, urban studies 23,
  36n1
post-tourists 33–4
Potsdamer Platz, Berlin 202, 204,
  206–10, 212, 245
public–private partnerships, Berlin
  202, 203

quality of life, local residents 31–2
Quebec *see* Montreal

Rada, U. 211, 212
railways, Australia 136–7
regulation
  and Australian Gold Coast
    133–40
  of cities 8–9, 242
  labor market 9–10, 121–3, 146–7,
    160–4, 179–80, 242
  local 89, 113–14, 123
  and museums 230–2
  politics of 247–8
  resistance to 33–5
  of tourism industry 10, 147
  tourist enclaves 28–30
  types of 6–10
  of visitors 7–8
  see also regulation theory
regulation regimes 14
regulation theory 2–6, 55–6, 67–8,
  92, 146–7, 162–4, 239–42
relational theory, of tourism 56–9
residents
  friction with visitors 88
  impacts of tourism 248–50
  tourist activities 31–2, 244
  see also synergy of uses and
    users

resistance, to tourist enclaves 33–5
resort cities
  Australia 126, 128–31
  definition 5, 16n1
Rijksmuseum, Amsterdam 223
ritual inversion theory 56–7
Rojek, Chris 23
Roost, F. 30
Rotterdam, tourism planning 31

San Francisco 9
Sassen, S. 30, 32
scale 10–11, 77, 91, 240
Schaustelle Berlin 203–6
Schmidt, Benno C. Jr. 97
Scott, A. J. 220
security issues, mega-events 39–50,
  250–1
September 11, 2001, impacts of 7,
  107–8, 123, 130–1, 150, 197,
  250–1
Serota, Nicolas 225
shopping centers 28
shops, museums 225–6
Small, Bruce 133
soccer *see* World Soccer Cup
social capital 93
social inequality 92–3
social movements
  Amsterdam 81–3
  Barcelona 116–17
social structure, changing 242–4
Sorkin, Michael 23
Spain
  tourism development 114–15
  see also Barcelona
spatial inequality 92–3
spatiality, urban tourism 30–3
staged authenticity theory 56, 57
Stone, C. N. 161, 164n3
Sudjic, D. 222, 226, 231
Sunshine Coast, Australia, tourism
  urbanization 126, 128–31
sustainable tourism 59–60
Sydney, Australia
  Sydney Opera House 228
  tourism 129–31

synergy of users and uses 12, 102, 245–6

Tate Modern, London 222, 225, 229–30
terrorism, threat of 7–8, 250–1
Time Warner, Harlem 100–2
Tourism
  benefits of 232, 248–50
  critical theory 54–6
  definition 3–4, 243–4
  development 103–4
  future 252
  gentrification 103, 249
  images, construction of 26–7, 207–8
  impacts of
    Amsterdam 87–8
    Barcelona 117–19
    Berlin 210–11
    Gold Coast 134–6
    Harlem 103–4
    Mexico 191, 193–4, 196–7
    Montreal 168–70
    Venice 66
  labor force *see* labor market
  prospects and limits 250–1
  resistance to 33–5, 103–4
tourism industry 4
  regulation 10
  types of establishments 150–1
tourism urbanization
  Australia 126–40, 248
  definition 5, 126
"tourist bubble" 9, 16n1, 61
  see also tourist enclaves
tourist enclaves
  construction of 25–7
  definition 23–5
  regulation 28–30
  resistance to 33–5
  spatiality 30–3
tourist-historic cities 5, 9, 16n1
tourists
  regulation of 7–8
  rights of 8, 16n2
  vs. visitors 3

transnational urbanism 12, 242
transportation 246
trend-setting, Harlem 97–8
TrizecHahn 159
Turner, L. 54

unionization, tourism labor force 157–9, 162–3, 174–7, 179–80
United States
  Grand Tour 25–6
  labor market regulation 9–10, 146–7
  Millennium celebrations 48
  minimum wage 181nn7–9
  museums 230–1
  September 11 impact 251
  unionization 175–6, 179–80
  urban decline 27
Universal Forum of Cultures (2004), Barcelona 120
Universal Studios, jobs 159
Upper Manhattan Empowerment Zone (UMEZ) 95–6, 97–8
urban competition 244–6
urban entertainment destination 100
urban marketing, Berlin 201–6, 210–15, 245
urban regeneration
  Barcelona 117–19
  museums as anchors of 229–30
urban regime
  in Berlin 215–16
  theory of 161, 164n3
urban spatiality 30–3
urban tourism
  definition 128
  see also tourism urbanization
Urry, J. 65

van den Berg, Leo 31
Van Gogh Museum, Amsterdam 223
Vancouver, tourism planning 31
Venice
  tourism impacts 5, 248
  tourism regulation 63–7, 67–8
visitors 3

wages, tourism employment 156,
173–4, 179–80, 181nn5–9
Withey, Lynne 25
workers in tourism industries 145–6
World Financial Center, New York
City 29–30
World Soccer Cup (France, 1998)
41–6, 48–50, 241
World Tourism Organization (WTO),
tourist definition 3

World's Fair
1893 (Chicago) 26, 27
1967 (Montreal) 168
Wu, C. 225, 226

York, museums 233

Zukin, S. 210, 220